Naturalism and Social Science

Themes in the Social Sciences

Editors: *Jack Goody & Geoffrey Hawthorn*

The aim of this series is to publish books which will focus on topics of general and interdisciplinary interest in the social sciences. They will be concerned with non-European cultures and with developing countries, as well as with industrial societies. The emphasis will be on comparative sociology and, initially, on sociological, anthropological and demographic topics. These books are intended for undergraduate teaching, but not as basic introductions to the subjects they cover. Authors have been asked to write on central aspects of current interest which have a wide appeal to teachers and research students, as well as to undergraduates.

First books in the series

Edmund Leach: *Culture and Communication: the logic by which symbols are connected: An introduction to the use of structuralist analysis in social anthropology*

Anthony Heath: *Rational Choice and Social Exchange: A critique of exchange theory*

P. Abrams and A. McCulloch: *Communes, Sociology and Society*

Jack Goody: *The Domestication of the Savage Mind*

Jean-Louis Flandrin: *Families in Former Times: kinship, household and sexuality*

John Dunn: *Western political theory in the face of the future*

Naturalism and social science
A post-empiricist philosophy of social science

DAVID THOMAS

CAMBRIDGE UNIVERSITY PRESS

Cambridge
London   New York   New Rochelle
Melbourne   Sydney

Published by the Press Syndicate of the University of Cambridge
The Pitt Building, Trumpington Street, Cambridge CB2 1RP
32 East 57th Street, New York, NY 10022, USA
296 Beaconsfield Parade, Middle Park, Melbourne 3206, Australia

First published 1979

Phototypeset in V.I.P. Palatino by
Western Printing Services Ltd, Bristol

Printed and bound in Great Britain
at The Pitman Press, Bath

Library of Congress cataloguing in publication data
Thomas, David, 1954–
Naturalism and social science.

(Themes in the social sciences)
Bibliography: p.
Includes index.
1. Social science.   2. Science – Philosophy.
I. Title.   II. Series.
H61.T48   300'.1   79-14223
ISBN 0 521 22821 2 hard covers
ISBN 0 521 29660 9 paperback

Contents

v

Contents

Preface

I would like first to acknowledge some old debts. Ian Hacking and David Papineau initially taught me philosophy and helped me to become clearer about its point. My earliest study of the philosophy of social science was encouraged by John Dunn and Michael Pickering, whose examples confirmed my suspicion that it was possible to do fruitful work on the borderlines of philosophy and social science.

Mary Hesse was my research supervisor; anyone familiar with her work will recognise her influence at many points in this book. Geoffrey Hawthorn commented carefully and sympathetically on successive drafts. Martin Hollis and Bernard Williams examined my doctoral thesis (on which chapters one to four are based) and I have used several of their suggestions. I spent a year as a student of Steven Lukes; chapters two and four, on which I was working at the time, benefited from his criticisms. David Lazar supplied me with a thorough critique of chapters three and four. My views on the philosophy of science have been clarified by conversations with Neil Williams.

I have learnt much from all the above people. None of them would agree with all that I have written; some would agree with very little. It goes without saying that the remaining deficiencies are mine alone.

I am grateful to my former employer, the National Coal Board, for granting me a week's special leave in order to finish this book.

An article based on chapter two was published in *Inquiry*, 21, 1978. I am grateful to the editor and publisher of *Inquiry* for permission to use that material here.

Finally, I would like to thank Diane Swansborough, who gave me much support and encouragement during the writing of this book, and to whom it is dedicated with gratitude and affection.

Introduction

vuruvuvuruvuvuvuvuvuvuvuvuvuvuvuvuvuvuvuvuvuvuvuvuvuvuvuvuvuvuvuvuvuvuvuvuvuvuvuvuvuvu

Any major development in the philosophy of science has implications for many other philosophical concerns. The theory of knowledge, ethics and the philosophies of art and religion, for example, have been profoundly affected by changes in our understanding of science. Of course, the influence is not simply in one direction; the philosophy of science has itself been moulded by ideas from these other domains.

Some people might find this claim of reciprocal influence between distinctive philosophical areas surprising. One proposition that would be uncontroversial, however, is that the philosophy of social science has depended on developments in the philosophy of science. Each philosophy of science sets narrow limits for what is acceptable as a philosophy of social science. Yet a philosophy of social science is formulated normally after the main ideas of the parent philosophy of science have been exhaustively studied; and often after it has become evident to specialists in the philosophy of science that there is something wrong with the model of science in question.

The philosophy of social science, then, typically has the fate of being behind the times and on the point of change, a fate which is depressing only if we want cut and dried intellectual answers. This means that this book's central question is both familiar and novel. I am concerned with whether the study of human society can satisfy natural scientific methodology. Throughout I pose the question in the following terms. Can social study conform to a *naturalistic* methodology, that is replicate the methodology of natural science? Is *naturalism*, the doctrine that there can be a natural scientific study of society, correct? *Anti-naturalism* is the view that there cannot be a study of society modelled on natural science. *Non-naturalistic* social studies are based on methodologies other than that of natural science, but are not necessarily committed on the issue of whether there can also be a naturalistic social science. Hermeneutic methodologies claim to sustain types of non-naturalistic study.

These issues are familiar in that they have always been fundamental

1

to the philosophy of social study. They are novel because there are many naturalisms, since there are many philosophies of natural science which might serve as models for the study of society. Those who ask whether social study can model itself on natural science use an identical set of words to pose a changing question. Failure to understand this leads repeatedly to the plea that we should forget the whole issue, a plea which is always ignored.

I cannot hope to set out in full the philosophy of science which I assume in my discussion of naturalism. To do so would not only require a separate book, but also involve much superfluous discussion, because the philosophy of science disputes issues, such as whether or not it is essential for theories to be interpreted by means of models, that do not have to be settled for my purpose.

My strategy is to borrow, as the content of the naturalism I will discuss, the key ideas from recent philosophy of science. This philosophy of science contributed to and developed from the demise of the strongly empiricist philosophy of science which held sway roughly until the mid-1950s. As a term of convenience, we can call this new philosophy of science the 'post-empiricist' philosophy of science.[1]

The key ideas I borrow are uncontroversial ones within post-empiricist philosophy of science. They are uncontroversial in that most disputants within contemporary philosophy of science accept them in some form, and in that they could be abandoned only in the context of a movement to an entirely different philosophy of science. Feyerabend's more Feyerabendian statements, for example, are uncontroversial in neither of these senses.

The two following points indicate the nature of the background philosophy of science I will assume in my discussion of naturalism. First, to call a study a science implies that there is an empirical constraint on the acceptability of its statements, that the testing of its statements against the world is at least one strong criterion for the acceptance or rejection of those statements. Secondly, scientific theories are much more holistic structures than was previously realised, in a sense which includes the point that the meaning of a term is partly determined by its relations with other terms in its theory; and, partly in consequence of this holism, there is no absolutely pre-theoretical observation language relevant to the conduct of science. In saying that a term's meaning is partly determined by its relations with other terms in its theory, we mean that limitations are placed on the sense and reference of terms used within a theory. The limitations occur because the term's sense and reference are modified as a result of

[1] Dispassionate accounts of recent developments in the philosophy of science are to be found in Achinstein (1968), Shapere (1966), Sheffler (1967) and Williams (1977).

the term coming into logical contact with other terms in the theory. These modifications provide, for example, new criteria for the identification of and new expectations concerning an object. This contextual view of meaning leads to a holistic interpretation of theoretical structure and then to the denial of existence to a pre-theoretical observation language, once it becomes apparent that there is no basis for holding that some terms derive their meaning in isolation from other terms. In particular, there is no basis for believing that any term is meaningful in virtue of an immediate relationship with the extra-linguistic world in abstraction from other terms in the language. It follows that there is no statement concerning which the decision about truth-status is independent of assumptions about other statements' truth-statuses.

With this insight, the issue that dominated empiricist philosophy of science – the analysis of the observation terms and statements which were held to be in an immediate relationship with the world – has to be re-stated. For since we no longer acknowledge pre-theoretical observation statements, we cannot study the nature of observation statements or their relations with theoretical statements. The resolution of this issue in any case looked increasingly unlikely from within empiricist philosophy of science, because many different grounds were adduced for distinguishing observation and theoretical statements, all of which were vague and most of which were in conflict with one another. In contrast to empiricist approaches, it became clear that what were considered absolutely empirical terms have their meanings partly determined by their relations with other terms in the theory, including terms in the most abstract reaches of the theory. What relatively empirical statements claim is, likewise, in part a function of the other statements in the theory.

There is thus a real sense in which the statements in a theory stand or fall together. In considering any statement within a theory, we must consider the relations of that statement with other of the theory's statements and, in principle, with the whole theory. How precisely we are to analyse the sense in which statements are dependent on one another is, however, a problem for current philosophy of science; it turns, in part, on our initial formulation of the critique of pre-theoretical observation items. This is a large area which I cannot enter here.

We started from the empirical point that a scientific theory is about the world. We then criticised the empiricist interpretation of this claim, namely that there are some terms and statements whose meaning is given immediately by reference to the extra-linguistic world in abstraction from all other terms and statements. These two starting points for post-empiricist philosophy of science encapsulate its fundamental promise and dilemma: it seeks to be empirical without being empiri-cist. As a first approximation, the claims that a scientific theory is about the world and that it should be considered as a whole unit, can be combined in the view that it is the theory as a whole that is assessed for correspondence with the world. This view indicates the right direc-tion, but does little more than that. The problem of how post-empiricist models of science can be empirical is the most basic issue facing current philosophy of science. It is an unresolved issue and it is one which we will continuously run up against in this book.

The term 'theory' has already occurred a great deal in these opening pages. It is necessary to say something about it, because it is a key term in this work. Three separate points ought to be noted in arriving at an understanding of what a theory is. First, there is much to be learnt from empiricist philosophy of science in the analysis of the internal structure of a scientific theory. It depicted a scientific theory as a layered struc-ture, with the higher level statements incorporating and explaining those on the lower levels. There is a reciprocal evidential relation between the layers, in that higher level statements might stand as support for lower level statements and vice versa. As an ideal, the language of a theory should be formalised and the links between the layers deductive.

If we keep in mind the ideal typical nature of this account – that, for example, no empirical theory is fully axiomatic or deductive – we can put it to good use in understanding scientific theory. What we must and can discard, for reasons already indicated, is the idea that there is an absolute break in a theory's structure between the theoretical and pre-theoretical terms and statements. This idea is not essential to analyses of different levels in a scientific theory's structure. All such accounts presuppose is a notion of *relatively* theoretical and *relatively* empirical terms and statements.

This leads to the second point about theories, which I have already discussed. The notion of theoretical terms and statements cannot be invoked in absolute contradistinction to the empirical. The meanings of *prima facie* empirical terms and statements are partly determined by the meanings of all the other terms and statements in a theory. There is no absolutely pre-theoretical observation language; in analysing the meanings or judging the claims of relatively empirical terms and statements, we constantly return to the avowedly theoretical.

A tension exists between the first, layered view of theories and the second, holistic view. In contrast to the layer model, the holistic view lends itself to a network model for scientific theory, in which there are no hierarchical relations between terms and statements in the theory. Investigations into the possibilities, if any, of reconciling layered and network accounts form a major part of current philosophy of science. Suffice it here to say that there is a chance of reconciliation if we accept that any designated hierarchical relations are not absolute. That is, which items are designated 'high level' and which 'low level' depends on what we are studying and when we analyse the theory in question. Nevertheless, as long as we accept these qualifications on delineations of levels within a theory, it remains possible and useful to talk of higher and lower level items.

Yet, and this is the third point, we need a clear way of distinguishing the relatively empirical from the relatively theoretical. To rest with the claim that all terms and statements are equally theoretical creates more problems than it solves. We need to be able to distinguish a relatively empirical layer as a way of accounting for the fact that scientific theory makes statements about the world. The sorts of question to be posed in deciding which terms and statements are relatively theoretical are as follows: how systematic are they, in the sense of which layers do they subsume and explain? How general and idealised are they? What relations of testability do they bear to other items in the theory? Can they be abandoned without fundamentally revising the theory? What are their relations to the terms and statements with which the theory appears to confront the world more or less directly? These different criteria may often yield different judgments as to the relative theoretical load of an item in a theory. One criterion applied to an item at different times for different purposes might even produce different answers. This is to acknowledge that the designation of one item as 'theoretical' and another as 'empirical' is relative, provisional and shifting within the context of a theory, as are even the most gross functional differentiations between, for example, explanation and classification.

This interpretation of theory allows us to talk sensibly of everyday actors' theories, commonsense theories and implicit theories. They comprise a network of terms and statements, internally related, not in an isolatedly immediate relationship with the world. Moreover, commonsense statements which are relatively systematic and general can be loosely delineated. Where commonsense theory differs from scientific theory is in terms of the first point I made about theories. Virtually by definition, commonsense theories are not rigidly structured, formalised or deductive. Nor do commonsense theories adopt movement towards more rigid structure as a controlling methodological ideal; in many ways, this prescriptive formulation is more important than a descriptive account of the point about lack of structure, because most natural scientific theories also, as a matter of fact, lack rigid structure. These ideas are central to chapters two and three.

A key aspect of the assumptions I use is that they rest on a notion of a unified, holistic theory. Just as it is difficult to give identity criteria for natural languages, so too the decision as to where one theory ends and another begins is not governed by explicit criteria and is often fairly arbitrary. The philosophy of science I adopt requires theoretical holism, because it stresses how terms and statements, previously considered to be common between theories, are structured by specific theoretical options. Theoretical holism might be held more plausible of natural than social science, since natural scientific theories tend to be more explicit and formalised. However, for reasons that should become apparent in chapter four, theoretical holism is relevant to social science because of the extreme difficulty in giving an account of a relatively empirical layer which might be common between two social scientific theories.

I do not claim that natural scientific methodology is the only possible model for social study. Various types of study of society are feasible. History, the study of literature or journalism might be taken as its model disciplines. This suggestion is clearly complicated, however, by the fact that there is methodological uncertainty about the proposed alternative model disciplines, as is evident from the debate that followed Hempel's (1959) attempted extension of a naturalistic model of explanation to history. Even despised journalism sustains its methodological controversies: Wolfe (1973) describes how a 'new journalism' arose out of, *inter alia*, a critique of the accepted notions of the given and of an objective point of view.

More generally, different studies of man could be constructed on the basis of different aims, methodologies and epistemologies. Different conceptions of the status of the student of society might be crucial in this respect. There is a broad division between those studies where the student is seen as an observer and those where he is seen as a participant. Most naturalistic methodologies assume the observer model of the student, while some hermeneutic methodologies use the participant model. This distinction cannot be made in terms of the distinctive objects of social study: for instance, the naturalistic student can 'observe', in the sense relevant to science, 'meaningful' social entities as well as physical objects (*pace* Earle, 1952–3), and a naturalistic social science can admit 'intentional categories' (*pace* Dunn, 1978). The observer and the participant are differentiated, not by the objects they can recognise, but by their different methodologies, aims and criteria of knowledge. The participant's distinctive aims are, first, to acquire the practical and cognitive social skills of the people of his study and, secondly, to enter into full interaction with these people, modifying himself and them in the process.

The fashionable view that a naturalistic methodology based on the student as observer has to 'objectify' the actor under study in some pernicious epistemological-cum-moral sense is mistaken. Certainly, the actor becomes an 'object' of social science in the trivial sense that he is studied and discussed in social scientific theories. But the actor is not necessarily reduced to an 'object' by naturalistic social science in two more interesting senses which are fundamental to the vague protest of 'objectification'. First, the social scientist need not (though he might) conclude that the actions he studies are out of the control of their supposed agents; Hollis's claim, in *Models of Man*, that a naturalistic social science cannot have a theory of the active subject is wrong in this respect. Secondly, the social scientist need not treat the actors' conceptual systems as different in principle from his own. Both these points are themes of this book. They will be discussed mainly in chapters two and three; in chapter three, I will also say a little more about the observer and participant models of the student of society.

It is also a reasonable view that the tradition of modelling social study on natural science has been an unhelpful one. This issue has to be argued again for each new philosophy of science. I wish simply to defend naturalism, which is the doctrine of the possibility of a natural scientific study of society, and to draw out some of the implications for social science if it were to adopt certain views in current philosophy of science as its naturalistic methodology. Only in drawing out these implications do I set forth prescriptions and even then the prescriptions are conditional, not categorical. That is, some of my arguments are of the form: one must hold certain views, *if* one wishes to adopt from the philosophy of science the naturalistic methodology in question. In defending naturalism, I am bound to criticise those elements of anti-naturalism which imply the impossibility of naturalism. But how one might compare the various methodologies of the study of man directly, if at all, is something I do not discuss. Suffice it here to make two points.

First, an advocate of a naturalistic social science would emphasise features such as the unification of knowledge (by means of generalisations, explanations, predictions, etc.) which would be yielded by a powerful naturalistic theory, as against the fragmented insights of non-naturalistic approaches. I suspect that non-naturalistic approaches are not merely fragmented. They are non-existent, in that no satisfactory account of a non-naturalistic social study has been given and no substantive body of non-naturalistic social studies exists. But it would take another book, on non-naturalism and social study, to support this suspicion properly.

Secondly, an element in the comparison of the various

methodologies would be the elucidation of the different interests on which the types of social study are based. That would be to show, for the level of methodology, what will be a central thesis of my discussion of values in social science: namely, values have a foundational role in the formation of the human studies. In *Knowledge and Human Interests*, Habermas analyses the different sorts of interests that may underlie naturalistic and non-naturalistic methodologies. From this book's point of view, Habermas's empirical-analytic, historical-hermeneutic and critical sciences are three *alternative* possible ways of conceptualising the study of man. On a more empirical level, Hawthorn's *Enlightenment and Despair* advances hypotheses about the political conditions of the presence of sociology in France and Germany, where there was a need for a moral science of social progress to mediate between anarchy and reaction; and of the absence of sociology in England, where liberal reformism had practical strength. Hawthorn appears, however, to make two doubtful assumptions: first, that sociology's basic value commitments are always liberal and reformist, and, secondly, that sociology experiences rapid development only when these value commitments are threatened.

This work, then, is doubly conditional. I argue that *if* my background philosophy of science is accepted and *if* the project of a naturalistic social science is deemed possible and fruitful, then social science should take the lines I sketch out. In fact, a certain tension is revealed between the body of this work and an antecedent of the condition governing it. For, as I have already indicated, I repeatedly run into a problem which is shown to be highly intractable, namely the key issue facing modern philosophy of science, that of giving an account of science's claim to be empirical. It may be, as I moot in the Conclusion, that setting out modern philosophy of science's implications for social science helps us to see that modern philosophy of science is itself ultimately untenable.

I focus, within the philosophical framework I have just described, on the problems posed by meaning and value for naturalistic social science. This focus arises from my belief that meaning and value are the areas where the most serious arguments against the possibility of a naturalistic social science, and where the most interesting implications for social science of the naturalistic methodology I adopt are located. My concentration on issues of meaning and value results in several traditional problems of the philosophy of social science (e.g. methodological individualism, the psychology–sociology and history–sociology relations, functionalism) being tackled only indirectly or in passing. Besides repeating the positive reasons for the focus I have chosen, I would justify these omissions by arguing that the problems concerned are not central to the question of the possibility of a naturalistic social science. They deal directly with the distinctive subject matter of social study (e.g. whether it is directed to social or individualistic entities), not with the philosophical status of that study. However, I will discuss these problems where I consider them to have *prima facie* damaging implications for the project of a naturalistic social science.

I discuss meaning and value in chapters two to five. Chapter one asks whether social science can replicate the internal structure and central achievements of natural scientific theories. It thus treats issues such as the possibility of empirical generalisations, theories and predictions in social science. Chapter one is in a sense ground-clearing, allowing me to dismiss certain topics from the discussion of naturalism, before moving to the deeper problems of meaning and value. But in another sense it is a fundamental part of this work. For my analyses of meaning and value are designed to show that, although there are senses in which social science is distinctively concerned with meanings and values, there is no reason why social study should not be scientific, if our model of science is derived from recent philosophy of science. Having established this point, social scientific theories are then free to model themselves on the kinds of aims and internal structure discussed in chapter one.

Some of the analyses of science I appeal to in chapter one were achieved before the more recent work in the philosophy of science which I assume as an overall background. This discrepancy in models of science is not serious for two reasons. First, recent philosophy of science stands in the empirical tradition, so it is not surprising that there are areas of agreement between it and the work of the previous generation. Secondly, perhaps a more precise way of making the same point, the strongly empiricist philosophy of science of the previous generation concentrated on the internal structure of scientific theories, often, moreover, on the structure of the relatively empirical layers of theories. Recent philosophy of science has shifted attention to an overall characterisation of the nature of scientific theory, without having to disagree with all of the detailed analyses of the previous generation. We can expect, for example, to find in Hempel much that is still interesting and sound on explanation.

Writers in the philosophy of social science should be self-conscious about the nature of the philosophy being undertaken and the status of the claims being made. To say that this is a work in the philosophy of social science is in a sense ambiguous, because there are two kinds of philosophy that are relevant to social science. The first might be called 'methodology', by which I mean what typically falls under the heading of the philosophy of science: namely, reflection on the structure and methods, whether of construction or of validation, of scientific theories in general. For many purposes, methodological reflection can be thought of as second-order, in that most scientists need not engage in it during their scientific work. This may not be the case, however, with natural sciences at the frontiers of research, where, for example, the nature of experimentation and of theory and the aims of explanations may become live issues. It certainly is not the case with social science, which has always been subject to methodological controversy. This work presupposes the relevance of methodology to social science, in the sense that the outcome of methodological debate will substantively affect the conduct of social science. But the very methodology whose relevance to social study I support, the natural scientific one, sets limits to the implications that methodological controversy carries for social scientific conduct. It is characteristic of natural scientific methodology that it is sensitive to the boundaries between methodology and substantive scientific theory, and that it invokes those boundaries in order to dissolve what have been thought to be methodological issues. This is a strategy I will follow at times.

Methodology has always to state whether it is prescriptive or descriptive. Prescriptive methodology lays down standards which scientists are enjoined to follow. Descriptive methodology sets out the methodology adopted by successful science. A satisfactory methodology must, in fact, be both prescriptive and descriptive. This can be achieved by constructing a methodology which plausibly claims to exhibit the structure of successful science, and which then draws the reasonable conclusion that if science wishes success in future, it must continue to follow the methodology in question. Such an approach to methodology, then, rests on views about the history of the area of reasoning being investigated, views which can be supported only by the use of realistic examples. Part of my reluctance to make categorical claims about background philosophies of science stems from the fact that I am not able to make informed judgments about the structure exhibited by successful natural science.

A separate issue is the place of idealised prescriptions *within* the overall descriptive-and-prescriptive methodology described in the last paragraph. A methodology advocating prescriptions about scientific reasoning based on an analysis of the history of science may or may not decide that scientific reasoning is governed by norms, which, though unattainable, still constructively affect scientific conduct. The ideals that scientific theory should be fully formalised and that explanation should be fully deductive are possible examples. This point will recur in chapter one.

Methodology may be ideal-typical in a further sense. If a methodology is derived from judgments about the structure exhibited by the
best examples of scientific reasoning, then inevitably many other
examples of science will not fully replicate that methodology. This
clearly does not render either the methodology or the scientific
examples worthless. We will simply have a basis for suggesting
improvements in scientific reasoning. Many social scientific studies,
for example, are based on a mixture of assumptions from very different
theories, which – if my theoretical holism is adopted – must yield
confusion, not light. Similarly, at a higher level, many social scientific
works adopt a pernicious jumble of naturalistic and non-naturalistic
methodological approaches.

These senses in which a methodology may be idealised must be
distinguished from certain idealisations about social science's subject
matter, within which I develop the argument in chapters one and two
and which are parochial to my study. These idealisations are best
justified when I make them, but their basic point is to allow me to
discuss issues in the philosophy of social science in abstraction from a
full consideration of the problems of meaning and value, which I
broach in their entirety in chapters three and four. The problems in the
philosophy of social science are notoriously likely to become confused
with one another; the idealisations I make will, I hope, help in keeping
apart distinctive problems.

The second kind of philosophy relevant to the philosophy of social
science studies, not elements common to all scientific theories, but
features of a specific theory that differentiate it from other theories.
These features include the ontology and metaphysics of a theory. They
are not straightforwardly empirical, because they are part of the basic
conceptual scheme of a scientific theory and are the elements furthest
removed from the empirical constraint on the theory. But the
philosophical elements are not irrelevant to the lower level elements of
a scientific theory. On the contrary, a theory's philosophy structures
the development of that theory, not least because the meanings of the
philosophical terms partly determine the meanings of the lower level
terms. That will be one argument which I will defend when I write
about values; another will be that the philosophy of a social scientific
theory is inevitably evaluative.

Logical connections might be found between the actual forms of the
first type of philosophy (the 'methodology') and of the second (the
'metaphysics') assumed by a specific scientific theory. For instance, the
change from one scientific theory to another might involve a change in
ontology so profound that a change in method (for example, from
deductive to inductive) is also required. Whether or not science has

11

ever experienced a methodological-cum-metaphysical shift, however, such changes must be very rare. For in talking about shifts in methodology, we mean changes in the forms of scientific reasoning: not just a replacement of a preferred model of explanation (e.g. the mechanical one), which is a matter of the types of entities and relations satisfactory explanations should refer to (i.e. ultimately a matter of ontology), but a shift in what it is to be a scientific explanation as such. If science has any general demarcating features, they would be found in its methodology; so there are limits to the extent we could change our methodology while at the same time continuing to do science.

The view that science has a metaphysical layer is a thesis within methodology. It is a thesis usually adopted by post-empiricist philosophy of science; and, in my opinion, philosophers of social science could usefully turn more of their attention to the metaphysics of social science.

I have not maintained the terminological distinction between 'methodology' and 'metaphysics' throughout this book. The context usually makes it clear whether I am discussing the general philosophy of social study or the philosophy of a particular scientific theory. In fact, my discussion of the metaphysical foundations of social scientific theories is concentrated in chapters four and five.

Finally, I must say a word about the examples I use. An important deficiency in much philosophy of social science is the token nature of its examples. An example can convincingly support a methodology's claim to have analysed the structure of successful scientific reasoning only if the example is realistic. Furthermore, appeal to token examples is a more serious fault in the philosophy of social science than in the philosophy of natural science, because the outcome of the philosophical debate (in both senses of 'philosophy') is likely to affect the substantive conduct of social science. But philosophers must first forgo the luxury of token examples, if they are to capitalise on the opportunity to be taken seriously by social scientists. I have tried to exemplify my arguments with more realistic social scientific examples than is usual in the philosophy of social science. (I intend, of course, to study only their formal properties, without committing myself to their theoretical or empirical adequacy.) I am nevertheless aware that the philosophy of social science cannot rest content with the kind of examples I give. A satisfactory philosophy of social science should be developed in conjunction with the study in depth of either a period in the history of social science or an area of social scientific work, in order to test conclusions reached on the philosophical level against actual social scientific practice. But that would be a project additional to the one I have undertaken here.

1

Complexity and social science

1.1. COMPLEXITY

In this chapter, I discuss some problems which provide no grounds for a philosophical distinction between natural and social science. In order to do this, I abstract throughout from two areas which pose serious, though not fatal, philosophical problems for the project of a scientific social science: the fact that the subjects of social science have meaning-ful theories about themselves and the role of value judgments in social science. I discuss these topics in the subsequent chapters.

Thinking in terms of the idealisations I have just proposed inevitably involves using an unrealistic picture of any actual area of social scien-tific work, given the way the social world in fact is. But my aim in this chapter is to dispose of certain problems irrelevant to the philosophical comparison of natural and social science, not to describe social science. Further, we can imagine a society where such an apparently unrealistic social science would be at home: a society where there are no major moral disagreements and where the actors' classificatory system (at least in the social area under investigation) is sufficiently explicitly defined and sufficiently uncontroversial for the actors to be unanimous in their classification of the items under study by the social scientist. Social investigation in a small isolated community or under Soviet Russian conditions may not be greatly misrepresented by these ideal-isations. Moreover, the 'end-of-ideology' theorists claimed to detect precisely such an emerging consensus in Western industrialised societies in the 1950s as a background for the demise of political philosophy and the possibility of political science. Similarly, though with the opposite overtones, Goldmann in *The Human Sciences and Philosophy* envisages the possibility of the closure of moral debate under the conditions of advanced capitalism.

For my abstraction from problems of meaning and value to work, the social scientist would have to be a member of the society under study. But his social investigations would not thereby be redundant. For we need not suppose that our ideally harmonious social actors are also ideally self-conscious about the social conditions and consequences of their actions. The social scientist (still thinking in terms of the agreed concepts and from the basis of the agreed values) may investigate, in Popper's phrase, the unintended consequences of the actors' actions, as well as the actions' social preconditions; he may also formulate relatively empirical generalisations about these conditions and consequences, which may be substantiated by being strictly tested in a variety of situations or by being derived from a confirmed and suggestive theory; and, on such a basis, he may predict what the actors would do either in basically similar or in superficially very dissimilar circumstances, depending on whether or not his empirical generalisations are supported by a theory. Such, at least, is what I will argue.

The philosophical problems which this chapter treats, then, are grouped under the headings 'empirical generalisations', 'theory' and 'prediction'. My claim that they are irrelevant for a philosophical distinction between natural and social science is just that no philosophical argument can establish that social science may not meet the toughest demands of the philosophy of science on these points; there are no *a priori* objections to social science developing in a naturalistic direction, if social scientists so desire it. Repeatedly, my argument reaches the philosophical dead-end marked by the conclusion that only the future will reveal whether social science will in fact develop along lines set out by naturalistic models.

I should indicate how I intend to differentiate problems of complexity from those problems, especially of meaning, with which I am not now dealing. Take, for example, MacIntyre's (1972) arguments about the limitations of generalisations and predictions in social science. MacIntyre holds that, since the actors' beliefs are partly constitutive of their practices and institutions:

we cannot ever identify a determinate set of factors which will constitute the initial conditions for the production of some outcome in conformity with a law-like regularity. To claim that we could identify such regularities and such sets of factors would be to claim that we can understand what occurs in politics independently of a knowledge of the beliefs of the agents, for it would be to claim that the beliefs do not play a causal role in political outcomes (p. 22).

In abstracting from considerations of meaning in this chapter, I will consider this claim only if it is interpreted in a contingent, not a logical, sense: that is, only if it is read as the view that actors' beliefs may introduce a complicating factor into social investigation – and perhaps as intractable factor, as some have argued of reflexive predictions – but not a factor of a different kind to other putative complicating factors (e.g. the historical nature of social institutions). The issue then becomes whether there are complexities in the social scientific subject matter profound enough to sustain anti-naturalism.

'Complexity' is my topic because this term best encapsulates those problems (other than those associated with questions of meaning and value – I will not make this qualification again) which have been held to face the establishment, testing and development of social scientific theories. The spectre of the complex nature of the data runs through J. S. Mill's discussion of the human sciences in *A System of Logic*. Mill's conception of this complexity depends on his notion of the 'Plurality of Causes', the multitude of causal factors acting upon any social object. Mill argues that social phenomena conform to fixed laws, but that there is

no hope that these laws, though our knowledge of them were as certain and as complete as it is in astronomy, would enable us to predict the history of society, like that of the celestial appearances, for thousands of years to come. But the differences of certainty is not in the laws themselves, it is in the data to which these laws are to be applied (1865, p. 461).

For, unlike the situation in astronomy, the circumstances determining social phenomena are innumerable and constantly changing. True, the relevant factors change according to causal laws, but the operative causes are too many for their consequences to be precisely calculated. Mill applies this general problem of complexity in social scientific data to each of his direct inductive canons of observation and experiment, since it is not possible that 'effects which depend on a complication of causes can be made the subject of a true induction by observation and experiment' (p. 466). Thus, the relevant factors in social scientific studies are too numerous to be ascertained and noted, and in any case too rapidly in flux to provide the necessary stable conditions for experimentation and for the separation of causes from contingently accompanying factors.

The problem of complexity recurs in more recent writings on social science. For example, Hesse (1972) in presenting her learning machine model of science writes that:

we know what some of the conditions of successful learning are. There must be sufficient possibility of detailed *test* to reinforce correct learning; the environment must be sufficiently stable for the self-corrective learning process to *converge*; and there must not be such strong action by the machine on the environment that either it exhibits no convergence, or what it learns is just an artefact of the machine itself (p. 289).

She argues that the last condition cannot be fulfilled by a study that involves strong reciprocal interaction between the student and the studied, as is encouraged by hermeneutics, and – more importantly for our present purpose – that the social world may as a matter of fact be too complex for the first two conditions to be satisfied.

Similarly, Homans (1967) holds that social science's subject matter is intractable on two grounds. First, it is neither suitable for precise, quantitative treatment, as is physics, nor sufficiently integrated for the all-or-nothing conditional statements of, say, physiology (e.g. the kidneys are necessary for the body to function). Secondly, social scientific objects are historically determined in a pervasive and radical manner. It is not that there are many variables in social science, but that the variables are instantiated in large numbers of people and groups, each with their own history, thus producing complex and specific configurations.

So, in talking about complexity, I mean the problems of deciding which factors are causally relevant and which irrelevant to a certain outcome in the social world. These problems are endemic in social science, so it is held, because: of the difficulties of observing the phenomenon under study in an environment that is relatively isolated from the complicating effects of other potentially causally relevant factors; the phenomenon and causal conditions that we are interested in are changing constantly as a result of interaction with all the other causal factors in the social environment; one of these complicating causal agents is the beliefs of the actors themselves, which, in an apparently particularly vicious situation, may be (causally efficacious) beliefs about the study of them being pursued by the social scientist.[1] A radical conclusion from these points is that the possibility of either isolating or knowing that we have isolated relevantly identical instances of a social object under study is so limited that all social phenomena must be considered unique, thus precluding any social scientific generalisations. More cautiously, it is concluded that social scientific generalisations will always be vague, imprecise, non-universal, etc., and that they will always be *de facto*, rather than *de jure*, because (given the changing environment) they will never be more than summations of past observations. This is what I take the problem of complexity in social science to be. I am not going to indulge in a discussion of whether social science is more 'complex' than physics in some intuitive sense of the word. Such discussions, like those of comparative 'easiness', are excuses for garrulous statements of personal prejudices. Nor am I trying to set up a criterion of when something is a science in terms of its number, nature or subject matter of laws and theories (a project which Morgenbesser [1972] shows to be

---

[1] I will deal with the fact that actors may have beliefs about the study, experiment or prediction in which they feature–in short, the problem of 'reflexivity'–in section 1.4.

fruitless). I wish to demonstrate only that if these problems of complexity exist, they are not philosophical ones.

1.2. EMPIRICAL GENERALISATIONS

We can discuss empirical generalisations in social science independently of the question of the content of these generalisations. Even Runciman (1970), who adheres to a strong psychologism and who therefore says that there are no genuine social scientific laws, allows that there is 'no reason why sociologists, anthropologists and historians should be inhibited from large descriptive generalisations about social systems and their constituents' (p. 43). Runciman further holds that correlations of the form 'whenever X, then Y' discovered by social scientists might be termed laws 'in a loose sense', if it is the case both 'that the connection between X and Y is causal and also that this connection can be fairly precisely formulated' (p. 12). Runciman's first concession concerning 'descriptive generalisations' is sufficient for my present purpose, since these are what I mean by 'empirical generalisations'. His second point about 'laws' requires a discussion of theories in social science, which I attempt in the next section, because the surest and simplest way to adjudge that X and Y are causally related is if the statement connecting them can be derived from an acceptable theory.

The short answer to the question whether the existence of complicating factors precludes the possibility of satisfactory empirical social scientific generalisations is that the question is misconceived. It is only in the light of attempts to state generalisations and in the light of revisions of those attempts because of adverse evidence, that we decide what is and what is not a complicating factor. This point can be supported in two ways, the first of which is the standard argument in the literature.

The argument from complexity holds that social science finds it difficult to create or observe similar conditions and that, partly in consequence, it cannot isolate causally relevant from causally irrelevant factors. Against this view, Popper urges in *The Poverty of Historicism* that what count as experiments on or observations of similar conditions (and hence as the study of phenomena sufficiently isolated from complicating factors) is not decidable *a priori*, but is itself the result of experiment and observation. Experiment and observation tell us whether the position of the planets is a relevant factor in a physical experiment, just as they could tell us whether the exact number of glances exchanged in a psychological experiment affects the outcome of that experiment. Only in attempting to generalise about our phenomena will we be able to say whether two superficially dissimilar phenomena are in fact instances of the same generalisation produced in different initial conditions. Wide differences in the manifest characteristics and behaviour of a group of phenomena do not exclude there being a common set of variables that underlie and can be used to explain all the phenomena; to think otherwise is to make the cardinal confusion of generalisations with initial conditions (see Nagel, 1961, p. 462).

This confusion, together with the fallacy that two items have to be identical in all respects for them to be classified by the same term, results in Neurath's (1962, p. 26) claim that we cannot generalise about nor could we have predicted the Nazi persecution of the Jews, because no other persecution has reached such dimensions. In fact, the Nazi persecution of the Jews and, say, the European witch-craze cannot be deemed either absolutely similar or absolutely dissimilar. In certain respects (e.g. the latter was concentrated within short periods and specific localities, while the former was more systematic and diffuse), they are different. But simply *qua* instances of persecution, they could be classed together. More theoretically, they might both be partly explained as scapegoating reactions to economic malaise. Further investigations might also lead to the conclusion that, as a matter of fact, one (but not the other) could not be so explained, so that they would be judged different in this respect.

Those who think that the manifest dissimilarity of social objects represents a pernicious problem of complexity for social science commit the deep mistake of strong empiricism. Language and concepts mirror the world in a direct way, they assume, and since the social world is highly varied, the language of social analysis must itself be too varied for scientific purposes. But they forget that how we conceptualise the world depends on our theoretical interests. Take the concept of the firm. On one view, that firms are profit-maximising, the concept of the firm covers most multi-national corporations and corner shops, but not some nationalised industries (see Lipsey, 1974, pp. 204–6). On another view, that the firm in advanced capitalist society is a giant, highly integrated and technologically advanced economic institution, the concept of the firm covers most multi-national corporations and nationalised industries, but not corner shops (see Miliband, 1977, ch. 1). Are multi-national corporations more like nationalised industries than corner shops? Which concept of the firm is more useful for understanding society? These questions cannot be approached through naive gazes at the social world. They are meaningless unless we consider the different theories of the firm sustained by the different concepts.

We organise our social investigations, therefore, into similar and dissimilar explananda and explanantia and into relevant and irrelevant factors at least in part on the basis of, first, what features we are interested in studying, secondly, the presuppositions (whether theoretical or empirical) we bring to the study, and, thirdly, the revisions that our studies force on these presuppositions. Insofar as the critique of the project of separating out the complicating factors is based on Mill's canons, we can argue that they are too rigid and artificial for the empirical investigation of even natural scientific objects. Further, they 'presuppose what they do not supply, such rules as will help us to discern relevant and irrelevant points of contrast, guiding concepts which will organise our experience for us and make it amenable to causal explanation' (Ryan, 1970a, pp. 139–40).

These direct arguments can be reinforced by some fundamental considerations from the philosophy of language which relate our judgments of similarity to the laws we hold and thereby to our judgments of causal relevance. In *The Structure of Scientific Inference*, Hesse argues that the terms of a language are applied not only on the basis of observed similarities between the instances of the terms, but also on the basis of lawlike statements that are considered to hold of the terms' referents by the relevant language community:

As learning of the language proceeds, it is found that some of these predicates enter into general statements which are accepted as true and which we will call *laws*: 'Balls are round'; 'In summer leaves are green'; 'Eating unripe apples leads to stomachache' . . . Making explicit these general laws is only a continuation and extension of the process already described as identifying and reidentifying proper occasions for the use of a predicate by means of physical similarity. For knowledge of the laws will now enable the language user to apply descriptions correctly in situations other than those in which he learned them, and even in situations where nobody could have learned them in the absence of the laws, for example, 'stomachache' of an absent individual known to have consumed a basketful of unripe apples, or even 'composed of diatomic molecules' of the oxygen in the atmosphere (pp. 14–15).

In cases of conflict between the law-based application of a predicate and the similarity-based application of the same, we may, depending on the overall convenience and coherence of our system of laws, either retract the law's application to a sub-set of instances more closely related by similarities or extend the range of application of the predicate so that it conforms with our law-based knowledge. Hesse's example of the first type of revision is that of the retraction of the application of 'element' away from water, and of the second type that of the extension of 'mammal' to whales.

I do not need to take a position on the fundamental issue that distinguishes Hesse's and Goodman's views on similarity. In 'Seven

Strictures on Similarity', Goodman writes that a philosophical scrutiny of similarity leads either to its disappearance as a useful philosophical term or to the conclusion that it is explained by the very features it purports to explain (e.g. the possibility of predictions and inductive reasoning). Hesse, in contrast, sees a necessary role for recognition of primitive similarity: for example, judgments of similarity cannot be wholly dependent on what generalisations we hold, because recognition of primitive similarity is required to decide what counts as the next instance of a generalisation. The argument I have given against ruling out social scientific generalisations on the ground that social phenomena are not sufficiently similar, to the effect that what we judge to be similar depends on what social scientific generalisations we are considering, not vice versa, is powerful even if we accept only Hesse's limited critique of similarity. Moreover, it does all the work we require of it, if we conjoin the limited critique of similarity with the plausible claim that the important social phenomena (e.g. kinship structures, states, exercises of power, classes, etc.) are not the kind whose instances are reidentified mainly on the basis of primitive similarity, so little of substance can be learnt by social science from considerations of pre-theoretical similarity.

A more detailed study of generalisations is required, however, in order to show that they provide no ground for a distinction of type between natural and social science. My argument to this conclusion involves four claims: it is proper and sensible to espouse a naturalistic model of the nature and usages of a sound empirical generalisation; much social scientific investigation comprises the increasing approximation to this model; whether or not social science will approximate this model to a satisfactory degree is something that the future will decide; and in certain contexts and for certain purposes further approximation to this model is not required even for a naturalistic social science.

Natural science provides social science with an ideal model of an empirical generalisation as maximally universal, general and precise. These ideal demands can be justified by noting that the more a generalisation is universal, general and precise, the more it tells us about the world and the more easily it may be tested. The ideal of universality implies that the generalisations of social science should be of the form '*All* X are Y', not of the statistical form '$p\%$ of X are Y'. The ideal of generality states that a social scientific generalisation is better the larger number of types of social entities it applies to. The ideal of precision encompasses a number of demands, two of the more important being that the statements of relations between social factors should be in quantitative terms and that the terms used should not be vague. One source of vagueness may be that a term is used without a precise demarcation of boundaries along some dimension (e.g. age, number of inhabitants, income), so in studying, say, violence in cities, we may not be clear as to how a city is defined in terms of number of inhabitants. Another type of vagueness is the usage of a term that has a number of independent criteria of application: 'religion' can be given at least nine plausible conditions of application and most students of religion would be vague about what combination of conditions they considered necessary and sufficient for the application of the term (see Alston, 1964, pp. 87–8, and Achinstein, 1968, pp. 195–6).

Lessnoff (1974, ch. 3) is correct when he argues, first, that many social scientific generalisations are only loosely or implicitly quantitative (e.g. 'In industrial societies consumers' pressure-groups are never as effectively organised as some producers' pressure-groups'); secondly, that some social scientific generalisations lack both generality and universality (e.g. 'In contemporary Britain most trade unionists vote Labour'); and, thirdly, that in the statement of social scientific generalisations, generality, universality and precision are often *competing* ideals.

The kinds of problems faced in formulating generalisations in social science are indicated by Scriven (1959) in his critique of Hempel's account of historical explanation. Scriven writes that the generalisation adduced in explanation of a certain risky decision made by Cortes will either be adequate on Hempel's model but false (e.g. 'All confident wealth-seeking people undertake any venture which offers wealth') or be true but trivially formulated to cover the case in question and therefore inadequate on the grounds of generality (e.g. 'All confident people with Cortes's background of experience, seeking very great wealth, undertake any venture involving the hazards of this one, which offers very great wealth'). On this basis, Scriven argues a plausible case about the nature of the generalisations in fact used in historical explanation, depicting them as very different from the ideal scientific model. These generalisations are often hybrid, containing some universal and some statistical features, and they are sometimes truisms. But what they crucially share is 'a *selective immunity* to apparent counter-examples' (p. 464). That is, they state 'that *everything* falls into a certain category *except* those to which *certain special conditions apply*' (p. 466). They cannot be turned into unproblematic generalisations by listing the exceptions, because the exceptions are numerous and complex.

Scriven's analysis perhaps describes how historical explanations proceed at present. In the light of recent work on the role of *ad hoc* hypotheses in science, it may apply to all science. Moreover, it clashes

21

with an account of social scientific explanation-procedures as an increasing (if perhaps endless) approximation to Hempel's model only if Scriven argues (which he doesn't) that it is typically not a desideratum of historical explanation that we should be able to list as many of the required generalisations as precisely, generally and universally as possible. This latter suggestion is plausible only if we are explaining events and actions (e.g. the spilt ink-bottle staining the carpet) where refinement of our truism-based explanation adds nothing to our understanding of the explanandum, because we are certain that the explanandum falls within the scope of the covering truism. But if we are trying to explain, say, the putative fact that science develops more rapidly in democratic countries, the covering laws are not part of a common stock of truisms. They have to be formulated, tested and refined. Any other procedure is likely to result in writers offering their prejudices and preconceptions as explanations.

Thus, while the points made by Lessnoff and Scriven may illuminate the contemporary state of social science, they establish nothing about philosophical limitations on social science changing in the direction of the naturalistic model. No doubt, they point to the practical problems of social study: for example, in identifying the relevant variables and thereby eradicating the complicating inessentials in a social phenomenon (e.g. do we consider area of origin of subjects, as well as their class status, to be a significant variable in experiments on greeting habits in Paddington Station?); in reproducing conditions which by any standards are sufficiently similar for controlled observation (e.g. in anthropology and the history of ideas many facets of the social context may be relevant conditions); and in deciding just what are the generalisable elements in a given 'unique' situation (e.g. this point underlies the difficulty of experiments in Freudian psychology). But no one would want to doubt that social science has difficult practical problems in these areas. What those who wish to use the complexity of the social world to distinguish in principle between natural and social science have to show is that the programme of steadily sorting out the complicating factors is necessarily destined for failure.

It would be reasonable to agree that there are no philosophical barriers to a naturalistic social science, but to conclude that the practical difficulties are 'far more formidable than many mainstream social scientists realise' (Bernstein, 1976, p. 42) or to conjecture that the social scientific subject matter may in fact be too complex in some absolute sense for a naturalistic programme to succeed (see Hesse, 1972, p. 289). What conclusion one reaches here is fundamental to whether one pursues a naturalistic or non-naturalistic methodology. This issue cannot be demonstratively settled one way or the other. Its answer

immediate and long-term psychological damage caused by maternal deprivation in early infancy (see Ainsworth [1971] for the results of recent research). The shortest (i.e. most imprecise, though also most general) statement of Bowlby's conclusions could be formulated as follows: maternal depravation in early childhood tends to affect adversely the development of children, and the extent and irreversibility of the adverse effects are directly correlated with the length of deprivation. This statement has received continuous corroboration from such studies as: direct comparison of deprived and non-deprived groups, the non-deprived groups being selected to resemble the deprived groups in such features as class background as closely as possible; historical research into the family histories of adolescents and adults with certain sorts of behavioural problems; follow-up studies of maternally deprived children; and experimental studies on the behaviour of maternally deprived animals. This summary statement has also been made increasingly precise by the researches of Bowlby and others; or, to put it differently, the complex nature of the activities subsumed under the basic statement of the maternal deprivation hypothesis has been progressively broken down, so what factors are relevant and what relevance they have are now much clearer. I will give one example of this progressive precision in results.

The notion of 'maternal deprivation' has been split into three types: type (*a*), gross discontinuity in the mother–child relationship (e.g. mother or child in hospital); type (*b*), insufficient interaction between mother and child (e.g. mother at work or mother with many children); type (*c*), 'bad' mother (e.g. mother gives contradictory signals to the child). It is now recognised that Bowlby's original work concentrated on type (*a*) deprivation to the neglect of types (*b*) and (*c*). Yet type (*a*) deprivation does not necessarily imply type (*b*) deprivation because of the possibility of substitute mothers. Recent research has also suggested that 'anti-social' activities, especially juvenile delinquency, are to be correlated with type (*c*) deprivation, rather than with types (*a*) and (*b*). More precisely again, type (*c*) deprivation has been analysed into three further categories with which three types of anti-social activities are correlated: (i) rejection by parents tends to unsocialised aggression; (ii) neglect by parents tends to socialised delinquency; (iii) repressive environment tends to neurosis. On this basis, it was concluded that Bowlby's original conjecture about the intensities of type (*a*) deprivation – namely, that partial type (*a*) deprivation produces anti-social activities (e.g. stealing) and complete type (*a*) deprivation produces asocial activities (e.g. withdrawal) – had to be modified. Further examples of the more precise statements of different effects following on different ages and lengths of maternal deprivation could be cited. They would show that reduction in the complexity of the subject matter and increasing precision in the statement of results are effects of careful research. Clearly, many of the notions used require still greater refinement. It would also be utopian to envisage a time when the correlations postulated would be universal, rather than statistical in form. These points preclude any complacency about the present state of social science. But neither is there reason for despair about social science's ability to approximate increasingly the ideal scientific models, even if it never attains them.

Finally, let us look at the most radical conclusion that can be drawn from the complexity argument: that the impossibility of either isolating or knowing that we have isolated relevantly identical instances of a social object under study means that all social phenomena must be considered unique, thus precluding any social scientific generalisations. Everything I have said so far is neutral as to whether social science is 'idiographic' or 'nomothetic', if that distinction is taken to indicate a difference between studies which are primarily concerned, on the one hand, with the understanding of individual phenomena or, on the other, with the formulation of systems of laws. Runciman's point in *Sociology in its Place* that the idiographic–nomothetic distinction is an *intra*-disciplinary one is correct: studies in both physics and sociology can have as their prime concern the investigation of either an individual phenomenon or a generalisation. The distinction is also a relative one in that no single object, in physics or social science, could be exhaustively explained, if an exhaustive account required the complete explanation of *all* the characteristics manifested by the object (see Hempel, 1959, p. 346, and Weber, 1949, p. 169).

Nevertheless, there may be a loose sense in which readers and writers of social science have a special interest in the 'irrational realm of unique individuality' (Popper, 1952, p. 245), simply because they are concerned with *human* phenomena. Typical contributions such as anthropological surveys of individual societies or Goffman's (1973) case study of a single American mental hospital indicate this interest. But the point remains that the naturalistic way of understanding the individual case is to describe it so that it is covered by generalised statements. Weber recognised this in arguing that, though the goal of social science is 'knowledge of an historical phenomenon, meaning by historical: significant in its individuality' (1949, p. 78), laws are required as means to this end, if not as an end in themselves.

There may be other ways of studying and understanding the unique case. One of the fundamental differences which Habermas draws between naturalistic and hermeneutic methodology is that the basic direction of thought in the former is from the particular to the abstract, while this direction is reversed in the latter (1972, pp. 162ff. and 263ff.). As I said in the Introduction, I am concerned neither to compare naturalistic and non-naturalistic methodology, nor to comment directly on non-naturalistic methodology.

If it were alleged that it is impossible to describe a 'unique' social object in such a way that it is covered by generalised statements, we could repeat our critique of the arguments from complexity and similarity of conditions, and our defence of the possibility of social scientific generalisations. It is only in the light of social investigation that we decide which aspects of a phenomenon are 'unique' and which aspects fall under variables and generalisations we are interested in. The notion of uniqueness cannot be invoked to ban social scientific investigation. Further, even if the picture of explaining all aspects of an object is an unrealisable ideal in social science (as it is in physics), it is a picture which can regulate social scientific work. The explanation of a single object can gradually be made more comprehensive. The tentative production of generalised statements and variables from the study of 'unique' phenomena is one aspect of current social scientific work. Goffman's study of a single mental hospital in *Asylums* leads directly to generalisations involving the variable 'mental hospital', and more interestingly to generalisations incorporating the more general variable 'total institution', which has mental hospitals as only one of its many kinds of instances, together with, for example, prisons, monasteries, boarding schools and army barracks.

These points apply even if we are trying to understand those most unique entities, people, and even if our approach is based on a strong assertion of the importance of individuals. Whyte opens *Street Corner Society* with the credo: 'In this exploration of Cornerville we shall be little concerned with people in general. We shall encounter particular people and observe the particular things that they do' (p. xix). Whyte's book is full of generalised conclusions arising out of the study of individuals, however. For example, he suggests many hypotheses about the behaviour of individuals in general social positions such as gang leaders and one of his basic conclusions is that Cornerville suffers not from a lack of organisation, but from an organisation which does not mesh with wider social structures. The work is not idiographic in any interesting philosophical sense. Rather, it adopts a distinctive theoretical perspective, in which the social positions adopted by individuals are important; Whyte theorises social structure in terms of the interaction of individuals, as is clear from passages such as: 'The stable composition of the group and the lack of social assurance on the part of its members contribute toward producing a very high rate of social interaction within the group. The group structure is a product of these interactions' (p. 256).

Sometimes the idea that social objects are unique is made dependent on the idea that they are constantly changing. The historical nature of social objects may be held damaging to the possibility of social scientific generalisations on two grounds. First, the point, after all, is not that social objects change, but that they change rapidly and continuously. Even if this claim is true, the threat it purports to present to social generalisations is one we have already argued to be philosophically empty. For rapid and continuous change is not even *prima facie* recalcitrant to scientific study unless the change is produced by or is composed of a multitude of factors. Under this interpretation, then, the argument from history is just another form of the main argument from complexity.

Secondly, it may be argued that a social scientific theory must represent the social situation of its time, but since society is always changing, we are never going to have a general theory of social systems. Marx's and Weber's models of capitalism, for example, were theories of the early, primitive capitalism that they knew, whereas by our time 'the structures and functions of society *have moved beyond the model*' (Lewis, 1975, p. 111). This is an ambiguous and curious idea. Of course, if social systems are the subject matter of social science, then any relevant change in social systems must lead to some change in social scientific accounts. This is another way of saying that social science must pay attention to its data. The strong value dependence of social science, which I discuss in chapter four, may also lead us to expect social scientific theory to be restructured by each generation. But these points have nothing to do with the uniqueness of social phenomena or the impossibility of generalisations. If Marx's and Weber's theories are theories simply of primitive capitalism, then they are deficient from the point of view of generality. Merely to say this, however, is to indicate how their theories can be revised in the direction of greater generality. We can now develop a more general theory of capitalism that encompasses primitive and advanced capitalism.

To summarise briefly this discussion of generalisations, we should note that no philosophical argument shows it to be impossible for social science increasingly to approximate the ideal model of an empirical generalisation as maximally universal, general and precise. Certainly, it is neither possible nor desirable from the point of view of furthering scientific knowledge that social scientific statements should fully satisfy all three desiderata all of the time. This can be established even without invoking the true point that universality, generality and precision are often competing ideals. Maximum universality and generality might in principle be attained, but it would not always be desirable to do so. Universality requires that our generalisations are not statistical. The centrality of statistical laws in many physical theories suggests that the universality of generalisations is not a necessary condition of a scientific theory. Whether or not there is some reason for concluding that social scientific generalisations must be of statistical form, attaining universal generalisations will nevertheless continue as a methodological ideal for social science. How general our statements should be depends on what level of scientific theory they are intended for. If we wish to talk about children who have suffered maternal deprivation of a certain type, at a given age and for a stated length of time, then our statements about them will be less general than if we wish to talk about children who have suffered maternal deprivation as such. But clearly there is a place for statements of the former kind in scientific theories of maternal deprivation. I have tried to refute arguments for the claim that social science must remain at a low level of generality, and my defence of the possibility of theory in social science will also be implicitly directed to this issue. Finally, precision is an ideal that is not absolutely attainable, since there may always be demands for further clarification of concepts or greater accuracy of measurements. But this is a point common to all scientific work, and the impossibility of social scientific statements either being made increasingly precise or being sufficiently precise for the purposes of the investigation at hand has not been established.

1.3. THEORIES

Arguments from complexity in social science have usually been directed against the possibility of satisfactory *empirical* generalisations and against the ability to pursue an inductivist methodology. They have not been central to the debate about whether theories are possible in social science. This is not surprising, because the notion of complexity is ultimately about the complexity of the social world itself. Hence, this notion is particularly problematic for statements such as empirical generalisations that purport to correspond with the world in a fairly direct way, and for a methodology that wishes to construct more general scientific statements out of low level statements about the world. Methodologies that emphasise the prior role of theoretical over empirical statements in a science – holding, for example, that theoretical statements are basic to the scientific aims of the unification of knowledge, explanation and prediction – can suggest that we may fortunately light on a more or less true theory, within whose concepts and statements the empirical complexities fall into place; though even a deductivist may be faced with the problems of complexity when it is finally a matter of ascertaining whether the social world is as the low level statements of his theory say it is.

I will not develop this idea here. Rather, I will meet directly the arguments that anti-naturalism puts up against theories in social science. Writers who doubt that social science can achieve satisfactory empirical knowledge also tend to question the role of scientific theories in social science. In this and the next section, then, I am using the issue of complexity as a means to branch out into the discussion of certain philosophical arguments which suggest that social science cannot replicate the structure of a scientific theory.

In talking about theories as opposed to empirical generalisations in social science, I am not committed to the existence of a clear-cut and absolute distinction between theoretical and empirical entities, predicates and statements. It is sufficient for my purpose to accept a relative analysis of the empirical or the factual, whereby, within the context of a scientific theory, factual statements are lower level statements, with little systematic import for other statements in the theory, closer to the observational constraint and hence more likely to be revised in the face of recalcitrant experience. Given recent critiques of the theory–fact distinction, we can hold that some statements are more factual than others, and even this only within the context of particular scientific theories.

What I must maintain if this discussion is to have a point is that – even given a relative theory–fact distinction – the theoretical items have different functions from the factual items. Writers on social science have been alive to the new possibilities brought to a domain by theoretical statements. These possibilities may summarily be divided into two kinds.

First, theories bring the possibility of more powerful explanations. In *The Nature of Social Science*, Homans argues strongly that social science no longer needs to prove itself in the discovery of empirical facts and correlations, but rather to engage in the enterprise of explaining these discoveries, thereby demonstrating their significance, through their derivation from systematic theory; though I shall later criticise Homans's account of what that systematic theory should be. Grounding empirical generalisations of human behaviour in theory is the main way of showing them to be statements of causal relations and of distinguishing *de facto* trends from scientific laws.

Secondly, theories unify our knowledge. They do so in the course of fulfilling their first function of explanation, for it is the role of theories to provide the explanation of a whole range of empirical explananda. This is one point behind Wright Mill's claim in *The Sociological Imagina-*

tion that no amount of minute 'abstracted empiricist' studies of small-scale milieux can combine to create a sociological theory. In unifying our knowledge, theories extend the significance of empirical results and facilitate more fruitful research.

With few exceptions, the need for the theoretical organisation of social scientific results is acknowledged. I exclude from the exceptions writers such as Merton (1964) who argue that for the immediate future social science must be content with laws of the 'middle range'. I exclude them because they have no objection in principle to theories in social science, but hold that it is bad policy to rush the postulation of social scientific theories. But included in the exceptions must be those (for example, the post-Wittgensteinians and adherents of hermeneutics) who argue that naturalistic theories must use criteria of the identity of actions other than those used by the agents of those actions, but that, since agents' meanings define the subject matter of social study, naturalistic theories necessarily suggest inadequate accounts of the agents' actions. Such views, which depend on a philosophical view about meaning in social science, will be studied in chapters two and three.

Well, are there theories in social science? This question should be taken in two parts. First, are there theoretical terms purporting to denote (relatively) unobservable entities in social science? There are two kinds of answer to this question, both of which are affirmative, but only one of which is helpful.

The first – unhelpful – answer is that of the methodological individualist. Popper argues in *The Poverty of Historicism* that most social scientific concepts, even that of a war, are theoretical constructions used to interpret our experience, in that they 'are the results of constructing certain *models* (especially of institutions), in order to explain certain experiences' (p. 135). This answer is unhelpful in at least two ways. First, any plausibility in the individualist's claim that concepts such as 'society', 'group', 'class', etc. are theoretical concepts comes from thinking about the role of these concepts exclusively in social scientific contexts, while ignoring their place in everyday thought. Clearly, there is sense in saying that 'society' as used by certain social theorists is a (relatively) theoretical term, given that it is embodied in some explicit system of laws (e.g. 'All societies are stratified') which partly determines its criteria of application. But in terms of being embodied in an explicit system of laws, 'society' as used by ordinary actors is not theoretical, though it certainly has vague and implicit constraints on how it is applied in everyday speech. That is, in certain contexts and depending on our definitions of 'theoretical', both individualist and non-individualist concepts are theoretical; in other contexts, neither are. For example, if our notion of the theoretical depends on an item finding a place in a hierarchically structured cognitive system, then concepts used in everyday contexts, whether individualist or non-individualist, are likely to be relatively untheoretical.

Secondly, the individualist's claim rests fundamentally on the contention that no statements involving social concepts are directly testable. This claim is false if we interpret it to mean that only physical behaviours, not social actions, are observable. We can observe someone cashing a cheque just as directly as we can observe a human being passing a piece of paper across a block of painted wood, etc. True, we need to know certain social rules in order to observe a cashing-action but this is just like knowing what counts as a physical object against the background of a specific natural scientific theory. The claim is also false if we take it to mean that individuals' actions are observable, but the actions and effects of social institutions are not. We can observe a macroscopic social phenomenon without having to observe the whole of it. We could have seen the Vietnamese war by seeing a battle between the Americans and the North Vietnamese, just as we can see a star by seeing an aspect of it. Moreover, for certain purposes we can identify an institution with its parts. That notoriously theoretical entity, the University of Cambridge, can at certain times and for certain purposes be identified with a meeting of the Council of Senate.

The helpful, important affirmative answer to our question involves simply noting that terms such as 'maternal deprivation', 'class', 'anomie', 'alienation', 'ideology' and 'oedipus complex' are theoretical social scientific terms, 'theoretical' here being understood in a relative sense.

The second question to be asked is: does social science possess theories, in the sense of structured systems of statements incorporating these theoretical concepts from which empirical generalisations can be derived and thereby explained? As an example of such a theoretical system, we can take Merton's (1964) reconstruction of Durkheim's explanation of the differential Protestant–Catholic suicide rate, which reads:

1. Social cohesion provides psychic support to group members subjected to acute stresses and anxieties.
2. Suicide rates are functions of *unrelieved* anxieties and stresses to which persons are subjected.
3. Catholics have greater social cohesion than Protestants.
4. Therefore, lower suicide rates should be anticipated among Catholics than among Protestants (p. 97).

Here statement 1 can be considered to be theoretical, statement 4 the empirical explanandum and statements 2 and 3 the bridge statements.

Clearly, empirical indices are required for the concepts of social cohesion, psychological stresses and psychic support, but whether these can be given satisfactorily is a contingent question to be left to research. The theory will also need support that is independent of what it at present explains. But, after all, Durkheim did not use the theoretical term 'social cohesion' only to explain the Protestant–Catholic suicide rates. Besides entering the explanation of other suicide rates (e.g. married–single rates and various occupational rates), it played its part in his theories of the division of labour and the decline of religion. It is not to the point to say, what is certainly true, that Durkheim's sociology is deficient. I instance his work only as an entirely fallible example of a social scientific theory which invokes more than an isolated theoretical statement in order to explain more than a single explanandum.

Certainly, social scientific theories are unlike fully formalised physical theories. But the latter can, as I have argued for empirical generalisations, be taken as an ideal towards which social scientific theory can advance. Brown (1968, pp. 185–6) argues that attempts to construct formal calculi from already existing social scientific theories have been helpful to those theories by revealing their defects, such as the absence of crucial assumptions or of measurable variables. Jarvie (1972, pp. 16–17) suggests that this is the sole purpose of full axiomatisation in any science. An example is Hempel's (1971) formalisation of functionalism which demonstrated the need for the assumption of a finite set of functional equivalents for any item being explained; in this case, however, it is probable that the difficulty posed for the theory is insuperable.

Other examples of mainly non-quantitative, occasionally ambiguous and not fully deductive theories – but theories, all the same – could be given using terms such as 'rules', 'conflict', 'interaction', 'impression-management', 'mode of production' and 'charismatic authority'. But I will illustrate the role of theories in social science in another way. Let us compare the answers of a theoretical social science and a non-theoretical discipline, such as journalism, to the same question. Two social scientists, Young and Willmott (1966), and one of the great journalists, George Orwell (1975, pp. 60–4), try to answer the same question: why do former slum-dwellers not like living in Corporation estates?

Orwell notes that although the physical standards of the estates are far superior to those in the slums, the new inhabitants of the estates complain about the bad conditions of the houses in them. Orwell argues that they are 'rationalising' deeper grievances. One such grievance is that life on the estates is more expensive than life in the slums.

More important, in Orwell's opinion, is the bleak atmosphere of the estates. They are built 'in a ruthlessly inhuman manner' and are 'soulless', with, for example, 'dismal sham-Tudor' pubs. The estates are replete with petty restrictions on such things as the decoration of houses and the keeping of pets, restrictions which witness the fact that, 'owing to the peculiar temper of our time', in order to secure slum-dwellers decent housing 'it is also considered necessary to rob them of the last vestiges of their liberty'.

Orwell pictures the estates as unfriendly, lacking in the slums' human warmth and with a meanly bureaucratic atmosphere. The overall image that Young and Wilmott present is very similar and they also give an account that transcends the actors' self-understanding (this point will be important in chapters two and three). But notice the different way in which Young and Willmott's picture is constructed. Much of their book is devoted to establishing the nature and functions of the strongly mother-centred extended kinship structure of the slums. They argue that a place in such a kinship structure provides one not only with the friendship of its other members, but also with a framework for meeting a wider set of people who are not members of the family. They further suggest that one's acquaintance set is a function of the interrelated factors of the strength of the kinship structure and the length of residence in a place. On this basis, Young and Willmott hypothesise that the key change in moving from the slums to the estates is the break up of the mother-centred kinship structure. This produces loneliness amongst the estates-dwellers, both directly through the loss of family and friends and indirectly through the loss of the framework for meeting people.

Young and Willmott's and Orwell's accounts differ in ways we would expect from our discussion of empirical generalisations. Orwell's version is less precise, more impressionistic, though simultaneously more evocative, both in its use of terms ('sham-Tudor') and in its hints at deeper explanations ('owing to the peculiar temper of our time'). Similarly, Young and Willmott are more concerned to support their thesis with clear empirical evidence: for example, they compare their work on the kinship structure of Bethnal Green with research on slums in other towns. But the difference which bears on the role of theories is that Young and Willmott's analysis depends on a theory of kinship. In place of Orwell's diffuse characterisations ('inhuman', 'soulless'), we receive a precise account of the main factor in the estates-dwellers' discontent, an account which is grounded in the hypothesis that 'the stressing of the mother–daughter tie is a widespread, perhaps universal, phenomenon in the urban areas of all industrial countries, at any rate in the families of manual workers' (p.

196). Young and Willmott enlarge the significance of the study of the estates-dwellers' discontent by seeing the discontent as an instance of a theory of kinship structure in industrial society. More generally still, their analysis would draw indirect support from any general theory of the importance of kinship in social structure. Thus, what may have seemed a parochial problem of British town planning receives systematic importance once it is explained in terms of a social scientific theory.

I want briefly to consider a view which implies that natural and social scientific theories are radically dissimilar in respect of the status of their underlying theories: namely, Homans's psychological reductionism. Homans claims that he is strictly not a psychological reductionist, because 'reduction implies that there are general sociological propositions that can be reduced to psychological ones' (1964, p. 817), while he suspects that there are no general sociological propositions true of all social systems. This is certainly a distinctive form of psychologism. But it is still a reductionism, differing only in that it is not social *generalisations* that are to be reduced.

I mention *Homans's* psychological reductionism advisedly. For Mill's associationist psychologism, Bowlby's original Freudian and later bond-based psychologism, Runciman's psychologistic call for a sophisticated psychology which we do not yet possess and even a thoroughgoing behaviourist psychologism do not introduce the problems for social scientific theory arising from Homans's claim that the psychological grounding of social science is familiar, 'part of the traditional psychology of common sense' (1967, p. 40). Homans's claim implies that the basic principles of social science have to be simply recognised, not discovered. An example of these principles is: 'Men are more likely to perform an activity, the more successful they perceive the activity is likely to be in getting [a] reward' (1964, pp. 16–17).

Such principles cannot be dismissed as merely tautologous, since the example I gave could be falsified. Of course, the theorist might render the statement unfalsifiable by, for example, a defensive redefinition of 'reward', but that is another issue. Rather, the decisive objection to Homans's account is that if these are the theoretical statements of social science, then all the work expected of theories remains to be done. No social phenomenon could be explained by these principles without many intermediate statements about, for instance, forms of socialisation in the relevant society. These intermediate statements may be relatively theoretical (e.g. about forms of prevailing ideology) or relatively empirical (e.g. about the inadequate attention pupils receive in schools with a pupil–teacher ratio of 40:1). Homans might counter by saying that these statements cannot be scientific. But it is precisely this book's intention to disprove that position.

To close this discussion of theory in social science, we should note that it has often been held that models and idealisations are at least of great value in facilitating the development of a scientific theory. A theory interpreted in terms of a model is said to yield predictions in areas other than those hitherto observed. Idealisations are statements about entities or events which could not exist, such as ideal gases and perfectly straight lines. They purport to simplify the statement of the theory, allowing us to explain observed instances by the discovery of initial conditions that account for the deviation of the observed phenomenon from its ideal behaviour as postulated by the theory.

The point to be made is simply that social scientific theories are full of models and idealisations. Their models (e.g. the biological model of society in certain functionalist theories) have been unsuccessful by natural scientific standards. But this is to state the fact, which no one doubts, that social science is not yet massively successful. I will say more about models and predictions in the next section. Social scientific ideal types cover the full range of generality, from, for example, 'the gang leader in Cornerville', through 'the profit motive', to 'the socio-economic class' and Weber's (1968, pp. 5–6) ideal types of action. An early realisation of the role of idealisations in social science was demonstrated by Weber's (1949) classic discussion of ideal types, which was vitiated only by the ironic belief that they are peculiar to social science.

1.4. PREDICTIONS

The idea that science should be able to predict novel phenomena is important in many methodologies. Popper's falsificationism holds a theory's ability to generate novel predictions to be a key sign that it is falsifiable. Lakatos's methodology of research programmes is less restrictive than Popper's philosophy in allowing theories to interpret discordant evidence in an *ad hoc* manner without ceasing to be scientific, even if that evidence strikes at the heart of the theory and even if the theory clings to *ad hoc* solutions for a long time. This very concession, however, produces a need to distinguish in some way between relatively sound and relatively unsound research programmes. To this end, Lakatos postulates the fact that one research programme predicted a piece of evidence, whereas another interpreted it *post factum*, as basic to the judgment that the first is progressive relative to the second (see, e.g., Lakatos, 1972). In Hempel's deductivism, with the isomorphism of explanation and prediction, a criterion for the judgment that we have a complete explanation of a phenomenon is that prior derivation from the explanatory laws and initial conditions would have allowed us to predict the phenomenon. Moreover, in the standard account of prediction, any limitations on the possibility of social scientific prediction are likely to be limitations on the crucial possibility of social scientific laws, because predictions follow straightforwardly from a conjunction of initial conditions and lawlike statements. In fact, many of the points that would normally be invoked in an analysis of social scientific predictions (e.g. similarity and uniqueness) have been discussed in the preceding sections.

In *Models and Analogies in Science*, Hesse analyses the demand for predictions into three senses:

1. That general laws already present in the explanans have as yet unobserved instances. This is a trivial fulfilment of the requirement and would not, I think, generally be regarded as sufficient.
2. That further general laws can be derived from the explanans *without* adding further items to the set of correspondence rules. That is to say, predictions remain within the domain of the set of predicates already present in the explanandum. This is a weak sense of predictivity that covers what would normally be called *applications* rather than extensions of a theory (for example, calculation of the orbit of a satellite from the theory of gravitation but not extension of the theory to predict the bending of light rays).
3. There is also a strong sense of prediction in which new observation predicates are involved, and hence, in terms of the deductive view, additions are required to the set of correspondence rules (pp. 175–6).

All discussions of prediction in social science have been in terms of the 'trivial' sense 1. To support my claim that social science possesses theories and empirical generalisations (albeit rudimentary ones in need of constant revision), I should produce examples of predictions in social science that satisfy senses 2 and 3 – or to be realistic, given the admitted primitive state of social science, sketches towards predictions in senses 2 and 3.

Hesse says that a theory which can sustain only sense 2 predictions possesses 'weak falsifiability', while sense 3 predictions correspond with a situation of 'strong falsifiability'. She writes that if we explain a set of observation statements containing only predicates of type O by a formal theoretical calculus, then there is no rational basis for deriving predictions from the theory about observation statements containing predicates of types other than O, say P: the theory can accommodate only sense 2 predictions and is weakly falsifiable. On the other hand, if we explain the O-statements by a theory which contains both Ps and theoretical predicates of type T, then predictions will be derivable from the theory about O- and P-statements: the theory yields sense 3 predictions and is strongly falsifiable. Hesse argues that formalist interpretations of theories cannot provide a rational justification for the introduction of P-predicates (and hence sense 3 predictions and strong falsifiability), while accounts which require theories to be interpreted by a model can do so. She further suggests:

whether a theory is required to be falsifiable in the strong sense will depend on the initial complexity of the correlations in the observation language. If this contains only the predicates of ordinary language, and prescientific correlations between them, it is likely that weak falsifiability will not be sufficient for a genuine theory . . . If, however, the observation language is already complex – if it is, for example, the language of classical physics – then it is possible that the formal theory may go on for a long time providing interesting correlations between new observational situations which are still described by the same predicates (p. 47).

I will now give social scientific examples which are sketches towards the satisfaction of prediction in senses 2 and 3. *Sense 2*: Marx's theory of ideology might be stated in its most condensed form as: modes of production determine ideological forms. Without adding any new postulates or correspondence rules (here, what are to count as modes of production and ideological forms), the theory can be extended in its applications, as sense 2 prediction requires. We might, for example (using all the terms in a technical Marxist sense), study which forms of ideology are determined by those modern modes of production in which a country's economy is a mixed capitalist and socialist one or in which the bourgeois and proletarian classes of a single country (e.g. France) are together exploiting another country (e.g. Algeria). Such studies are new applications in that these modern economic forms were not envisaged at the time of the formulation of the Marxist theory of ideology.

Moreover, Hesse grants that a theory which is only weakly falsifiable might yet be adequate if its observation language is 'already complex', rather than containing merely 'the predicates of ordinary language, and prescientific correlations between them'. 'Complex' may be meant here in ways (e.g. necessitating quantitative correlations) which preclude Marx's theory of ideology from satisfying this demand, but I do not see why it need be. In fact, the terms 'politics, laws, morality, religion and metaphysics' and 'primitive communist, slave-based, Asiatic, feudal, bourgeois, socialist and communist' are sufficiently complex in their connotations and correlations to 'go on for a long time providing interesting correlations between new observational situations which are still described by the same predicates'. An example of an attempt to establish such correlations outside the spheres with which Marx was concerned is the various Marxist attempts to link modes of production with forms of natural scientific knowledge.

Sense 3: An example in which a social scientific theory sustains sense 3 predictions and hence strong falsifiability is provided by the biological model of society. This can be reconstructed in Radcliffe-Brown's way (1965, pp. 178–80). We wish to explain the existence of social structures, that is the fact of continuities within societies despite continuous changes of its constituent members. We employ a biological model, in which the crucial analogical point is that organisms have physiological structures. But in employing the biological model, we notice that physiological structures contribute to the satisfaction of a general need of the organism, namely the maintenance of life. By analogy, we postulate social needs (this analogy, then, provides the basis for the introduction of the P-predicates), such as the maintenance of order and the catharsis of individual grief through collective activity. At this point, we are on the road to a general and strongly predictive functional theory. We have moved from our attempts to explain certain recurrent social structures to the prediction that in every society we will find structures which will maintain order and relieve individual grief and which will service any other social needs we may detect.

I have tried to show that social science can run before I have proven it can walk, because discussion of social scientific prediction always centres on the possibility of prediction in the 'trivial' sense 1. I know of three arguments (other than those appealing to factors of complexity which I have already discussed) which would impugn the possibility of any kind of prediction in social science, none of which is cogent.

First, it may be argued that the fact that social science does not successfully predict the future indicates a flaw in the very project. This is an instance of the general argument from present difficulties to conceptual impossibilities which I have been attacking throughout this chapter. In this case, the argument fails to note that successful predictions are not categorical, but conditional on a knowledge of initial conditions. Without there being anything in the logic or epistemology of social science that precludes the possibility of social scientific predictions, it may be that our empirical social scientific knowledge is simply not sufficient to carry out predictions. The economic prediction of a year's output, for example, may be inaccurate if a major strike is not foreseen. We are similarly ignorant of many situations in the natural world. The initial conditions are too complex for a physicist to predict the path of a falling leaf (see Nagel, 1961, p. 461).

Ignorance of the conditional nature of predictions is a feature of the uncritical extrapolation of trends, which is common in social science and which often leads the project of social scientific predictions into

disrepute. Trends are accidental generalisations which are contingently true of a certain time and place, whereas logically sound predictions require laws which sustain counterfactuals. Popper (1961) correctly states that prediction through the extrapolation of trends, as
opposed to law-based prediction, is blind to the point that trends exist
only in specific initial conditions and that logically sound predictions
are dependent on these conditions being predicted too. But this is not a
criticism of social scientific predictions as such. Rather, Popper's
analysis sensitises us to the distinction between sound and spurious
predictions, a distinction which turns on what statements we use to
support predictions. As an example of a formally sound social scientific
prediction, Durkheim's theory of suicide would predict a tendency
towards increased rates of suicide in Catholics, if independent meas-
ures indicated a decrease in social cohesion among Catholics.
Moreover, trends such as suicide or population rates may be used
pragmatically for successful (though not logically justified) predictions
over short periods or if they have been detected in numerous
instances. An example of the latter would be the utilisation of a population trend observed in many advanced industrial societies, even if we
are not sure which aspects of these societies the trend is correlated
with. Finally, there is no rigid division between giving further information about a trend and that trend assuming the status of a law. Providing information about a trend will typically include stating the necessary and sufficient conditions for the existence of the trend, though
deriving the trend from a system of laws remains the best way of
showing that it is not accidental.

Secondly, it is sometimes held that social science cannot produce the
weakest kinds of prediction because it is unfalsifiable. This chapter has
argued that social science can progressively improve its theories and
generalisations in the face of evidence. Let us take the example of
Marx's theory of ideology again, since it is often thought of as a
paradigm of unfalsifiability. One set of data that has been urged
against the Marxist theory of ideology is the fact that certain ideological
forms have not changed as a result of changes in modes of production.
This is a clear counterexample to the theory. Now the Marxist might at
this stage, as many have done, introduce the notion of 'ideological
survivals'. This term could be used in either of two ways. It might be a
blanket *ad hoc* term applied to all embarrassing examples and without
explanatory import. Such a move would render the theory unfalsifiable. Undoubtedly many Marxists have defended Marxism as received
by trying to neutralise empirical criticism. The place of the term 'revisionism' in Marxist pejorative vocabulary witnesses this anti-empirical
trait, for from the point of view of scientific progress revisionism

should be 'the highest virtue rather than the greatest crime' (Botto-more, 1975, p. 21). But this is a point about Marxists, not Marxism, because an alternative reaction would be to postulate an empirical theory of ideology+survivals. For example, ideological forms survive changes in the modes of production if they either are not directly related to the needs of a specific mode of production (e.g. mathematical theories) or are given a new function in the new mode of production (e.g. works of art). The continuing prevalence of religion in the Soviet Union is a *prima facie* counterexample even to the theory of ideology+survivals. But, in Popper's terms, this is to suggest that the theory is false, not unscientific. Generally, in both natural and social science, there is always a choice of revising a theory in an *ad hoc* or in a progressive way. The claim that all social scientific theories are always revised in an *ad hoc* way merely indicates ignorance of the social scientific literature.

Finally, there is the problem of reflexive predictions. In social science it may happen that, by way of the subjects in question coming to hold a belief about a given prediction and acting on that belief, the social scientist's prediction becomes a causal factor in the area he is studying. This problem would arise even in our ideally harmonious society, where the social scientist and actors share a classificatory system and so where problems of different classifications and evaluations do not arise.

I will argue that the reflexivity of social scientific predictions is not philosophically important on four grounds. First, there is the point that analogous limitations on prediction exist in natural science. This claim can be supported by many standard examples, such as a thermometer measuring the temperature of an object together with the thermometer's temperature. But let us use Popper's more systematic analysis in 'Indeterminism in Quantum Physics and in Classical Physics'. His study establishes an analogy between the reflexive limitations of a mechanical predictor and of the social scientist. It is only an analogy, not an identity, because the crucial mediating factor of actors' beliefs is absent from the mechanical situation. But there is a genuine analogy in that, in both the mechanical and social scientific cases, the activities necessary for making the prediction (e.g. collecting information and propagating the prediction) tend to ensure that not all predictions can be entirely successful.

Popper argues, then, that real prediction, as opposed to the ideal prediction of some Laplacean demon, is impossible even from the assumptions of classical physics for certain mechanical systems. It is impossible in that, even if one of the predictors can carry out each prediction task, there is no single predictor which can carry out every prediction task. No mechanical predictor can fully predict its own closer environment, because no predictor can be fully self-predicting, so no predictor can know all the initial conditions (which in the case of its closer environment crucially include its own states) relevant for predicting its closer environment. Popper claims that no predictor can be fully self-predicting on the ground that it can completely describe only its own past, not its present or its future. For while it can describe all its states up to time t, it cannot describe its state at t (including its describing activities) before t itself has passed. Further, a predictor C may receive full information about its own immediate past, but the receipt of this information will change the predictor's state, a change which will destroy the completeness of the information and hence its value for all possible predictions. Another predictor C^+ may ingeniously foresee the distorting effect of providing C with information about itself. Instead of providing C with accurate self-information, C^+ may give C such information that will induce C to predict for itself a certain t state and that simultaneously interferes with C so as to bring C into the state predicted at t. But C^+ cannot achieve this by giving C complete information about C's states. For on the previous argument C's self-information cannot include a description of the possession of that same self-information, so C's self-knowledge must remain deficient for some possible self-predicting tasks.

Secondly, it is suggested that the possibility of actors' invalidating predictions about themselves is essential for human freedom. Determinism in social science can take the form only of an after-the-event explanation. If social science purported to predict the future, it would necessarily be false to the elements of creativity, choice and intentionality in human affairs.

This issue has too many aspects to study in a short space. At the least, we would have to dissect the various senses of freedom. Here it is enough to note the distinction between freedom as unpredictability and freedom as being in control of and responsible for our actions. Even if a person's actions are completely predictable, he may be free in the sense of being in control of and responsible for his actions.[2] To think the contrary is to confuse determinism with fatalism. If a person is determined in the sense that all his actions are predictable, it does not follow that anything he does, thinks or chooses makes no difference, which is the fatalist thesis. Indeed, part of the data necessary for the observer to predict a person's actions may be knowledge of the

---

[2] For a systematic statement of this view, see MacKay (e.g. 1960 and 1971). MacKay also criticises the identification of freedom with unpredictability. He does so, however, on the basis of certain assumptions – for instance, the radically different natures of the observer's and the agent's languages – which I do not wish or need to make.

very factors – the person's intentions, decisions, creativity – which enter the traditional account of what it is to be free in the sense of exercising responsibility and control. Weber (1949, p. 124) makes this point when he writes that freedom in the sense of unpredictability characterises the insane, not the ideally rational and self-controlled person. The complementary thesis that an actor's reasons, motives, intentions etc. – the constituents of free action – can be considered part of the causal universe by a social scientific theory will be defended in chapter three.

What I have said is neutral on the question of whether a social scientific theory may treat these constituents of human freedom as unimportant. A social scientist may believe that reasons, choices, decisions, etc. are always derivative explananda in social theory, never significant explanantia. Loosely, this is a belief which distinguishes the Althusserian and Goffmanesque visions of human action. But it is an issue firmly rooted within the confines of the metaphysics of substantive social theories, not one to be settled on the level of social scientific methodology. The fact that social theorists may hold different views on freedom in this sense is an example of metaphysical debate within social science, which I discuss in section 4.6.

Thirdly, the idea that the reflexivity of a social scientific prediction *invalidates* that prediction misunderstands the conditional nature of prediction, which derives from the conditional nature of the laws that sustain predictions. A prediction states that a certain situation will obtain, if a prior situation obtains. Should that prior situation not arise, then the question of whether the prediction is true or false is not even posed. Thus, if the initial conditions which a prediction mentions do not contain the actors' beliefs about the prediction, then whatever happens as a result of the actors' beliefs about the prediction renders the original prediction inoperative, not valid or invalid.

Having understood the conditional nature of predictions, the reflexivity of social scientific predictions – and this is the fourth point – can be treated as one more initial condition that social science must elucidate. To revert to the notion of complexity, reflexivity is one more complicating factor in social science. But complications, I have argued, should invoke empirical study, not despair. The very realisation that social scientific predictions are reflexive is an empirical advance, the prediction, we may say, that the propagation of some predictions will have certain effects. In this case, we should aim for social scientific laws and predictions whose antecedents take note of actors' reactions to social science. In doing so, we move away from Popper's fully engaged predictor towards a Laplacean social scientific predictor; though the

Laplacean social scientific predictor may remain an unattainable, if epistemologically cogent, ideal.[3]

Of course my discussion of reflexive predictions has been disingenuous. The reflexivity of predictions is only a philosophically serious topic if it is also argued that the mediating factor of actors' beliefs introduces not just one more complicating factor, but a difficulty of principle into social science. But to say this is to indicate that the meaningful nature of human actions, not the reflexivity of predictions, is the fundamental issue. The question of reflexive predictions cannot settle our attitude to naturalism. Rather, what we think of reflexivity depends on what we think of the project of a scientific study of meaningful action. If we consider the latter to be possible, then reflexive predictions are a minor complication; if impossible, then they involve a difficulty of principle. It is to this more fundamental problem of meaning in social science that we must now turn.

[3] See Simon (1971) for a neat proof of the fact that, in principle, it is possible to make a correct prediction of the outcome of a two-party election, even given interference by the prediction on the voting.

Common sense and social science

2.1. COMMON SENSE

The nature of the problem of meaning in social science is unclear. It is one of the intentions of chapters two and three to disentangle the various issues involved. Schematically, these issues may be grouped under three headings: the nature of the language of social scientific theories, the fact that actors have meaningful theories about themselves, and the relationship between social science's and the actors' theories. While chapter three will tackle all three issues, this chapter deals mainly with the last issue and conceptualises the actors' theories as the common sense with which the theories of social science are contrasted.

I approach the problem of meaning in social science in two stages. The first stage, in this chapter, retains some aspects of the idealisation with which I opened chapter one. The second stage, in the next chapter, will drop all artificial restrictions on the kinds of problems that a social science may face and so will allow a discussion of the question of meaning in social science in its most general forms.

These remarks can be clarified by examining the vague term 'common sense'. In posing the problem of the social science–common sense relation, three different types of common sense may be at issue: (i) the common sense of the social scientist's own home culture (e.g. British middle class); (ii) that of the actors' culture (e.g. Nuer or Welsh working class); (iii) that of the social scientist's audience (e.g. professional social scientists). I will not consider (iii). Furthermore, I will assume the identity of (i) and (ii), namely that the social scientist is investigating a group of actors whose common sense is basically the same as that in his own home culture. This assumption of course makes the analysis *prima facie* irrelevant to all anthropology and much other social science. It can be defended on two grounds, however. First, the simplifying assumption of identity between the common senses of the actors and the social scientist allows us to pose the problem of the social science–common sense relation in its simplest form, that is, without having to consider the problems that arise for the relation between the social scientist's and the actors' theories in the anthropological situation of radical conceptual disparity. Secondly, having clarified this simplified problem we may then consider the question of extending the analysis to the general situation where (i) does not equal (ii), which is what I will do in chapter three.

It is clear, then, in what ways I am retaining certain aspects of the idealisation of chapter one. I still assume that the social scientist's and the actors' classifications are not radically different; in other words, that they share a home culture. But I also forgo some aspects of the rigid chapter one idealisation. Specifically, in posing the problem of the social science–common sense relation, I now admit that the subjects of social science have meaningful theories about themselves. Further, I now acknowledge and discuss the fact that the social scientist and the actors use different concepts and make different statements, albeit within the same home culture. This fact may also be stated in terms of the social scientist having two cultures: the social scientific culture and his native culture. In this chapter, the remaining idealised aspect is the assumption that the social scientist and the actors under study have the same native culture. I depart from the full chapter one idealisation in recognising the problem of the nature of conceptual agreements and disagreements between the social scientist's professional and native cultures. In loosening the idealisation in this respect, I will have to reconsider certain things I said about theories in chapter one in order to study the relationship between a social scientist's theoretical and commonsense concepts.

My usage of 'common sense' conflicts with the standard understanding in two ways. First, I consider common sense only from the point of view of its cognitive aims and purposes. Clearly, common-sense statements may have purposes other than that of stating claims to knowledge; but, for that matter, so may scientific statements. There is no reason why we cannot develop a theory of common sense in its purely cognitive role.

Secondly, I deny the assumption that there is a shared universal common sense. I give a formal definition of common sense which allows different groups of actors to possess different common senses and, to reiterate, I am concerned only with a common sense that is shared by the social scientist and the actors under study. I define 'common sense' as the concepts and the methods used to generate statements from those concepts that are accepted by the majority of the social actors under study at a given place and time. In short, common sense is the actors' conceptual scheme. On this definition, it follows that a social scientific investigation that concludes not-p when the majority of actors believe that p is not necessarily contrary to common sense. The reason for accepting this counter-intuitive consequence is that no philosophical issues concerning the relation of the social scientist's and actors' theories arise until social science begins to depart from the concepts in terms of which actors understand and act upon reality. There are two relevant ways in which p may be denied, the first of which is not contrary to common sense, as I have defined it, while the second begins to be. The first remains within the conceptual scheme in terms of which p was stated, and implies that the person who stated p has made a mistake, perhaps in observation, but that his basic conceptual scheme is satisfactory. This is an uninteresting denial of p for our present concerns. The second type of denial of p is a first step towards the propagation of an alternative conceptual scheme to that in which p was formulated. This is the type of denial of p that I am here concerned with. For example, p may be the statement that the better educated are more likely to become mentally ill in times of stress. This statement might be denied, first, on the basis of a commonsense understanding of 'mentally ill' and the discovery that it is as a matter of fact false, and, secondly, on the basis of a movement to a non-commonsense concept of 'mentally ill'.

2.2. SOCIAL SCIENCE AND COMMON SENSE INTERACT

Given this notion of common sense, I will now state what I take to be the correct view on the social science–common sense relation. The arguments I here summarily give for this view will become clearer when I criticise contrary views on the social science–common sense relation in the remainder of this chapter.

The conceptual schemes of social science and common sense interact. This interaction can both be established as a matter of fact by research in the history of social science and be supported philosophically as an implication of the naturalistic methodology I have been assuming throughout. I concentrate on a philosophical discussion of the problem.

To establish the interaction thesis for the social science–common sense relation, we must argue two points. First, it is at times rational for common sense to develop as a result of the effect of social science on it. Secondly, it is at times rational for social science to develop as a result of the effect of common sense on it. The second point is the more counter-intuitive. If we can give it substance, we will have given content to the vague idea that social science should somehow learn from common sense. I divide each strand of the argument into arguments concerning refutation and arguments concerning meaning.

(A) That social science can rationally affect common sense: (a) Argument concerning refutation: This argument has conventional and exotic forms. The conventional form makes the standard point that social scientific advance can demonstrate the inadequacy of commonsense concepts and beliefs, as, for example, did Marx in criticising contemporary views of the nature of historical change. The exotic form of the argument is Feyerabend's thesis (see 2.4.c), plausible if segregated from his anarchistic methodology, that an aspect of the replacement of one theory by another in science may be the change in associated common senses. (b) Argument concerning meaning: A theoretical science can deepen our understanding and change the connotations of a set of commonsense concepts x, y and z by showing that these concepts can be placed in the same context, precisely that of the theoretical system in question. This theoretical context unifies x, y and z in demonstrating that statements embodying them separately can be explained in terms of the same set of principles. The provision of theoretical groundings for a commonsense concept also involves at least the provision of new criteria for the identification of and new expectations concerning that object. For example, Lukes's work *Power*, if accepted, would extend the range of our conceptions of power and provide us with new expectations concerning the exercise of power.

(B) That common sense can rationally affect social science: (a) Argument concerning refutation: At least one prime factor in the development of a scientific theory is its relation with experience. Even if corrigible, the domain of experience possesses an initial credibility as compared with the hypotheses of theoretical science. Hence, a basis for the development of theoretical science is given by the comparison of the implications of the theoretical system with statements about experience. In social science, the actors' experience gives rise to and is structured by the categories of common sense as I have defined it. It is therefore rational to utilise the statements of common sense in the criticism of social scientific theories. It is of course impossible to legislate rules for every research situation which would establish when common sense should give way in the face of social science or vice versa; this is the most important issue that arises for practical methodology from the social science–common sense relation and it cannot be settled *a priori*. (b) Argument concerning meaning: Just as the meanings of commonsense concepts are changed by being incorporated into a theoretical context, so too the meanings of theoretical terms are clarified and extended when statements embodying them are used to explain statements composed of commonsense concepts that the theory had not previously covered. Meaning relations do not flow in only one direction. There is a constant mutual adjustment between the interpretations of theoretical science and of commonsense theories.

The close relation between social scientific and commonsense concepts implied by the interaction thesis does not mean that there is no distinction between the two types of concepts. My definition of common sense and the interaction thesis imply that the set of commonsense concepts is not identical with the set of social scientific concepts. Moreover, scientific concepts tend to be more precise, more abstract and ideal, more systematically organised and more methodical in their facilitation of prediction and explanation, than commonsense concepts (see Körner, 1970, ch. 4). But none of these points suggest that there is a difference in kind between scientific and commonsense concepts, a difference which might support either of the two opposed views that social science must always or should never break with common sense.

I will now discuss some possible views on the social science–common sense relation and criticise each in the light of the interaction thesis. The chapter will have five more sections, four of which will deal with distinctive views on the social science–common sense relation: section 2.3, social science must break with common sense; section 2.4, social science must be based on common sense; section 2.5, social science and common sense are incomparable; section 2.6, social science and common sense are identical. The last two views have not often been held, but they are interesting because they both imply the impossibility of posing the basic question of the relation between social science and common sense. Within the views discussed in sections 2.3 and 2.4, I make a further distinction in terms of the grounds that are adduced for holding that social science must break with common sense or the contrary. Are there grounds of the kind (*a*) that are independent of the nature of social science and common sense and yet can be used as a basis either for the decision that social science should break with common sense or for the contrary? For example, are these grounds such as an increase in explanatory power, in truth-content, consistency, generality or simplicity, grounds which do not decide essentially between the two opposed views? Or, are the grounds of the kind (*b*) that either of the two views follows essentially? In short, is it a contingent fact that either social-science-as-broken-with-common-sense or social-science-as-based-on-common-sense corresponds with social reality? Or is the criterion of corresponding with social reality internal in some sense to either social-science-as-broken-with-common-sense or the contrary?

I present each view by means of a discussion of a single writer.

Sections 2.3 and 2.4 are sub-divided into three parts: elucidation of the different types of grounds that may be given for each view via a discussion of a single writer (sub-sections a and b, as indicated above, each of which ends with a short critique of the writer in question), followed by some general remarks (sub-section c) on the overall view in the light of the interaction thesis. Sections 2.5 and 2.6 are also based on the analysis of a single writer and I conclude section 2.6 with a short discussion of the views expressed in sections 2.5 and 2.6 taken together. Finally, section 2.7 takes ethnomethodology as an example of a school whose analysis in terms of the preceding classification is fruitful, though complex.

I will not draw systematically on the philosophy-common sense debate, because there are large areas of dissimilarity between the philosophy–common sense and the social science–common sense discussions. For example, two of the features held to characterise the common sense of the philosophy–common sense debate are irrelevant to the common sense of the social science–common sense relation. Namely, commonsense statements should be believed because no attempt to criticise or prove them can operate from more clear or more certain premises than the statements themselves, and commonsense beliefs are not actively entertained, but assented to only if doubted (see Grave, 1967, p. 156). Moreover, a key consideration in the social science–common sense issue is the purportedly scientific nature of social science, a consideration absent from the philosophy–common sense question.

2.3. THE VIEW THAT SOCIAL SCIENCE MUST BREAK WITH COMMON SENSE

2.3.a. On external grounds

Durkheim in *The Rules of Sociological Method* argues that each new science must leave behind the 'crudely formed concepts' that men possess of the science's subject matter prior to the constitution of the science itself. People always have such rudimentary precursors of a science, because 'thought and reflection are prior to science, which merely uses them more methodically'. When we come to think scientifically about an area, we run the risk of confusing our elementary ideas of that area with the area itself, because our ideas are, as it were, closer to us than the reality they purport to describe. This confusion is dangerous because unscientific concepts are designed for pragmatic purposes, not for the purpose of finding the truth. The necessity of leaving such prejudicial idols behind is common to all sciences, but particularly important in social science. For people possessed ideas on such things as law, morality, the family and the state before the emergence of social science, since these ideas are necessary conditions of human existence. Far from prescientific ideas containing the key to the reality of things, 'they are like a veil drawn between the thing and ourselves' (p. 15). Durkheim exemplifies his attack on a 'science' that 'proceeds from ideas to things, not from things to ideas' (p. 15) by demanding that we cease, as social scientists, to use certain prescientific concepts, such as those of the state, sovereignty, political liberty, democracy, socialism and communism.

A variant on this view, which Durkheim advanced in other works, is that a scientific social science, once constituted, can react back on common sense and change it in the image of the new social science. This variant remains a species of the view that social science must break with common sense provided that common sense is given no role – indeed, is seen as a hindrance – in the original constitution of social science, and that the subsequent relation between social science and common sense is held to be one-sided: social science leads to rational change in common sense, but not vice versa.

This stance on the social science–common sense relation remains the orthodoxy in social science. For example, Roberts (1972) opens a discussion of comparative politics's need for strict conceptualisation by stating that there has been a long-term debasement of political terminology, involving the stretching of common concepts to the point of imprecision and their contamination by usage in value contexts. In consequence, Roberts doubts the utility of such concepts as fascism, imperialism and self-determination, and warns of the phobia against neologisms.

But merely to render old concepts more precise is not a sufficient reason for the methodological postulate of the need to break with common sense. The criterion of precision provides a difference in degree, not in kind, between commonsense and social scientific concepts. The discussion in section 1.2, to the effect that appeals to precision cannot preclude the situation where it is rational to use relatively imprecise concepts, was based on the assumption that precision is a relative, not an absolute, criterion. Moreover, until the new concepts are embodied in a workable theory, our understanding of them rests on our prior understanding of the old concept that they supplant. For example, the concept of democracy, being deemed imprecise and value-laden, is broken down into the circumscribed, technical concepts of representation and participation. But until we evolve a theoretical language in which these technical concepts find an autonomous role, explaining them

51

to the neophyte will always assume his commonsense understanding of democracy.

Turning from the question of precision (and ignoring the problem of value which is irrelevant here) to the role of theory, we can substantiate the need for social science to break with common sense. The two main functions of theory, as I noted in section 1.3, are to facilitate explanation and to unify our knowledge. These functions are linked because the theoretical unification of knowledge reveals connections between classes of relatively empirical events, with statements about these diverse classes of events being derived from the more abstract statements. With this understanding of theory, we see that social scientific theory is essentially contrary to common sense. For it must link, so as to explain, empirical concepts and results that had not been linked before. Take as an example Merton's reconstruction of Durkheim's theory of suicide, which I used in section 1.3. The point of Durkheim's theoretical apparatus is to extend the significance of an originally isolated empirical finding, namely one about the differential Protestant–Catholic suicide rate. By means of the theoretical terms 'social cohesion' etc., the differential Protestant–Catholic suicide rate is linked, because it is explained by the same theory, to statements about other phenomena, such as differential suicide rates in married and single people. The full theoretical apparatus ('social cohesion', 'psychic support', 'stresses and anxieties') has been extended to explain obsessive behaviour, morbid preoccupations and other maladaptive behaviour (see Merton, 1964, pp. 97–8). The theoretical term 'social cohesion' functions also in Durkheim's theories of the division of labour and of religion. So, the commonsense understanding of concepts such as suicide rates and religious adherence has been deepened by the postulation of a set of theoretical concepts which link and explain sets of phenomena, presented in terms of the commonsense concepts, which had not been coherently linked before. Moreover, this process is in principle open-ended. We can extend our understanding of any commonsense concepts x and y, and simultaneously of our newly constituted theoretical terms, by showing that they can replace 'Catholics' and 'Protestants' in our original commonsense statement.

2.3.b. On internal grounds

Althusser's philosophy is a philosophy of levels and of breaks between the levels. For Althusser, rigorous thought is endangered if distinct levels, whether in theory or in reality, are collapsed into one another. Such reductions are effected by simply not making the necessary distinctions (e.g. by not separating historical and dialectical materialism) or by specifying a common essence for the separate levels (e.g. by holding *praxis* to be what is common to all the levels). We are interested in one specific break which Althusser postulates between two of his levels: 'the opposition that separates a new science in process of self-constitution from the prescientific *theoretical* ideologies that occupy the "terrain" in which it is establishing itself' (1969, p. 13). This break from ideology is not of mere historical interest to the science concerned. In the first place, as the last quotation suggests, the science must operate on the terrain which it has wrested from ideology. Secondly, ideology remains a constant 'threat' (1975, p. 90) to scientific development.

Have I forgotten common sense in emphasising Althusser's thesis of the science–ideology break? No, for Althusser's concept of ideology includes that of common sense as I have defined it, so to break with ideology is typically to break with common sense. For example, Althusser follows Lenin in holding that the spontaneous ideology of the proletariat – i.e. proletarian common sense – produces utopian socialism, trade-unionism and anarchism, but not scientific Marxism. Marxism, far from being an expression of the proletariat, is developed outside the proletariat and then 'imported' into that class (1975, pp. 140–1). The main positive and negative functions of ideology for Althusser belong precisely to the domain of common sense. Positively, ideology is necessary for all social formations because it is the mode in which people live their everyday actions. Negatively, ideology threatens the theoretical labour necessary for science through the transparency or obviousness of ideological thought-expressions. In contrast to ideological givenness, scientific method is defined as: 'the method which brackets sensory appearances, i.e. in the domain of political economy, all the visible phenomena and practico-empirical concepts produced by the economic world (rent, interest, profit, etc.), in other words, all those economic categories from . . . "everyday life" ' (1975, p. 83).

Althusser gives an elaborate description of the process of the initial break of science with ideology and the subsequent development of science in 'continuous' (1969, p. 170) struggle with ideology. He characterises scientific development as a process of production, carried out on raw conceptual material (which in *For Marx* is termed 'Generality I'), by means of the determinate theoretical system of a given science ('Generality II') and resulting in a theoretical product ('Generality III'). The discontinuities in the formation and development of a specific science are in the first instance discontinuities in the conception of that science's object. The theoretical object (i.e. the concept of the real object) is continuously transformed, while the real object is unchanged. This process establishes that knowledge of the real object is continuously deepened by the reorganisation of the theoretical object, and that the transformation of knowledge is not just a subjective change of viewpoint or paradigm, because it is constrained by the real object. Each science constructs its specific conceptual apparatus, as the theory of its specific object. Althusser defines a theory as 'the system for posing problems in a correct form', that is as a 'problematic' (1975, p. 155). He holds that the introduction of a new concept of an object does not merely add one more concept and one more answer-to-a-problem to a pre-existing list of concepts and problem/answers, 'like an unexpected guest at a family reunion'. Rather, it involves 'a transformation of the *entire* terrain and its *entire* horizon, which are the background against which the new problem is produced' (1975, p. 24).

But now we have lost our problem and this loss is not an innocent one. Why must science break with ideology and common sense in order to constitute itself and why must it continuously renew its initial struggle against ideology/common sense in order to develop? We are told that while an ideological concept 'really does designate a set of existing relations, unlike a scientific concept, it does not provide us with a means of knowing them' (1969, p. 223); the relations which ideology expresses as existing between people and their world are at least in part 'imaginary' (1971, pp. 153 ff.) Yes, but why? We are told that, while there are real problems prompting an ideological problematic, the ideology is not conscious of them, but instead produces answers to a set of false problems; correspondingly, non-scientific problematics lack real objects. Again, why? Why are the problematics of the subject and of idealism illusory? Why is there no object corresponding to the concepts of the value of labour or of empirical history? If we are told that their illusoriness and falsity are defined in relation to the theory that broke with them, then that would be circular. Shortly, I will argue that Althusser's account of the need to break with ideology and common sense *is* circular. But we must note first that Althusser is aware of this point, and this awareness, together with the claim that such circularity is unimportant, partly constitute the originality of his philosophy.

The circularity, then, consists in the fact that justifying the break between science and ideology/common sense turns on the postulation of the truth of science and the falsity of ideology, while the reason for the latter postulate is precisely that science has broken with ideology. In a move which Lecourt (1975, p. 12) calls 'materialist', Althusser posits the truthfulness of scientific practice as beyond doubt. Theoretical practice, through the production of the concept of a real object, appropriates the real world. To doubt this is a mistake for two reasons.

First, there is no basis for a detailed study of the relation between thought and the real, given that they are distinct systems. The thought system has, as we have seen, its own structure, with its specific raw material, means of production and product. This product, knowledge, is a result of a process which 'takes place entirely in thought', constituting a distinctive system which is articulated as a whole onto other systems (1975, p. 42). Hence, 'we can admit no *one-to-one correspondence* between the different moments of these two distinct orders [i.e. the real and the thought orders]' (1975, p. 47). Secondly, once scientific practices are constituted 'they have no need for verification from *external* practices to declare the knowledges they produce to be "true", i.e., to be *knowledges*' (1975, p. 59). Philosophy should analyse the forms and mechanisms of the production of scientific knowledge, not ask for a guarantee of the possibility of knowledge. This search for the forms and mechanisms of scientificity becomes for Althusser the search for the specificity of the Marxist dialectic, since 'Marx's requirements restate in a new domain the requirements which have long been imposed on the practices of those sciences which have achieved autonomy' (1975, p. 184). These requirements are twofold and both of them differentiate science from ideology. First, as I have noted, scientific method should bracket everyday ideological concepts. Secondly, scientific theory should be a systematic appropriation of its object, systematic in that it links the underlying essences of all the bracketed phenomena.

The circle is now complete. Science must break with ideology/common sense because the former is posited as true and the latter as false. But insofar as any content is given to the concept of science, it is defined as not-ideology/common sense. For the Althusserian, all questions have been answered; for the non-Althusserian, they have not even been posed.

2.3.c. Criticisms

We should retain from the view under discussion the basic belief that social science can break with common sense, because it does so. We should discard the underlying assumptions that the social science–common sense relation is always unidirectional and that social science breaks with common sense once and for all.

We can achieve the required discards by pointing to two mistakes of strident Durkheimianism and to the correct interaction thesis. First, we must note that the domain of common sense is the basis for our initial understanding of theoretical concepts and for many checks or tests of a theoretical interpretation of a phenomenon. Even if we take social scientific entities such as modes of production, the unconscious or anomie to be directly observable, we will have to learn the conditions of application of terms referring to these entities via our knowledge of a previously existing common sense: e.g., with the unconscious, via our understanding of talk about dreams, slips of the tongue, desires, guilt, conventions, etc.

Secondly, common sense does not form a single unchanging whole which can be left behind by science once and for all. Historians of science have shed light on the mutual dependence of scientific theories and their associated common senses. For example, in *The Origins of Modern Science* Butterfield analyses the need for the scientific revolution to institute new commonsense concepts of motion, breaking with the then dominant Aristotelian ones. Moreover – and here is the crucial point – common sense changes as a result of theoretical scientific advance. I will return to this point, but I have already outlined a prime mechanism of this change in talking about the interplay which occurs between the theoretical and commonsense domains when a new theoretical interpretation is introduced.

2.4. THE VIEW THAT SOCIAL SCIENCE MUST BE BASED ON COMMON SENSE

2.4.a. On external grounds

The view that there are cognitive standards defined independently of our concepts of social science and common sense which, as a matter of fact, sustain a judgment in favour of common sense is part of conventional anti-social science wisdom. It is more difficult to find arguments from people who have thought about social science for this position. But it has at least one champion in Homans, whose work I briefly discussed in section 1.3.

Homans holds that the crucial test which propositions of social scientific theory have to pass is whether they can sustain precise, testable, deductive, explanatory schemata. Homans believes that the generalisations which can underpin such schemata in social science are all propositions of behavioural psychology, including learning theory and decision theory. He states that these propositions have proved their power in explanations in everyday life, historical explanations and explanations of institutional phenomena, including such entities as rules and norms.

Homans further argues that social science must be clear about the nature of its axiomatic propositions, that is, the propositions of psychology:

The propositions are not new, in the sense that they were once unknown and have had to be discovered. Though the language in which psychologists state them is unfamiliar because it aims at precision, their content is not. When we know what they mean, they do not surprise us, though some of their further implications may do so . . . Indeed they are part of the traditional psychology of common sense (1967, p. 40).

The commonsense nature of the axiomatic social scientific propositions implies a basic difference between natural and social science, for the principles of social science 'do not have to be discovered but, what is much more difficult, simply recognised for what they are' (1967, p. 73). The difficulty follows from the fact that theorists are contemptuous of systematically stating and developing truisms. Blinded by the fact that the basic natural scientific propositions are discoveries, they conclude that either social science is not scientific or its principles are not psychological truisms and remain undiscovered.

A full evaluation of Homans's specific view is a matter for social scientific theory, not philosophical analysis, and is therefore beyond the bounds of this book. For Homans supports his view on contingent grounds. He admits the possibility of social scientific propositions which could not be explained psychologically and which possessed greater explanatory power than the psychological propositions. He says that this is a contingent question, which cannot be settled *a priori*. I will shortly argue that, in general, sociology cannot be satisfied with a basis in common sense. But a critique of Homans's specific thesis concerning the power of behavioural psychology requires a venture into substantive social scientific theory which I cannot make here.

Suffice it to note that the critical philosophical point I made in section 1.3 against Homans is again relevant. Namely, Homans's account of social scientific theories leaves all the work expected of such theories to be done. No social scientific phenomenon could be explained by behavioural psychology without many intermediate statements (about, for example, modes of socialisation), some of which would be statements of theoretical social science. Hence, the problem of the relation of common sense and theoretical social scientific statements would be re-introduced.

2.4.b. On internal grounds

A theorist who believes that social science should be based on common sense because of certain features of the internal natures of social science and common sense is Peter Winch. Winch holds that social science should not transcend the actors' commonsense understanding of their actions. Winch's basic reason for this thesis is what he takes to be an essential fact about the relation between human action and commonsense theories. Namely, it is definitional of actions that they should be conceptualised in terms of the actors' theories, so we must base ourselves on the actors' theories in analysing their actions. It is admissible for the social scientist to give us more information than the actors could give us, but not to engage in a theoretical restructuring of the actors' accounts.

Winch's views are best discussed in the context of the more general debate on meaning in social science, that is, of the situation where the social scientist's and actors' common senses may be radically different. It is for this reason that I will not consider Winch's views until the next chapter.

Let me just note here what will be a central theme of the next chapter: it is important to accept the possibility of the social scientist breaking with the actors' conceptual scheme. When the social scientist shares the same culture with the actors, he may accept the actors' accounts, as the interaction thesis allows. But when the social scientist and the actors are from entirely different cultural backgrounds, the social scientist will often reject the actors' descriptions and explanations, suggesting instead his own interpretation of the object under study.

I must leave these as unjustified assertions until the next chapter. As a defence of the bald assertion that social science can break with common sense, I will for the moment simply discuss an example from social science which seems to support the contrary view. In a paper on anthropological linguistics, Hale writes:

Many important aspects of the structure of a given language are essentially beyond the reach of the scholar who is not a native speaker of it. Even where insights of great importance have been contributed by non-native speakers to the study of English, for example, it is possible to argue that the insights are based on intuitions which, in all essential respects, closely approximate those of a native speaker (1972, p. 386).

Mentioning his own studies of the syntactical area 'dealing with phenomena of pronominal reference and deletion of coreferential elements in complex sentences', he confesses his 'absolute dependence on the searching introspection of a native speaker' (p. 387).

The status of these problems is revealed, however, when Hale writes that this dependence on native intuitions, together with the proliferation of research interests in linguistics, has produced 'a serious problem of logistics', which 'is greatly reduced if the linguist and the native speaker are the same individual' (p. 387). Logistics, not logic, as Hale remarks, because the philosophical issue – whether social science can break with common sense – has been pre-empted by the phrase 'pronominal reference and deletion of coreferential elements in complex sentences', a phrase whose home is in the linguist's, not the native's, culture. It may be that a linguist has to refer to the native speaker in order to decide what can be correctly said in the language under study. But, in linguistics, this is a point about the source of the data. When the linguist moves to the level of classification and explanation, he may introduce terms and ideas (about, for example, the origin and structure of language) from outside the conceptual scheme of the native speaker – even if, which is precisely the idealisation I am making in this chapter, the linguist is a native speaker.

2.4.c. Criticisms

We must retain the central insight of the view under discussion in this section – that social science often refers to, learns from and incorporates actors' theories – without going to the extreme of holding that social science cannot transcend actors' theories. The short way to avoid the latter pitfall is to state that social science can break with common sense, that common sense changes, and that it often changes as a result of the action of social science. More positively, we must see how the continual possibility and occasional necessity of going beyond common sense can be reconciled with an understanding of scientific theory.

Some of Feyerabend's arguments in *Against Method* for the possibility of and occasional necessity for a scientific critique of common sense are useful here. Feyerabend advocates theoretical pluralism, appealing to the usual empirical desiderata of scientific method. He maintains that theories can be irrefuted and even irrefutable not because they are in perfect agreement with the world, but because the factual statements in terms of which the theory is supposedly to be tested are themselves theoretically contaminated. Hence, 'the evidence that might refute a theory can often be unearthed only with the help of an incompatible alternative' (p. 29).

On this basis, we can understand why the criticism of common sense should be so strategically important to Feyerabend's pluralism. A new theory may seem unpromising because it clashes with the received common sense. This common sense is not, however, to be taken as an impartial arbiter because, as we have seen, it may be structured by the assumptions and concepts of older theories. Indeed, the new theory may be required in order to reveal that the received common sense, far from being a direct reflection of the world, involves specific theoretical opinions. Feyerabend's discussion of Galileo is intended to establish such points. Galileo, Feyerabend claims, both revealed and implicitly criticised the accepted 'natural interpretation' of motion, according to which all motion was operative. Galileo first asserted his premise of the motion of the earth and then asked what changes in common sense would remove the conflict between this premise and the interpretation by received common sense of such facts as that a stone falls straight to the ground. Galileo answered in terms of a new natural interpretation of motion, according to which only relative motion is operative. Feyerabend concludes that Galileo's oblique method of revealing the received common sense by developing an alternative is correct, because we can neither analyse nor criticise a common sense directly, since to do so would require the use of concepts or percepts from the common sense under study; that the new common sense should be allowed to develop before it is criticised, in order that we can evolve such normal features of a theoretical system as sensory reactions in terms of its categories prior to comparing it with familiar idioms; and, generally, that Galileo had the correct attitude to 'natural interpretations'. Namely, we should not call abstractly for their removal or retention, but engage in a critical discussion 'to decide which natural interpretations can be kept and which must be replaced' (p. 73).

The close links between the theoretical and commonsense domains, as well as the possibility of rejecting any particular commonsense concept or statement, can also be grounded in Hesse's philosophy of language, which I noted in section 1.2. In the terms of her analysis, if we defend and extend the application of the theoretical law (as opposed to the commonsense predicate based on pre-theoretical similarity), we would have modified an element of common sense by theoretical science. If, conversely, we defend and extend the application of the commonsense predicate, we would have modified an element of theoretical science from the basis of common sense.

2.5. THE VIEW THAT SOCIAL SCIENCE AND COMMON SENSE ARE INCOMPARABLE

The view that social science and common sense are incomparable is, perhaps surprisingly, rarely to be found in writers concerned with social science. It can, however, be supported through some of the points made by Ryle in *Dilemmas*. These points are central to the many fashionable intellectual compatibilisms; we are concerned here with the compatibility, because of incomparability, of social science and common sense. Ryle attempts to resolve the dilemmas that arise, he claims, when types of thought and evidence appropriate to one sort of questions are offered as answers to an entirely different sort of questions. Such dilemmas are not substantive ones, requiring more facts for their resolution. Rather, disputants caught in them talk at cross-purposes with one another, because they falsely believe that they are producing rival answers to the same questions. The dilemmas are therefore to be dissolved by philosophical analysis of the conceptual confusion that sustains the puzzles.

Ryle does not discuss the social science–common sense relation explicitly, and there is no guarantee that he would consider these two domains incomparable, as he does the other pairs of domains whose attempted conflict he thinks results in conceptual confusion. But there is enough material in his book to construct an ideal type for the view that social science and common sense are incomparable.

Ryle argues that a clash between a scientific theory and 'common knowledge' is an example of conceptual confusion, because the scientific theory and the common knowledge are based on different interests and are answers to different questions. For instance, the economist is not trying to characterise Ryle's brother. Rather, he 'is offering an account of certain marketing-tendencies, which applies to or covers my brother insofar as he concerns himself in marketing matters. . . . We cease to think either that my brother is a well-camouflaged Economic Man or that the economist is asking us to believe in fables' (p. 70). Likewise, our platitudes about perception neither agree nor disagree with physiological theory: we do not check our reply with a physiologist, if asked whether we see a tree, just as we do not need to check economic theory in order to decide whether Ryle's brother invests wisely or not. Scientific theory should be seen as allowing, not prohibiting, statements in the everyday domain which the particular scientific theory is also about, 'in a rather artificial sense of "about" ' (p. 80): 'the logically necessary silence of physical formulae about mahogany and oak or about colours and tastes need not be construed as proclaiming a shut door. It can be construed instead as proclaiming a wide-open door' (p. 84). Similarly, we might suppose, theories of class consciousness do not prohibit, but allow all the complexes of attitudes, dress, behaviour, manners, etc. which constitute everyday class consciousness. So, scientific theory leaves undecided the truth-status of any specific commonsense statement. Far from clashing with common sense, scientific theory requires that some (unspecified) statements not in scientific theory are true, for two different sorts of reasons. First, and this could be a point either about how we go about checking scientific theories or about the structure of the world, 'the very fact that some statement in physical theory is true requires that some statement or other (it cannot be deduced which), about such things as chairs and tables are true' (p. 79). Secondly, people are such that technical concepts have to be learnt via a grasp of untechnical concepts: 'It is quite false that people could, even in Utopia, be given their first lessons in talking or thinking in terms of this or that technical apparatus. Fingers and feet are, for many special purposes, grossly inefficient instruments' (p. 35) as are, we may add, commonsense intuitions of society.

I will make some critical remarks about Ryle's argument at the end of the next section. The views in this and the next section will both be dismissed for the same basic reason – their implausibility with respect to the history of social science.

2.6. THE VIEW THAT SOCIAL SCIENCE AND COMMON SENSE ARE IDENTICAL

This view differs from the view, noted in section 2.4, that social science should be based on common sense. This view holds that social science and common sense are identical in the respects (e.g. method or conceptual structure) relevant to a philosophical analysis of these two thought systems. The weaker view that social science should be based on common sense can accept that social science may diverge from common sense in certain relevant respects. But it must argue that social science should relate back to common sense, for example, by a translation of social science into common sense or by making common sense the seat of an incorrigible quasi-observation language for social science. Winch, for instance, holds that any distinctive social scientific statements must be translatable into the statements of the actors under study, in a way that parallels the purported relation between philosophical analysis and the pre-philosophical understanding of what is being analysed in classical analytical philosophy.

Few writers on social science have argued the identity of social science and common sense. In a crude form, it is part of conventional anti-social science wisdom, like the crude form of the external version of the view that social science must be based on common sense (see 2.4.a). A basis for a sophisticated version of this view emerges if we read Foucault's rich work with the sole concern of isolating his position on the social science–common sense relation. Such a reading is difficult to perform, for the good reason that Foucault maintains the identity of science and common sense.

In what sense he argues for their identity becomes clear if we consider the framework category of *The Order of Things*, namely the *'episteme'*. The *episteme* is the object of an investigation that analyses 'an epistemological space specific to a particular period': that is, the shared 'rules of formation', found in widely different disciplines, but used in each 'to define the objects proper to their own study, to form their concepts, to build their theories' (p. xi). Foucault also calls the *episteme* the 'historical *a priori*' (p. 158) and defines it as the overarching determinant of a period's possibility of thought. It is unnecessary for our purpose to exemplify Foucault's detailed analyses of an *episteme*. As a way of conceiving its overarching character, let us just note that it determines for its epoch such basic elements as the fields of knowledge and the relations between objects and their representation, and the conceptions of the role and character of language, nature and man.

The Archaeology of Knowledge, which has been seen as a movement away from *The Order of Things*, retains the category of the *episteme* in the notion of the positivity of a discourse, which is again called the 'historical *a priori*' (p. 127). *The Archaeology of Knowledge* is indeed a more Althusserian work than *The Order of Things*. It emphasises the rigidity of different levels in any structure and the discontinuity between these levels. It also criticises the notion of a total history which tries to isolate a unifying essence for an epoch, a critique which reads like a direct attack on the concept of *episteme*. On this basis, we might wonder whether Foucalt wishes to posit social science and common sense as distinct levels in the later book. Several features suggest a negative answer. First, circumstantially, Foucault is concerned to dissolve the unities of traditional concepts – which might include the unities of science and common sense – while Althusser is never so happy as when he is reifying traditional concepts into irreducible levels. Secondly, below the unities of the book and the *oeuvre* which he criticises, Foucault finds the unity of discourse. This unity involves various relations across domains, including 'relations between groups of statements . . . (even if these groups do not concern the same, or even adjacent, fields; even if they do not possess the same formal level . . .)' (1974, p. 29). Thirdly, the discourse has the same role as the *episteme* in *The Order of Things*. Thus, Foucault analyses discourse as a system of rules of, first, the formation of objects, concepts and theoretical strategies and, secondly, their dispersion into the different regions of the discourse.

Given the concept of *episteme*, we can understand Foucault's view that in any age, no matter what distinctions we introduce into human thought and practices, we find a basic unity by isolating that age's *episteme*. Foucault at times qualifies the exclusive rights of the *episteme* as a generator of an age's statements. He mentions survivals from previous *epistemes*, such as natural magic after the seventeenth century. In *The Order of Things*, literature and madness are generally exempted from determination by the dominant *episteme*. We can note, however, first that these qualifications are unexplained by Foucault and, secondly, that they are in any case marginal.

Foucault's thesis of underlying unity embraces any distinctions we may make between the specialised/scientific and the everyday/common sense. Thus, the *episteme* unifies not just theoretical disciplines, but also everyday practices, such as economic ones, for

A money reform, a banking custom, a trade practice . . . are all based upon a certain ground of knowledge . . . In any given culture and at any given moment, there is always one *episteme* that defines the conditions of possibility of all knowledge, whether expressed in a theory or silently invested in a practice (1970, p. 168).

The change from the Classical to the modern theories of language is a change not only in the intellectual conception of language, but in 'the whole mode of being of language' (p. 281), a change which is signified to language users by 'the radical and immediately perceptible obsoleteness of the language one has been using' (p. 282). *Madness and Civilisation* is a massive testimony to Foucault's belief that specialised thought systems share the same structure as everyday thought and practice. The specialised images of madness in psychiatry change according to such variables as whether madness is conceptualised by the common culture as at the centre or at the limits of society, as tragic or moral, as excluding reason or as the reverse face of reason, as a possible partner in dialogue or not, as *sui generis* or as merely one amongst other incapacities (such as poverty) requiring confinement, and as illness or not. As Foucault summarises *Madness and Civilisation* in *The Archaeology of Knowledge*, the discursive practice at the root of modern psychiatry 'is not only manifested in a discipline possessing a scientific status and scientific pretensions; it is also found in operation in legal texts, in literature, in philosophy, in political decisions, and in the statements made and the opinions expressed in daily life' (p. 179).

The identity that Foucault claims to discern between science and common sense is, then, an identity of conceptual basis, of deep conceptual structure, not necessarily of how people talk. *Within* an *episteme*'s conceptual structure, specialised disciplines may have pretensions to being different and superior to common sense. These pretensions are signalled by the specialised discipline being located in a different site from its everyday correlate – in an economics department, rather than in a bank or a supermarket, for example. Thus, Classical natural history claims to be a 'well-constructed language' which reveals the continuities of nature in ways that escape the spontaneous ordinary language of the Classical *episteme* (1970, pp. 145–8). But any differentiation within the *episteme* remains precisely *within* the conceptual unity which is the very nature of the *episteme*. The same point applies to Foucault's isolation of a scientific realm within an *episteme*. Scientific statements are a sub-group of the totality of statements which as a whole are generated by the formation rules of the *episteme*/discursive formation. The totality of generated statements, whether scientific or not, is regarded as constituting a unified corpus of knowledge, governed by a single criterion of knowledge, for the *episteme* constitutes its own validity as knowledge (see 1970, p. 365, and 1974, pp. 61 and 181–2).

The contrary views outlined in sections 2.5 and 2.6 share the feature that were we to accept either of them, discussion of the social science–common sense relation would be impossible. For there can be no conceptual relations between social science and common sense if they are either incomparable or identical. These views are therefore natural limiting positions for any classification of the social science–common sense relation.

It is possible to make purely philosophical criticisms of these two views. We might ask Ryle how social science and common sense can be about the same domain in any sense, and how he can make comparative judgments (e.g. technical versus untechnical) between the two, if they are incomparable; and Foucault faces the problem of how an *episteme* could ever break down if there are no internal tensions within it. But these two views are best evaluated by the history of social science. Unlike the views discussed in sections 2.3 and 2.4 which are prescriptive, the views now in question are descriptive.[1] Certainly, the views that social science should be based on or should break with common sense might be stated descriptively; and, conversely, the views that social science is incomparable or identical with common sense might be stated prescriptively. I consider the former in their prescriptive versions because powerful (though ultimately not powerful enough) philosophical arguments exist for both, irrespective of considerations about the history of social science. The latter, in contrast, would be eccentric to the point of absurdity if advanced in purely prescriptive form: that, no matter what the previous nature of the social science–common sense relation might be, social science and common sense ought to be either incomparable or identical.

Rather, the views advanced in sections 2.5 and 2.6 should be judged by answering the historical question: have the conceptual schemes of social science and common sense been either incomparable or identical? It is a fair bet that the answer would be negative: that, as against Ryle, we would discover rational interaction between social science

[1] At a fundamental level, the very possibility of differentiating descriptive and prescriptive approaches to the problem presupposes that our identification of social science prior to posing the social science–common sense relation does not refer in any way to common sense. As I indicated in the Introduction, my conception of social science is ultimately ostensive. The good social science of the classic writers exemplifies what I mean by social science. On this basis, we can ask non-circular questions about the actual and rational relations of social science and common sense.

and common sense; and, as against Foucault, occasional conceptual disparity between the two domains. This is only a guess about the history of social science. But it is a guess which is supported by the philosophical arguments for the view that social science and common sense interact. This is the most satisfactory of the views on two general grounds. First, it represents an extension of the relevant elements of post-empiricist philosophy of science into the philosophy of social science. Secondly, it portrays social science as an enterprise which both profits continuously from the conceptual scheme of the actors under study and yet can move beyond that scheme, if necessary.

2.7. AN EXAMPLE: ETHNOMETHODOLOGY AND THE SOCIOLOGY—COMMON SENSE RELATION

Ethnomethodologists and writers influenced by ethnomethodology adopt a complex position on the sociology–common sense question in terms of the above classification. This complexity does not imply that there is a weakness in my classification of views on the sociology–common sense relation, only that care is required in its application. Ethnomethodologists are committed variously to the views illustrated in sections 2.4.b, 2.5 and 2.6. My contention is that ethnomethodology's instability on the sociology–common sense relation suggests that the nature of this relation is a critical question for ethnomethodology. The variety of the positions it takes is an index of the fact that ethnomethodology is most at home in the view that sociology must break with common sense (an option it does not explicitly embrace), but that certain of its constituent theses prevent it from recognising this point.

Ethnomethodology advances the view of the at least partial identity of sociology and common sense (i.e. a variety of the view discussed in section 2.6) in the first instance as a critical point against professional sociology. In *Abandoning Method*, one of whose sources is phenomenological sociology, Phillips writes that the rules of sociology which determine its problems and acceptable solutions 'include not only formal procedural rules but the commonsense theories and methods that the sociologist must consult and utilise when faced with numerous choices and decisions in his inquiries' (p. 119). Commonsense conceptions enter essentially into sociology, because sociology's explicit procedural rules are not sufficient to determine a proposition's cognitive status: for example, they are not sufficient to determine when a proposition under study is supported by the previous results in an area. Similarly, Garfinkel emphasises in *Studies in Ethnomethodology* that typically commonsense methods of organising accounts determine the results of professional sociology: for instance, documentary interpretation in questionnaire and interview analysis. But Garfinkel does not restrict his claim to professional sociology, as opposed to ethno-methodology. Documentary interpretation as a method is character-ised by such features as continuous temporal restructuring, with the meaning of any item being continuously re-interpreted in the light of preceding and successive items. Garfinkel holds such a method to be integral not only (unconsciously) to interpretations achieved by lay actors and professional sociologists, but also (consciously) to ethno-methodological work. Thus, Garfinkel's study of Agnes, an intersexed person, is characterised by a developing awareness on Garfinkel's part of what his research problem is, ending, ironically and inconclusively, with the realisation that Agnes had been practising a massive dissimu-lation.

Yet another strand in ethnomethodology suggests that ethno-methodology and common sense are incomparable, the view illus-trated in section 2.5. Here, sociology and common sense are related only in that the latter is 'sociology's programmatic topic' (Garfinkel, p. 75). Everyday actions and commonsense accounts of those actions are ethnomethodology's unique subject matter, because of lay members' indifference to them. Thus, the staff of a bureau which determines if a death is suicide found it 'incongruous' to study the processes whereby they arrived at the decision of 'what really happened' (pp. 7–8).

But why are commonsense and ethnomethodological accounts incomparable? To understand this incomparability, we have to intro-duce the basic ethnomethodological concept of the radically contextual 'indexical expression'. Garfinkel defines them as expressions

whose sense cannot be decided by an auditor without his necessarily knowing or assuming something about the biography and the purposes of the user of the expression, the circumstances of the utterance, the previous course of the conversation, and the particular relationship of actual or potential interaction that exists between the expressor and the auditor . . . Indexical expressions and statements containing them are not freely repeatable; in a given discourse, not all their replicas [i.e. further tokens of the same type] therein are also transla-tions of them (pp. 4–5).

Garfinkel sees indexicality as central to actors' accounts, as when the staff of the suicide classification centre decide the status of deaths by means of the specific 'this's' of the case at hand: 'they have to start with *this* much; *this* sight; *this* note; *this* collection of whatever is at hand' (p. 18). Further, Garfinkel asserts that in sociology no convincing distinc-tion between objective and indexical expressions has been made and no programme for substituting occurrences of the former for occur-rences of the latter has been achieved. Garfinkel entrusts the method of 'documentary interpretation' with the task of constructing generalised patterns out of indexical particulars. It does so 'by treating an actual appearance as "the document of", as "pointing to", as "standing on behalf of" a presupposed underlying pattern' (p. 78). But documentary interpretation is not a final answer to indexicality. On the contrary, it too is riddled by an essential indexicality, given that 'not only is the underlying pattern derived from its individual documentary evidences, but the individual documentary evidences, in their turn, are interpreted on the basis of "what is known" about the underlying pattern. Each is used to elaborate the other' (p. 78).

The relativistic implications of ethnomethodology's contention that both actors' and sociologists' accounts contain indexical expressions are clear. The meanings of items in a system governed by indexicality are essentially contextual. Hence, items cannot be compared across contexts, for it is not certain that – even if physically identical – they would share the same meaning. In particular, items cannot be compared across the three large-scale contexts of (*a*) actors' accounts and practices, (*b*) professional sociologists' accounts and practices, and (*c*) ethnomethodologists' accounts of (*a*) and (*b*). But to suspend judgment of commonsense claims is equivalent in practice to accepting common sense's criterion of truth and judgments as to which statements are true. This is seen in McHugh's (1971) attempt at a phenomenological theory of truth. McHugh's analysis of truth is interestingly similar to Althusser's – though Althusser, of course, does not share McHugh's relativism – and equally vacuous. McHugh holds that we cannot have a philosophical criterion of truth, but only a description of the procedures that exist for generating truth-claims. On this basis, McHugh and phenomenological sociology are committed to accepting all claims to truth at face value, whether they occur in the domains of common sense, traditional sociology or ethnomethodology.

Ethnomethodology cannot rest with the view that sociology and common sense are incomparable, however. In order to see why, let us return to the notion of indexical expression. This concept is held to apply to the situation where terms and assertions are not independent of their usage. But to state that meaning depends on usage is ambiguous between: (i) the meaning of the assertion/term is determined by some occasions of its use, but not necessarily by the particular occasion in question; (ii) the meaning of the assertion/term is determined by some occasions of its use, including the particular occasion in question; and (iii) the meaning of the assertion/term is totally determined by this particular occasion of its use. Possibilities (i) and (ii) do not preclude either this particular occasion of its use being used as evidence for or against statements in which the term is used, or this particular usage serving as a check on the correct application of the term, if it is the indexicality of a term (rather than an assertion) that is at issue. Possibility (iii) would prevent argument and it is to this interpretation that ethnomethodology is committed. But it does not prevent only arguments across the common sense–sociology–ethnomethodology divides. It also prevents argument within ethnomethodology. If all linguistic items change their meaning in different contexts, then the repetition of a term or assertion in the course of an ethnomethodological text is not in fact a genuine repetition. By reducing its unit of relativistic analysis to anything which can be identified as an individual item, ethnomethodology becomes enmeshed in an attempt to talk about the essentially unique, a project which we noted in section 1.2 to be fruitless.

Moreover, ethnomethodology's central claim that it studies the accounts given by members assumes comparability between the commonsense and ethnomethodological domains in two ways. First, ethnomethodology presupposes that it is talking about actors' practices and accounts. But if ethnomethodology and common sense were incomparable, ethnomethodology's claim to be describing everyday accounts could not be substantiated. This point suggests a deficiency in McHugh's formal and relativistic notion of truth. An element in ethnomethodology's claim to truth, which it assumes in its concrete examples, is that it corresponds in some sense to its object, namely, actors' accounts. McHugh's concept of truth provides no way of distinguishing between truth as ascribed to the derived statements of a purely formal, uninterpreted logical calculus with definite, but meaningless rules of inference, and truth as ascribed to the statements of a sociological theory. But there is a difference, and this difference is at least partly described when we say that sociology aims at an adequate depiction of its object. Secondly, ethnomethodology does not just talk about everyday accounts; it talks about them critically. The fact that ethnomethodology has a distinctive focus on everyday accounts, in that it makes explicit what is usually left implicit, does not imply that ethnomethodology's results cannot clash with the theories of everyday actors. Garfinkel mentions as one of the conditions for a jury to arrive at a correct decision that jurors should 'emerge from the inquiry with their reputations intact' (p. 108). This claim involves an account of juries' decisions given in terms completely different from those found in the ideology of the jury system and, no doubt, from those to be found in jurors' statements.

Some phenomenological sociologists have tried to give an account of the fact that ethnomethodology is comparable, and yet not identical, with common sense. Perhaps the clearest attempt is Douglas's 'Understanding Everyday Life', an essay which tries to argue the view that sociology should be based on common sense on internal grounds, but is prevented from doing so by the basic ethnomethodological assumptions.

Douglas holds that 'Any scientific understanding of human action, at whatever level of ordering of generality, must begin with and be built upon an understanding of the everyday life of the members performing those actions' (p. 11). That sociology is based on common-sense understanding is clear, for example, from the interpretation of surveys, which requires the sociologist's commonsense understanding of actors' responses.

But ethnomethodology does not just replicate the 'natural stance', the 'stance in which the everyday world is taken for granted as it is experienced in everyday life' (p. 14). Rather, ethnomethodology takes the 'theoretic stance', which is 'to stand back from, to reflect upon, to re-view the experience taken for granted in the natural stance' (p. 15). Douglas argues that both common sense and science take the usefulness and shareability of knowledge as their criterion of objectivity. Science, in which Douglas includes the theoretic stance, differs from common sense in having more objective, that is, more useful and shareable knowledge. And the 'greater shareability of scientific knowledge is achieved primarily by progressively freeing the knowledge of concrete phenomena from the situation in which they are known' (p. 28). A method of producing more objective knowledge is, for example, the provision of systematic evidence about research methods so we do not take for granted the commonsense procedures for inferring social meanings in interviews.

We begin to see why Douglas's approach is not a satisfactory example of the view that sociology must be based on common sense. Unlike Winch who sees sociology as developing the conceptual possibilities of common sense, Douglas holds sociology to be based on common sense only in that it starts from common sense. For Douglas, sociology develops by progressively freeing itself from the restrictions of commonsense thought. In fact, Douglas argues both that sociology must be based on common sense because of common sense's relation to sociology and that sociology should break with common sense.

Nor is Douglas's position a satisfactory explication of phenomenological sociology. Central to ethnomethodology, as we have seen, is the notion of indexicality. Douglas recognises this in his concept of the 'integrity of the situation', which is 'a specific form of the more general principle of the contextual determination of social events' and whose most important element is the 'contextual determination of meaning'. Douglas writes that, *pace* the sociologies which have tried to analyse away the individual differences of situations, 'once we make the commitment to retain, at least initially, the integrity of the phenomena, we have decided not to use such *ad hoc* procedures to eliminate from consideration the concrete differences in events' (p. 37). But Douglas's previous description of sociological objectivity conflicts with the integrity of the situation. Sociology becomes more objective, for Douglas, by freeing itself from the contextual aspects of situations. Phenomenological sociology would be locked in perpetual conflict with what is often claimed to be its sole topic and main source, namely common sense. Douglas does not flinch from this conclusion: 'there is an essential tension between the sociologist's new-found commitments to the integrity of the phenomena and to the theoretic stance' (p. 44). The point is that there is no basis in ethnomethodology for understanding this tension as fruitful. Indeed, fidelity to ethnomethodological indexicality precludes an objective sociology.

Ethnomethodology cannot find a site in the sociology–common sense debate because its relativist indexicality initially prevents it from giving an account of sociology's relation to common sense as other than that of subject to subject matter. Even in this role, ethnomethodology is unstable, since its intellectual practice is incoherent if it remains faithful to extreme indexical relativism. Douglas broaches the idea that phenomenological sociology stands, not just in a subject/ subject matter relation, but in a competitive cognitive relation to common sense. Retaining the commitment to common sense, Douglas wishes to say that ethnomethodology is based on common sense, and yet can improve it. But he is caught in the dilemmas that, with respect to sociology, either he succeeds in providing a site for this new sociology at the cost of abandoning such constitutive phenomenological notions as the indexical integrity of the situation, or he maintains the phenomenological commitments and then must fall back into the incoherence of an indexical sociology; and, with respect to common sense, he wishes to say that sociology can tell us novel and theoretically deep things about common sense, without rendering common sense vulnerable to criticism.

This analysis suggests that, given ethnomethodology's belief in the indexicality of common sense, ethnomethodology could present its own position coherently if it posited: first, the possibility of non-indexical thought; secondly, the fact that sociology is capable of this non-indexical thought; and, thirdly, that sociology in consequence attains non-indexicality by breaking cognitively with common sense, even if common sense were to remain its unique topic. This would propel ethnomethodology into a version of the view that sociology must break with common sense. It would not be that distant from the implicit criticism of common sense underlying much ethno-

71

methodological practice. Whether we would still have a distinctive phenomenological sociology in any sense, I will not discuss here; though the irony of the fact that ethnomethodology – with its pretensions to learning from common sense – is unable to conceptualise that side of the interaction thesis which emphasises the dependence of social science on common sense bears savouring.

3

Meaning and social science

3.1. MEANING

I now drop all artificial restrictions previously placed on the conceptualisation of social science and its objects. In this chapter, I try to understand the implications for the problem of meaning in social science of the full anthropological situation, the situation where the actor may possess not only theories about himself but also radically different theories from those of the social scientific observer.

The idealisations I made in the previous two chapters have facilitated the discussions of meaning and value I am about to undertake. For in chapter one, by abstracting from all problems of meaning and value, I showed how a number of issues which might otherwise have been confused with more fundamental questions are not of decisive philosophical relevance to naturalism. In chapter two, I showed how social science can at times break with, as well as at times be based on, actors' theories, even if those theories form part of the social scientist's home culture. The complementary themes that the social scientist may sometimes reject and sometimes accept actors' accounts – rejection is more likely, especially in the anthropological situation – will again be central to this chapter, though I will approach the problem in a different way. An element of this different approach is the argument that actors' theories are potentially scientific, and that therefore they can be entertained and either accepted or rejected by the social scientist in the same way as he would entertain the theories of another social scientist. In fact, the thesis of chapter two – that social scientific and commonsense theories interact and that they differ only in degree – itself supports the view that there is no radical heterogeneity between social scientific and actors' conceptual schemes.

In chapters three and four, I discuss what I take to be the two key areas in the defence of naturalism, namely meaning and value. Both have repeatedly been centres for anti-naturalism. With the recent critiques of functionalism and behaviourism in social science and empiricism in the philosophy of science, meaning and value are again of decisive importance for the philosophy of social science. I will argue that social science must note meanings and values in ways unnecessary for natural science, yet this fact does not impugn the possibility of a naturalistic social science. But I consider the point that social science must note values to be much more fundamental than the point that social science must note meanings. To understand why social science must be value-laden produces a radical revision of our conception of the nature of social science. I hope to show, however, that it does not necessitate a revision in the direction of anti-naturalism.

There is no more confused area in the philosophy of social science than that of the problem of meaning. Diverse anti-naturalistic writers argue that action is determined or is constituted by meaning. Yet the notions of meaning involved, and the relations postulated between meaning and action, are typically left unanalysed. These views are equated with the different position that the social is language-like. From both, hasty conclusions are drawn concerning the heterogeneity of social and natural science. So poor have most formulations of the problem of meaning been that writers concerned to defend a naturalistic social science have often missed the complexity of the issue at hand. This chapter analyses the various claims that social science is meaningful; suggests that there are senses in which social science must note meanings that natural science can ignore; and argues that this does not preclude the possibility of a naturalistic social science.

My study of meaning in social science concentrates on two paradigmatic relations that may be said to exist between the actors' meanings and other features of the social world, typically the actors' actions. These two relations I call the meaning 'determining' the action and the meaning 'constituting' the action; though I also discuss a further relation between meaning and action which I term the meaning 'classifying' the action. By the meaning determining the action, I indicate the belief that the meaning is a condition, necessary or sufficient, of the action. In turn, to say that the meaning is a condition of the action may be to say two broadly different things. First, the meaning is a scientific condition of the action; 'scientific condition' covers both causal relations and biological and mathematical functions, for example. Secondly, the meaning is a logical condition of the action, that is, a ground of or logically linked to the action. One of the purposes of this chapter is to argue that the first notion of scientific determination is coherent as an analysis of the meaning–action relation in naturalistic social science. By the meaning constituting the action, I indicate the stronger point that the meaning is an essential element of the action's identity. Here, the meaning is not just a condition of the independently existing

74

action. Rather, meaning and action are related in the following schematic way: 'meaning + . . . = action'. Of course, there may be other necessary ingredients of the action's identity: a physical behaviour may always be found on the left-hand side of the equation. But that question is not now at issue. The anti-naturalist's basic claim is only that meaning is always an essential part of an action, whatever else may be too. Another purpose of this chapter is to argue that the notion of meaning constituting action provides no decisive problems for naturalism and can be interpreted as an instance of the (scientific) determination of action by meaning.

Meaning is not a pre-occupation exclusive to philosophers. The claims that social science must explain action by its meaning or must show how action is constituted by meaning are central, whether implicit or explicit, to many studies in various social sciences informed by diverse theoretical traditions.

Thus, Taylor and Walton open a study of industrial sabotage by saying that they object to official statistics of industrial sabotage because

they simply give details of *actions*, whereas our central interest is in the *meanings or motives* which lie behind such actions. We categorise acts of sabotage, not under such behavioural headings as 'smashing conveyor belts' or 'dropping ball-bearings into cogs', but rather under meaningful and intentional headings such as 'attempts to reduce tension and frustration', 'attempts at easing the work process', 'attempts to assert control' (1971, p. 220).

More generally, social science's concern with meaning is revealed, for example, in Dahl's (1965, p. 11) definition of a social role as a pattern of shared expectations; in Evans-Pritchard's complaint against nineteenth-century anthropology that the facts analysed were 'often wrenched from the social contexts which alone gave them meaning' (1972, p. 39); and in Goffman's theories and empirical studies which attempt to show how understanding both what a social situation is and how it came about depends on understanding actors' impression-management, world-views, theories and meanings.

3.2. THE SOCIAL AS LANGUAGE-LIKE

In the course of arguing that integrity is as necessary a norm in social relations as truthfulness is in the use of language, Winch writes that there 'are important formal analogies between language and other social institutions' (1972, p. 70). Are there? And is there anything distinctively philosophical to be said on this topic? I will argue in this section that whether there are significant analogies between language and society is purely an empirical question, so philosophy has nothing to contribute on the matter. This is important because many of the fashionable comparisons of language and society seek to establish no more than that society is language-like in one of the three senses I elucidate below. These claims by themselves have no implications for the issue of social science's status *vis-à-vis* natural science. Such parallels prove philosophically interesting only if we argue in addition that the theory of language in question cannot be scientific. In this section, if any proposed theory of language has non-naturalistic implications which carry over into the theory of society that is to be modelled on it, I will indicate them and postpone consideration of them until section 3.4.

I will show, then, how various ways of claiming that the social is language-like are irrelevant to the question of the scientific status of social science. We can break down such claims into three general types.

(I) A theory of language ('model'), whether from linguistics or from the philosophy of language, may serve as a model for a theory of society ('explanandum'). Whether or not such a development is fruitful depends on the relative strengths of the positive, negative and neutral analogies between the two theories, and on how much of the neutral analogy eventually turns out to be positive; both of these issues are empirical. For the development of the explanandum on the basis of the model to be a scientific one, the relation between the terms in the model that are held to be analogous to terms in the explanandum must be deterministic in some scientific sense. There must also be no good reasons for denying that determinisitic relations of the same kind may exist between the terms of the explanandum (see Hesse, 1970, pp. 8–10 and 86–7).

Examples of the types of theories of language that are currently being used, either in whole or piecemeal, as models for the development of theories of society are Saussure's and Chomsky's analyses of the structural rules for the production of sentences, Grice's analysis of the meaning of sentences in terms of speakers' intentions, and Austin's and Searle's analyses of the force of speech acts. The proponents of Saussure's and Chomsky's theories usually take them to be scientific. For example, they are said to involve an element which is standardly considered to be incompatible with non-naturalistic accounts of social science. Namely, the fundamental explanatory features of the theories are below the consciousness of everyday actors. Insofar as this is the case, then we can assume that theories of society being modelled on them will themselves be scientific. In contrast, Grice's, Austin's and Searle's theories raise problems for the possibility of a scientific social study, because their theories of language are not developed as scientific theories. Indeed, some aspects of their theories could be held to preclude a scientific account of language and hence of any object whose theory was modelled on them. For instance, Austin (1962, pp. 102ff.) emphasises that the illocutionary act – which gives the force of a verbal utterance – is conventionally or constitutively, not causally, related to the verbal utterance. Similarly, Grice (1967, p. 46) argues that in an intentional analysis of meaning the intended effect resulting from the speaker's utterance should be not merely causally related to that utterance. Analogous points are made by writers concerned to emphasise the meaningful nature of social science's object. I will consider them in section 3.4.

As an alternative to taking individual theories of language as models for a theory of society, we may study the items that any theory of language has to explain and the elements out of which it must be constructed, and ask whether it is fruitful to look for analogous explananda and elements in a theory of society. These point-by-point analogies may be at the most general theoretical level (see, for example, Ardener's [1971, pp. xxxvi] suggestions as to how general Saussurean insights may be of use to social science). Or they may involve empirical details. Examples of questions produced by such considerations are: is there anything corresponding to the empiricist–rationalist debate about the nature of language acquisition in the theory of society? Is there a corresponding syntax–semantics distinction in the theory of society? Is the competence–performance distinction relevant to both domains? Can Frege's distinctions between the sense, reference and associated idea of a term in the theory of meaning be applied to the notion of the meaning of action? Is there a social analogue to the debate in the theory of language as to whether the basic vehicle for linguistic meaning is the word, the sentence or the whole language? Does a piece of social interaction possess temporal structuring similar to that of a sentence (e.g. is an action related to a previous action in the way that a word or phrase is related to the previous word or phrase?)? None of these questions have convincing answers at present. Their resolution may prove more fruitful for social science than the insights derived from the biological model of society; though we are certainly not yet in a position to compare the theories of language and biology as models for the theory of society, because the former has barely been developed as a model for social science. In any case, whether or not the linguistic model is fruitful is a matter for theoretical and empirical social science to decide. It is not a concern of philosophy. In developing the theory of language as a model for society we will certainly discover negative analogies between the two domains.

Perhaps areas of negative analogy are the inability to specify a reference for social action, the fact that meaning is more dependent on context in the case of a sentence than in the case of an action, and the sense in which more than one person is more essential to the production of an action than to the production of a sentence. Not only are these points a matter for theoretical and empirical (not philosophical) decision, but in discovering any negative analogies at all, we discover ways in which the social is not language-like, so any philosophical arguments that purport to show that the theory of language could not be scientific become thereby less relevant to social science.

(II) A second general way of claiming that society is language-like is to hold that the laws and structure of language and society are identical, not just analogous. Put in this general way, the thesis is barely intelligible. We can re-state it more modestly as the claim that a specific sector of social action has the same laws and structure as a specific sector of language. Once again, whether this is so is a social scientific, not a philosophical matter. It is a philosophically interesting position only if we produce an argument that the relevant sector of the theory of language is not scientific. An example of a claim of structural identity between aspects of language and society that has no such philosophical implications is the theory of communication which Leach proposes in *Culture and Communication*. Leach writes that many modes of cultural action in addition to speaking – including writing, musical performance, dancing, painting, singing, building, acting, curing and worshipping – communicate information. He concludes that 'at some level, the "mechanism" of these various modes of communication must be the same' (p. 16). Leach holds that the mechanism causally determines the production of these acts of communication. Two examples of structural mechanisms which Leach thinks are shared by language and non-verbal communication are the facts that all acts of communication are constructed by metaphorical transformation between one self-contained system of signs and another (e.g. physical objects representing the divine in rituals) and that the elements of a system of communication derive their significance not individually, but in patterns of binary opposition (e.g. red and green in traffic lights).

(III) An at present even more speculative way of holding the social to be language-like is to claim that, although language and society possess different laws at one level, at a more fundamental level their distinctive laws can be derived from the same theoretical principles. The term 'semiology' has been coined for this putative basic science of linguistic and non-linguistic communication (see Lévi-Strauss, 1974, p. 16). Again, such a position of itself has no implications for the scientific status of social study, unless we construct an argument about the non-naturalistic nature of the basic science of communication.

3.3. TWO VIEWS OF MEANING AND SOCIAL SCIENCE

Winch's *The Idea of a Social Science* sets out the idea that a grasp of the meaningful nature of social action leads to a radical anti-naturalistic revision in our understanding of social science. I will outline the main theses of this work which bear on the sense in which social action is meaningful and the implications that these theses possess for social science. I am not here interested in an exhaustive presentation and critique of Winch's views for their own sake. I use Winch's work as a foil to develop the correct position on the problem of meaning in social science, so I discuss what he says only where it is relevant to my theme.[1]

Winch terms a set of behaviours an action if it is given or could be given a meaning by its agent. The 'could be given' is needed to theorise the fact that we often perform an action without consciously imbuing it with meaning. All Winch demands is that some description exists of the action as an action which would be assented to by the agent.

Winch holds that we cannot understand the meaning of social action causally, for instance in terms of structures of past social interaction, because patterns of interaction depend on or are themselves constituted by meanings. Rather, meaningful behaviour is to be explicated as governed by rules, for only rules give determinate criteria of sameness and difference for meanings. Whether a set of behaviours means (= is the action) X or Y is decided by reference to the past rules, implicit or explicit, that have governed our usage of the concepts of X or Y.

These rules exist essentially in a social context. Winch's argument for the social nature of rules is a special case of Wittgenstein's critique of the possibility of a private language. Only in some social context can determinate sense be given to the notion of a correct and incorrect application of the rules, which is a necessary feature of a rule, for anyone must be in principle able to understand what acceptance of the rule implies.[2]

Winch denies that the relations between the social rules and the meanings they govern, between the meanings and the actions constituted by those meanings, between different instances of meanings and

---

[1] Peters (1969), Melden (1961) and Louch (1972) suggest positions on the meaning of social action similar to Winch's.

[2] Examples which Wittgenstein gives of how the social context is important in understanding a set of behaviours are to be found in his *Lectures and Conversations on Aesthetics, Psychology and Religious Belief* (p. 8) and *Zettel* (paras. 164, 350 and 374–8).

hence between different actions, are in any sense causal. Thus, although Winch writes that primitives' concepts can be understood only in the context of their way of life and makes it clear that he is happy to identify 'way of life' with 'social institutions' (1970, pp. 95–6), he denies that the relation between primitives' institutions and their concepts is a causal one. The model for all these relations is rather how ideas are related to one another: logically and internally. Ideas are the core of Winch's delineation of the basic object of social analysis, actors' actions; so Winch concludes, actions are naturally related to one another as ideas are to ideas.

Winch originally defines social actions in terms of actors' meanings. He then situates both actors' meanings and action in the particular social context of the agent. From these positions, Winch infers that social science's subject matter is defined by the criteria of significance of the actors in question, not by those of the observer. Hence, it is at least an essential part of social study that we understand the point of view of the members under study. Examples of how the imposition of the observer's categories may hinder understanding are to be found in Needham's claim that the validity of the distinction between belief and experience in anthropological work 'is to be determined by whether or not the people under study actually possess the idea of experience as we define it' (1972, p. 174); and in Evans-Pritchard's argument (1967a, pp. 315–16) that the central ideas of Nuer religion are essentially vague, so an anthropologist risks misunderstanding if he tries to be precise in his elucidation of the nature of the Nuer's *kwoth*, Spirit.

Winch holds that having identified social actions from the actors' point of view, the observer cannot then evolve a theory which negates that point of view. For if the observer denies the actors' theories which constitute their actions, he changes the criteria of identity of the objects under study; he thereby ceases to study what he set out to study. Malcolm exemplifies this thesis in *Dreaming* (ch. 13), with the claim that to identify dreams on the basis of rapid eye movements is to provide a different meaning for the notion of dreaming than is ordinarily accepted. That these two concepts of dreaming are not co-extensive can be seen in the case where on the rapid eye movement criterion a person is said to have dreamt, but on the ordinary first-person criterion this is denied.

Winch's second argument for the view that the observer cannot deny the actors' theories is that appeals to standards of reality and rationality cannot be made across languages or cultures. I do not discuss relativistic arguments directly in this chapter, though what I will say about theorising across contexts is relevant to them, and I will return briefly to the issue in the Conclusion.

By these points, Winch hopes to prevent social science from suggesting a theory which conflicts with the meanings constitutive of the actors' actions. Winch admits that the concerns of social science often necessitate a more sophisticated conceptual scheme than is to be found among everyday actors, but, he urges, the arguments just developed imply that the observer's conceptual scheme must be ultimately intelligible in terms of the actors' concepts. Failing such intelligibility, the question whether the observer has given an adequate account of the social object in question does not even arise.

The implications drawn by Winch from his argument for social science are, negatively, that social science must eschew scientific theories and cross-cultural research. A complex set of actions such as asceticism derives its meaning from a specific context, and to argue that there is one thing, asceticism, in different contexts is to court superficial understanding. Positively, Winch sees social science as contextual interpretation. To understand a situation we must come to view it in the actors' terms. We must grasp how the actors' meanings constitute the situation, and how they are internally related to each other and to the social context which gives them determinate sense. In hermeneutic terms, *verstehen*, the process of understanding the actors' viewpoint, is adequate as a methodology for the whole of social science.

Naturalism's basic strategy in criticising anti-naturalistic views of meaning is to urge that meanings are social scientific objects on a par with other social scientific objects. As a sub-set of the objects of social science, meanings do not pose special philosophical problems. A typical example of this approach is Brodbeck's 'Meaning and Action'. Brodbeck isolates four meanings of meaning. These are: the reference of a term (Brodbeck's 'meaning$_1$'); the significance of a term in virtue of the fact that the term's reference is lawfully connected with other things ('meaning$_2$'); what a thought intends or is about ('meaning$_3$'); and the psychological significance which a term or physical pattern has for an individual ('meaning$_4$'). She argues that only the first two senses of meaning are relevant for the philosophy of social science. Meaning$_3$ and meaning$_4$ may form part of the subject matter of a psychological or social science, but they do not structure the cognitive claims of those sciences: we can make meaningful$_{1,2}$ statements about meaning$_3$ and meaning$_4$. Moreover, these statements are objective, Brodbeck argues, for although mental events are ontologically distinct from physical events and statements about the two are not tautologically related, the efficacy of mental events in the world can be theorised by a complex re-description of them in terms of physical events. This re-descriptive strategy for maintaining the objectivity of social science rests on the

81

assumption that mental events are unobservable. This is one thing I will dispute in the following analysis, an analysis which must be more complex than Brodbeck's in order to show how Winch has exaggerated the implications of meaning for social science.

3.4. VARIETIES OF MEANING

3.4.a. Meaning and the language of social science

Let us first examine how social scientific language has meaning in ways similar to natural scientific language. In doing so, it is essential to emphasise more consistently than Brodbeck does herself the distinction which underlies her essay, namely between the language of a scientific theory and what the language is about.

We can accept Brodbeck's analysis of meaning$_1$, that social scientific statements are meaningful in that they purport to refer to things. Of itself, this clearly gives no grounds for distinguishing natural and social science. Brodbeck's meaning$_2$ is more problematical, however. She says that a term's meaning$_2$, the connection which a term's reference has with other things, is a matter of fact. But if we distinguish between the language of a theory and what the theory is about, we see that Brodbeck's claim is too simple. How what the term refers to, an object in the world, is actually related to other objects in the world is indeed a matter of fact. The importance of this point for an analysis of the meaning of scientific terms and statements appears more limited than Brodbeck thinks, however, given recent sensitivity to what previously appeared to be a mere platitude, namely that scientific statements are made in language. The systematic connections of one term with other terms in a scientific theory cannot simply be identified with the relations which exist between things in the world; the former are basically logical, the latter contingent. Here, then, is another sense in which meaning may be relevant to the philosophy of social science. In analysing a social scientific term, it will typically be necessary to study the meaning that the term has in virtue of its logical links with other terms in its home theory. Yet this second sense of the meaning of social scientific terms is common to an analysis of the meaning of natural scientific terms and therefore does not support an anti-naturalistic analysis of social science. Indeed, the extent to which the systematic links a term possesses are to be incorporated into that term's meaning is one of the currently unresolved issues in the philosophy of natural science.

A classic statement of the importance of internal links in a scientific theory is given by Quine (1961, pp. 42ff.). In his study of the concept of the unconscious, MacIntyre (1973, pp. 10 ff.) exemplifies how the meaning of a social scientific term can be understood only by stating its systematic connections with other terms in its theory. Similarly, Ollman (1971, pt. I) claims that the relations between elements of Marx's theory should be understood as internal. One of Ollman's arguments for this is the strong thesis, which goes beyond considerations of the nature of theoretical language, that Marx held the relations between things in the world to be internal too. I will discuss this strong thesis, as it has been interpreted by analytical philosophy, later in this section.

Noting the importance of the apparent platitude that scientific theories are formulated in language also encourages a convergence between the philosophy of natural science and the hermeneutic philosophies of social science which stress the role of meaning in social science. This convergence has been explicated by Apel (1967) from the direction of hermeneutics, and by Hesse (1972) from the direction of the philosophy of science. The need to understand an intersubjective language is recognised as a central feature of the philosophy of all science. This recognition underpins the point that the meanings of scientific terms are at least partly determined by internal connections within theory; a point which, in turn, allows us to apply to the philosophy of science such hermeneutic ideas as that the relation of the whole (theory) and part (meanings) is circular, and that no data are uninterpreted (atheoretical).

Brodbeck's meaning$_2$, that a term has significance in virtue of its referent's lawful connections with other things in the world, and the idea of the meaning of a scientific term which I have just noted, that a term's meaning is given by its interconnections within a theory, are closely related. This relation arises from the fact that the ultimate point of engaging in scientific work is to construct a scientific theory which, either in whole or in part, corresponds to the way the world is. The systematic connections between terms in a theory, then, are typically held to reflect the way the world is. Theories further purport to be explanatory, as well as descriptive. The contents of the statements which act as the lawlike premises in explanations vary, depending on such things as one's interests and the context of the matter at hand; they include empirical generalisations, functional laws and statements that a situation is an instance of a more general (deeper) process. Now, some authors talk of explanations as the meaning of the corresponding explananda. Thus, Lévi-Strauss (1974, p. 32) says that the meaning of the incest prohibition is to create social bonds between different biological groups. To label social scientific explanations 'meaningful' or 'interpretative' in a way which is meant to differentiate them from natural scientific explanations is mere confusion. At the level of social scientific language (that is, before we consider social science's specific objects), there is no reason why the form of explanation in natural and social science should not be identical. If we wish to use the rather quaint locution that the meaning of the incest prohibition is to create social bonds between different biological groups, then we are also entitled to say that the meaning of the thermostat is to control the temperature in the house.

A refusal to distinguish the form of explanation in social and natural science in terms of the notion of meaning carries over into a refusal to distinguish different types of explanation as meaningful or not. For instance, Mannheim in *Essays on the Sociology of Culture* argues that a historical analysis of an action's determinants is causal, whereas setting that action in a structural context in order to learn the event's function in the equilibrium of its whole system is meaningful or interpretative. We could speak like that, but there is no good reason to do so, because functional explanations are a type of satisfactory scientific explanation and, conversely, genetic explanations are relevant to 'understanding the real nature' (in some loose sense) of the explanandum. Moreover, both types of explanation occur in natural and social science.

There is a final sense in which by looking at the language of scientific theory we can show social science to be meaningful in exactly the same way as natural science. Some writers have argued the need for an interpretative, non-naturalistic social science on the ground that naturalistic social science must be based on objective 'brute data', that is 'data whose validity cannot be questioned by offering another interpretation or reading, data whose credibility cannot be founded or undermined by further reasoning' (Taylor, 1971, p. 8). Such data are held to be inadequate for conceptualising the interpreted and meaningful nature of the basic data of social science. Insofar as this argument depends on a point about the specific objects of social science, I will deal with it shortly. But insofar as it rests on a point about the nature of natural scientific theory, it is clearly mistaken. It is a platitude of post-empiricist philosophy of science that there are neither incorrigible nor theory-free (uninterpreted) basic data; not only are such data impossible, they are also unnecessary for objective science. Much hermeneutic writing on social study works with a naive contrast model of natural science, against which social accounts are held to be theory-laden and therefore 'meaningful'. Perhaps the current rapprochement between naturalistic and hermeneutic methodology will help to remedy this deficiency in the latter.

3.4.b. *Meaning and the objects of social science: subjective meanings*

When we turn to social science's specific objects, we can no longer rely on outlining the formal similarities between natural and social science in order to show that the latter is no more meaningful than the former. Rather, we must see whether the properties of social science's objects require a rejection of naturalistic methodology in social science.

The most important feature to note about social scientific objects is that, whether they are actions, institutions, belief-systems or people, what and how they are typically depends on the theories and beliefs of the relevant actors. In social science, unlike natural science, analysis of meaning is relevant to the object of study, as well as to the language in which the study is done. It is this fact which Giddens (1976, p. 79) suggestively calls the 'double hermeneutic' at the centre of social science.

I will divide actors' meanings into two categories: personal, subjective meanings and social, objective meanings. This distinction turns on the difference between the types of beliefs etc. which are likely to be held by individual actors or are actually in the consciousness of individual actors, and the types of beliefs etc. which can be isolated as part of the socio-cultural context, irrespective of individuals. It is a distinction only made for the convenience of analysis. I do not imply that there is a clear-cut distinction. Indeed, it may be impossible to make at all if the social constitutes and determines the personal or, conversely, if the social is reducible to the personal. But the distinction is useful for delineating two different possible types of meanings and for clarifying their relevance for social science.

By 'subjective meanings' I mean such entities as intentions, reasons, motives and purposes which actually or potentially are part of the actor's consciousness and which actually or potentially determine, constitute or describe the actor's actions. Insofar as the actor is conscious of the meanings associated with his actions, these meanings are subjective. However, conscious meanings are only a sub-set of subjective meanings. For an actor may act unself-consciously, yet be prepared to assent to a subjectively meaningful description of his action in retrospect, if he is pressed to do so. Some illuminating distinctions can be made between intentions, reasons, motives and purposes (see, e.g., Peters, 1969, chs. 1 and 2). But they are mainly irrelevant for my purpose. All I need distinguish is, first, a form of subjective meaning which would be offered by the actor, if an explanation were sought for an action: I will call this the *reason* for the action. Secondly, I will call the *intention* of the action that form of subjective meaning which states what the actor primarily conceives the particular action to be; the

85

intention is, as a matter of fact, more likely than any other type of meaning to be present in the actor's consciousness.

My strategy in the following is three-fold. First, I argue that most social scientific purposes and the study of most social scientific objects can be achieved without much note being taken of conscious subjective meanings. Secondly, I draw out the implications of the idea that reasons can be causal in an acceptable scientific sense. Thirdly, I suggest that intentions, though not causal, are to be understood as suggested classifications of actions, a necessary element in scientific reasoning; and social science need not (though it may) accept at face value the actor's classification of his actions.

In pursuing this strategy, I commit myself to two beliefs. The first is that it is fruitful to treat actors' accounts of their actions as rivals to social scientific accounts of the same. This is an assumption which is justified by the fact that actors typically classify and explain their actions, and that the social scientist's first task will be to understand these actors' accounts. Having understood them, the social scientist will decide whether they are plausible according to his theories of action, and thus whether they are to be accepted or rejected: that is, if these suggested classifications and explanations are to be taken as correct social scientific accounts or if they are to enter the social scientist's causal network only as items referred to by his theory. Secondly, I hold that this situation of rivalry between the actors' and observer's accounts can be plausibly described as one in which the actors' theories are potentially scientific. This second point is not so much an assumption of my strategy, as one of its conclusions. My analysis of actors' accounts is intended to show that there is no *a priori* reason why the elements of these accounts should not be treated as elements of scientific theories: that, for example, actors' reasons are attempts to state some of the causal conditions of actions. As such, actors' and observer's accounts differ in degree of scientific status, rather than in kind. The degree is measured by such desiderata of a scientific theory as the degree of structure and systematisation, which includes the requirement that the theory's basic statements should be able to explain a large range of types of phenomena. It could be argued that certain sorts of actors' accounts are not intended to be anything like scientific explanations and hence cannot be said to rival a social scientist's theory. I will return to this point in my discussion of the sociology of religion in this chapter's final section. There I will accept its substance, while arguing that from the social scientist's point of view, the non-scientific actors' accounts have been rejected as incorrect in a weak sense.

Certain types of actions are, as a matter of fact, carried out without the actor consciously imbuing them with subjective meaning. That sub-set of subjective meanings, conscious meanings, is therefore irrelevant to an account of those actions. Impulsive and routine actions are examples. If the former are mainly of interest to history and psychology, the latter are central to role theory and the sociology of organisations, whose point is to describe and explain how actions are routinised.

Winch can give an account of the study of actions which are not consciously meaningful to the actor. For Winch's constraint on the student's postulation of meaning is that the actor must assent to it, *if asked*. Similarly, Wittgenstein (see 1967b, paras. 295 and 301, and 1972, para. 54) allows the radical possibility that actors in a language-game might be able to continue a series of digits without there being a rule that they are following and without there being a reason why they continue in the way that they do. Wittgenstein's account is compatible with an observer watching the actors and constructing a rule which successfully differentiates what for them constitutes correct and incorrect continuation of the series. The observer's account is surely an improvement on the actors', an improvement in that it notes an element of the actors' activity about which they themselves were not self-conscious. It is likely that this improved account is in terms of concepts which the actors do not possess, since they have no need of such concepts, given that their activity is only implicitly governed by the rule in question.

But actions without conscious meanings cannot be assimilated by those versions of hermeneutics which see the meaning relevant to social science as the actor's conscious meanings. Thus, Collingwood says in his autobiography that you are thinking historically 'when you say about anything, "I see what the person who made this (wrote this, used this, designed this, etc.) was thinking" ' (p. 110). Collingwood's example of a historical object in this context is a general's carefully considered battle-plan. But the social scientist is equally likely to be concerned with the thousands of routine actions and utterances repeated daily by an actor.

Just as subjective meaning is not always consciously present even when the social explananda are actions, so too understanding as the empathetic reliving of actors' conscious meanings is necessary neither as a method nor as a goal of social theory. It is not the case that 'historical knowledge is the re-enactment in the historian's mind of the thought whose history he is studying' (Collingwood, 1970, p. 112). This approach is clearly irrelevant when the action under study was unaccompanied by conscious meanings and when, even though the action is consciously meaningful to the actor, the social scientist is not interested in its conscious meaning, but in such features as the unconscious conditions and results of the action.

Even if the social scientist is interested in an action which had conscious meanings attached to it, he need not relive those meanings in order either to understand or to explain that action. This is evident in biography, the epitome of personal history. Fiori (1970, pp. 69ff.) writes that Gramsci's actions on arriving in Turin in 1911 were determined by such aspects of his situation as that he was a hunchback, almost penniless, a brilliant student with a slight history of socialist activity, and had just arrived in the large industrial city of Turin from his backward rural homeland of Sardinia. Gramsci reacted first by almost completely withdrawing from social contact, and then by gradually joining in the work of the socialist party in Turin to the point of total immersion in that work. But precisely the opposite set of reactions would appear equally intelligible if, in order to explain Gramsci's actions, we had to create artificially in ourselves what we imagined were the conscious meanings appropriate in a hunchback, someone almost penniless, etc. This indeterminacy is not accidental. The method of empathetic reliving is ambiguous about whether the historian is supposed to imagine how he would feel in the given circumstances or how his subject felt (for the difficulties involved in both options, see Cunningham, 1973, pp. 105–6).

Certainly Fiori and his readers have to understand what such phrases as 'hunchback, almost penniless . . . ' mean in the referential sense of meaning. For this, it is not necessary to have had such experiences or even experiences like them. What one has to be able to do is to speak the relevant language. But understanding talk about mental states does not presuppose that we have experienced those states. Were such a presupposition involved, it would be impossible to account for a commonplace phenomenon, namely our ability to talk and to understand talk about experiences we have never had. Rather, on the basis of understanding the relevant characterisations, the historian suggests hypotheses, derived from his social knowledge including his theoretical social knowledge, about what would be the typical social reactions to and of a person who was a hunchback, etc., in order to try to explain the specific reactions of the individual under study. Some of the typical reactions he elucidates will be specific to the social context in question and will be explained as such, while others will be more general.

In any case, it is not clear that the empathetic experiencing of a thought or action analogous to the thought or action in question can by itself be an adequate method for social study. For it is not clear whether empathy is governed by rational criteria that determine which results of its usage are acceptable and which unacceptable. Empathy's indeterminacy goes beyond the ambiguity we have already noted of whether the historian is supposed to imagine how he would feel in the given circumstances or how his subject felt. Even given that this question has been resolved, how would we decide what are to count as experiences analogous to the experiences under study? Presumably, by evaluating the historian's work. But, in that case, his empathising is being controlled by the standard criteria governing historical evidence and explanations, not by any criteria peculiar to the method of empathy.

Nothing I have said denies that having performed actions similar to those under study may be helpful in analysing those actions. Perhaps, though it seems unlikely, only a socialist (or should we say: only a Marxist? or only a Sardinian? or only a hunchback?) could write a good biography of Gramsci. But this experiential understanding of the meaning of actions is certainly not necessary for the historian to give descriptive or explanatory accounts of the action in question. For in using his own experiences of similar actions, the historian is assuming that the agent's consciousness of the actions was similar to his own. This assumption, and hypotheses based on it, may turn out to be false. But the historian need not, in consequence, abandon his attempt to understand his subject. Rather, he could suggest other hypotheses about the actor's consciousness of his actions. Nor is the fact that the historian has had the relevant experiences sufficient for the acceptability of the historian's descriptive and explanatory accounts; clearly, because in evaluating the historian's work, as I have noted, we would look at the evidence he has given and the theory he has advanced, not at anything he may have told us about his own history. Thus, to understand conscious meaning in this experiential sense may be of heuristic value to social science. But it is neither necessary nor sufficient for a naturalistic methodology.

Any plausibility the empathetic methodology possesses is based on asking rhetorical questions which involve a caricature of historical practice of the 'How can we understand Hitler if we have not experienced ambition?' variety. To this we can counterpose our own rhetorical question, which rests on a more realistic view of historical study: namely, 'How can we understand Gramsci's actions if in order to do so we have to experience the mental states determined by being a hunchback, etc.?' Further, if experiencing such mental states were necessary to the historian, could only those who have also had such experiences understand the historian's work? *Verstehen* as empathy mistakenly assumes that understanding something requires its reproduction, a mistake which Rudner (1966, p. 83) terms the 'reproductive fallacy'.

There may be a kind of study of human experience which necessitates the reliving of that experience and whose result is as much the deepening of self-knowledge as the greater understanding of the experience under study. But if there is, it is perhaps the writing or study of literature. It is not social science.[3]

Moving away from conscious subjective meanings and the mythical re-living of conscious meanings, we come to what I have called reasons. Reasons are that form of subjective meaning offered by the actor, if an explanation is sought for an action. They may or may not be consciously entertained by an actor at the time of his action. I will draw out the implications of the idea that the reasons which actors offer or may offer to explain their actions can be causal in a scientific sense.[4] The reason–cause debate is so voluminous that the contrasting positions are now clearly drawn and it would be pointless to reproduce the debate here. The most interesting and powerful argument of those who deny that reasons can be causal is the 'logical connection' argument. Namely, the standard formulations of the reason and the associated action are logically connected and therefore cannot refer to two events that are only contingently related, the latter being a requirement of Humean causality. The strategy of those who argue that reasons can be causal is to show that, even if the standard formulation of the reason is logically connected with the standard formulation of the action, we can redescribe either the action or the reason in such a way that they are seen to be linked only contingently. Once this is done, we can produce two sets of independent evidence for the existence of the reason and its corresponding action. In other words, by redescribing the reason or the action, we can show that coming to have a reason and doing the associated action are distinct events. Having done this, we can ask the empirical question whether the reason in question is, as a matter of fact, the cause of the action in question.

More important for our purposes than the detail of this debate is to grasp the implications for social scientific methodology if we accept that reasons can be causal. First, there will inevitably be occasions when the elucidation of the actors' reasons furnishes a satisfactory

---

[3] Evans-Pritchard (1972, pp. 81 ff.) writes interestingly on the kind of personality that may be necessary to be a good anthropologist. See Cunningham (1973, pp. 105–6), Abel (1968), Nagel (1961, pp. 484–5) and Popper (1961, p. 138) for the argument that empathetic *verstehen* is of merely heuristic value; these criticisms of hermeneutic methodology are typically flawed by their assumption that *verstehen* can be interpreted only as subjective empathy.

[4] I thus side with Davidson (1963), Ayer (1967), MacIntyre (1970) and Keat and Urry (1975, ch. 7.2), against Peters (1969), Melden (1961), Louch (1972) and von Wright (1971, pp. 92 ff.).

explanation for social science of the action under study. An often unstated assumption in the argument that reasons cannot be causal (and one which will reappear in our discussion of constitutive rules) is a naive empiricism about what can and cannot be observed. Brodbeck counters the assumption that reasons are unobservable by arguing that mental states are redescribable in dispositional terms which are observable. More than this, as I argued in section 1.3, we can hold that within the relevant society's theoretical framework (and natural scientific observation is made against such a theoretical background) actions and reasons may be intersubjectively observable. Within the assumptions operative among men working on a ship, we can observe a sailor smashing some of the ship's property in order to reduce tension and frustration at work (see Taylor and Walton, 1971, pp. 227ff.).

Empiricist objections to reason explanations also tend to be too strict in their analysis of what statements can serve as deterministic laws and hence as elements of an explanatory system. Strict empiricism argues that only Humean lawlike statements are acceptable; on this view, lawlike statements are to be dissolved into assertions of constant conjunction and spatio-temporal contiguity. But several types of scientific laws do not fit this pattern, including statistical law and functional laws in the mathematical and biological senses. Statements of reasons would probably contravene the contiguity conditions (as do functional laws); but they are both generalisable, within the limits of the *ceteris paribus* clauses which characterise most scientific statements, and empirically testable. Note also that we do not need to invoke the idea that causality involves natural necessity in order to argue that reason explanations can function satisfactorily as deterministic scientific accounts. Clearly, however, the latter argument would be strengthened if we accepted the natural necessity analysis of causality.

Secondly, the fact that reasons are potentially causal underpins the possibility of a commonplace feature of social life, namely that we can disbelieve the actor's proffered reasons. Asking whether the actor's suggested reason really explains his action implies that the agent is not in a uniquely privileged position with respect to the determination of the cause of his action. This implication is intelligible if the actor's reason is potentially the correct account of the cause of the action, so stating the reason is to suggest one possible cause among many. But the ability to doubt the actor's reason is anomalous if act and reason are logically connected. If we discount the reason as the explanation of the action, we can still hold that some occurrence of subjective meaning (e.g. the actor thinking, consciously or unconsciously, that he was acting for such-and-such reason) was causally necessary for the action in the form in which it was produced. The issue between hermeneutic and naturalistic methodologies (at least with those versions of the latter that have a sophisticated understanding of what can serve as observational evidence) should not be posed as whether social scientific explanations must refer to meanings, but as whether social scientific explanations must be based on the acceptance of actors' meanings at face value, that is as correct explanations. The fact that the observer can (though he need not) disbelieve actors' accounts and produce an entirely different explanatory framework does not stop him from referring in his theory to actors' meanings as causal factors or as factors to be explained.

Thirdly, explanations in terms of the actors' reasons, though possible, are unlikely to be important for social science.[5] Even if explanations in terms of reasons are acceptable at a certain level, the social scientist is likely to push explanation to a deeper level in order to show how the existence of the reason is itself explicable in terms of structures of customs or institutions, not conceptualised by the actors' framework of subjective meanings. Moreover, explaining group actions by reasons is problematical, because it has to be shown that all the group's members acted for the reason in question. Social science tends to be concerned with classes of actions, not individual actions, so reasons are of interest only if they can be shown to be representative. Finally, the social scientific subject matter includes vast areas where reasons are not usually of any explanatory interest: for instance, actions' conditions and results, perhaps conceptualised in terms of action rates, which are beyond the conceptual range of actors' meanings. If there is to be an explanatory social science based on the study of meanings, then these meanings must be objective. We do not generally need to know subjective meanings in order to understand an action. What appears *prima facie* necessary is to grasp the social context, including the context of cultural meanings, against which the action is produced. It is indeed for such reasons that hermeneutics has moved from reliance on subjective empathy to commitment to objective *verstehen* (see Outhwaite, 1975, pp. 26ff.).

Before turning to objective meanings, we must look at how non-causal subjective meanings are relevant to social science. As I use the word 'intention', to give an action's intention is to state, not the cause of the action, but what the actor conceives the action to be. As with reasons, the intention may or may not be present in the actors' consciousness at the time of his action; though, as a matter of fact, intentions are more likely to be consciously entertained than any other element of subjective meaning. The Zande poisons the chicken to find

[5] See Brown (1968, chs. VI–VIII). Arguments against psychologism are of interest here: Evans-Pritchard (1967b, ch. II), Popper (1952, ch. 14), and Durkheim (1964, chs. 1–2).

out who is causing his illness. For the Zande, finding out who is causing his illness is what he is doing. Skinner (1972) illuminatingly compares giving the intentional meaning of an action with giving the illocutionary force of an utterance. We are not elucidating a condition of the action or utterance, rather we are stating what the action or utterance *is* for the agent. Skinner is also right in arguing that the discovery of intentional meaning can provide the social scientific observer with understanding in a non-causal sense. The Zande's action no longer seems entirely arbitrary when the poisoning of the chicken is described in such a way that we can grasp what the agent conceives the action to be.

But in virtue of the fact that intentional meaning is a form of subjective meaning and on the basis of the critique of subjective meaning already developed, it is certain that the provision of an action's intentional meaning can produce only limited understanding of that action and an understanding which is not even germane to many social scientific concerns. Moreover, the actor's intentional description of the action is by no means privileged. There is always an area of potential doubt in ascribing intentions and subjective meanings to an actor. This area of doubt is not just a matter of the radical philosophical uncertainty, due to the underdetermination of language by the world, at the heart of any theorising. It is rather doubt based on the opacity of subjective meanings. Intentions and subjective meanings are generally opaque to – and therefore always open to revision by – the actor, other actors within his cultural framework, and a student of society, whether working with a naturalistic or non-naturalistic methodology.

Thus, even within the actor's society's system of meanings the actor's description of his action may be rejected as neurotic, rationalising or obtuse. It is surprising that anti-naturalistic writers do not defend a student's right to disagree with the actor's self-interpretations. For non-naturalistic claims that the student's interpretations and the actor's self-interpretations do not differ in kind should be amenable to the idea that the student might offer alternative and better interpretations of the actors' actions, just because, on non-naturalism's view, the student is only another actor and social actors are constantly refining their interpretations of self and others. Few non-naturalistic writers are consistent on this point, with Taylor (1971, pp. 16–17) a rare exception. More importantly for our present purpose, the naturalistic social scientist is likely to describe the action in completely different terms. He may say that what the Zande is doing in poisoning the chicken is peacefully relieving aggression or maintaining the authority structure in his society. The actor's intentional description of his action classifies that action. The observer typically

offers an alternative classification of that action, because how he classifies cannot be detached from his further explanatory and theoretical
concerns. Fundamental to post-empiricist philosophy of science is the
idea that the conceptual network of a scientific theory is holistic. This
holism implies that the terms in which an action is classified and the
terms in which it is explained cannot have conflicting connotations.
We cannot both accept 'finding out the cause of an illness' as a correct
classification of an action – with the theoretical implications that such
acceptance entails (about, for example, the illness actually being
caused, diagnosed and cured in such-and-such ways) – and explain
that action in terms of the relief of aggression. Skinner ignores this
point. He sees no problems in superimposing deeper levels of explanation onto the actor's intentional description of the action, a flaw which
is central to most attempts to reconcile the causal and the hermeneutic.

The advocate of an anti-naturalistic methodology may argue that if
naturalistic methodology is so holistic, then that methodology cannot
be appropriate for social study. But this would be to miss the point. In
the first instance, I am analysing the implications which a specific
naturalistic methodology has for the conduct of social study, without
denying that there may be a viable non-naturalistic social study (e.g.
one committed to accepting the actors' accounts of their reasons and
intentions at face value). Secondly, I am defending this naturalistic
methodology against the criticisms of certain anti-naturalistic writers,
a defence which is intended to show precisely that this naturalistic
approach is a possible one.

The possibility of alternative conceptualisations of an action has
been ignored by recent philosophers of social science for two reasons.
First, the prejudice that alternative descriptions would involve the
progressive analysis down from the most inclusive (in terms of the
action's consequences) intentionalistic description of the action (he
moved his finger to pull the trigger to kill the prince to cause the war) to
the most exclusive intentionalistic description of the action (he moved
his finger to pull the trigger); analysis beyond that latter point, it is
held, would shift our focus from the domain of action to that of
movement (see von Wright, 1971, p. 67, and Rickman, 1967, p. 107).
What this argument misses is that alternative descriptions of action
may be given by means, not of shifts within the actor's framework, but
of the utilisation of an entirely divergent conceptual scheme. The rain
dance or the poisoning of the chicken or the ceremonial exchange of
gifts may be classified as actions 'intended' to express commitment to
group norms.

Secondly, the thesis that actors' conceptualisations are inviolable
has the same function in non-naturalistic arguments as the notion of a

basic observation language in empiricist social science. Whether or not a non-naturalistic social study requires some epistemologically privileged foundation, it has recently been realised that an incorrigible and atheoretical basis is both impossible and unnecessary for scientific theory. Hence, the idea that agreement with actors' accounts provides an absolute basis for the validation of social scientific accounts is neither useful nor required in naturalistic social science.

Post-empiricist philosophy of science leads us towards a wholehearted belief in the possibility and necessity of displacing the actor's by the observer's theories, including theories of subjective meanings. Compromise attempts to reconcile the actors' and observer's positions, by holding that the observer must work from the acceptance of the actors' intentional descriptions, have never taken seriously the problems inherent in combining two such potentially divergent theoretical frameworks. However, there must be *some* level of description about which the actor and observer agree, on pain of their failing to have theories of the *same* thing in any sense. The Zande and the anthropologist, for example, must agree that the Zande 'is poisoning the chicken', even if they disagree on everything else about this basic action, including further intentional classifications of the action. The trouble, of course, is to specify *what* level of description the Zande and the anthropologist must and do agree on. The terms in which the putative agreed description are phrased should not have concealed theoretical implications, for otherwise it is doubtful whether the actor and the observer are genuinely agreeing. But this would seem to disbar all terms we might actually want to use (do the Zande and the observer agree on what poisoning is, for example?). We are pushed towards postulating an observation language in a mythically immediate relationship with the world. In other words, we are forced back to an unacceptable empiricism. I will return briefly in the Conclusion to this issue.

3.4.c. Meaning and the objects of social science: objective meanings

Accepting the limitations of a social science based on actors' subjective meanings, let us consider the proposal that social science should involve the description and interpretation of the objective, social meanings which may bear on actions. By objective meanings, I refer to the meanings (languages, conceptual systems, theories, philosophies, moralities, etc.) that can be isolated in the actors' social context as determinants, constitutents or descriptions of the elements (actions, institutions, etc.) under study, irrespective of how individuals conceptualise those elements. Brodbeck ignores this level of meaning, but it is central to Winch's account for he holds that meanings are essentially social. Objective meanings escape those critical points directed against the purely individual nature of subjective meanings. Their elucidation is often genuinely explanatory. They are particularly likely to be explanatory of subjective meanings which we have isolated. We further explain the Zande's intention to harm his neighbour by setting it in the context of the full Zande witchcraft belief-system.

But the more general points I made against the view that the social scientist must accept at face value or even base his account on the actors' subjective meanings are also cogent against objective meanings.

First, the presence of objective meanings in a society might have conditions and results which are not objectively meaningful to that society. Theories of ideology and false consciousness presuppose this possibility. An interesting example of the contortions entered into by writers who both recognise this possibility and want to remain committed to the necessarily anti-naturalistic nature of social study is to be found in Mannheim's 'On the Interpretation of *Weltanschauung*'. Mannheim examines the types of meaning pertinent to social science. Mannheim calls 'objective meaning' a level of meaning similar to my notion of objective meaning. It is what is immediately understood as the meaning of an element under study by situating that element in its relevant context, irrespective of the thoughts of actors; we understand the objective meaning of a sentence by its place in the book of which it forms a part. Mannheim then argues that all objective meanings have 'documentary meaning', in that they indicate and are understood as manifestations of a deeper totality, which for Mannheim is always ultimately the age's *Weltanschauung*. It is symptomatic of a central flaw in non-naturalism – that the conditions of objective meanings may not themselves be meaningful to the society under study – that Mannheim sees the age's *Weltanschauung* as essentially objectively meaningless to it. For Mannheim, the *Weltanschauung* is thought only by historical study. Given this framework, the only reason why Mannheim does not hold that an age's *Weltanschauung* is a causal condition of objective meanings is his adherence to the dogma that any understanding of meanings is non-causal.

Secondly, we must again distinguish between the observer referring to the society's objective meanings as part of the explanation of certain characteristics of the society and his explanations coinciding with ones which could be given in terms of the society's objective meanings. That is, the observer might treat the objective meanings as causal factors, rather than as sound explanatory accounts.

Thirdly, a social scientific observer might propose theories which cannot be formulated in the objective meanings of the society under

96

study, in order to classify and explain the objects of his study differently from the classifications and explanations suggested by the objective meanings of the actors' society. The individual may describe his action as a protest against rising prices; that individual's society may describe the actions of many individuals as a demonstration or a riot; but the Marxist could describe them as a stage in the nascent proletarian revolution, as an instance of proletarian solidarity and as the way the proletariat improves its organisation and consciousness level, and he could have done so when none of the actors concerned conceptualised their action in such terms and when Marxism had no place in the objective meanings of the society under study. Objective meanings are useful to the social scientist as possible classifications and explanations of actions. He will certainly begin his work by noting them, not least because they operate on the actors he is studying. He may even accept some of them at face value, that is, as useful classifications and explanations. But he will reject most in favour of his more systematic theories; and nearly all objective meanings will figure eventually in his work, if he pushes his research to the deepest explanatory levels, as items to be explained, not as items that explain.

My argument would be opposed by Winch and other exponents of non-naturalistic social study on the ground that rules governing objective meanings *constitute* the actions and institutions under study. In *Speech Acts* Searle provides a framework for this position through his distinction between constitutive and regulative rules. Searle argues that constitutive rules do not just order pre-existing behaviour, but sustain the very possibility of engaging in behaviour: without the rules of chess, playing chess would be impossible. In this way they differ from regulative rules of pre-existing behaviour, for example rules about how to eat properly. In virtue of this feature, constitutive rules (again unlike regulative rules) provide the basis for descriptions of behaviour which could not be given in the absence of these constitutive rules: e.g. 'X voted for Y'. Searle believes that both the possibility of speaking a language and the usual performance of illocutionary acts are underlain by constitutive rules. He also holds that statements about social actions (e.g. 'X married Y') are typically not statements about brute, physical facts, nor are they reducible to such statements. Physical facts count as parts of social events only against the background of institutions. So, statements about social actions are statements about institutional facts. These institutions, Searle believes, are systems of constitutive rules, hence 'every institutional fact is underlain by a (system of) rule(s) of the form "X counts as Y in context C" ' (pp. 51–2). For instance, raising one's arm in a specific way counts as saluting in the context of an army parade ground.

The constitutive–regulative distinction helps to avoid the mistake of many of Winch's critics who read Winch as though he were talking of regulative rules. Searle's analysis of constitutive rules also accommodates the fact that particular actions may be possible only against the background of a specific social context with its appropriate language and objective meanings. Further, analysis of constitutive institutional rules of an action might feature in social scientific explanations of the action and, as such, enhance 'understanding' (in a loose sense) of that action.

But what is the methodological import of invoking constitutive rules as the explanation of an action? The constitutive rule is not a sufficient condition of the action. For only when certain other conditions obtain will the action be performed, despite the continuous existence of the constitutive rule in the society's objective meanings. What is being claimed is that the existence of a constitutive rule is a necessary condition of the existence of a corresponding action. It is one of the antecedents, though not the *only* one (this point damages Winch's view of social science as the explication of rules), of the occasion of an action. But if the constitutive rule is a necessary condition of a whole range of actions, then to state this fact is to explain those actions straightforwardly. This is not to suggest that in any actual case the relation between constitutive rules and actions is so simple. Rules and actions may form complex interactive patterns. But such patterns are precisely objects for social scientific analysis. They should not serve as an excuse for the groundless claim that language (in which rules are embedded) and actions are identical. Nor do I suggest that because constitutive rules may explain actions we have to rest content with this level of explanation. On the contrary, we may wish to explain the existence of constitutive rules in terms of deeper social features which are not themselves objectively meaningful. To maintain that objective meanings are fundamental is to propose a particular ontology for social theory. As such, the claim must be defended by showing that the theory with this ontology is more powerful than a rival theory constructed on the basis of a different ontology. The required defence would have to cope with idealist theory's *prima facie* difficulty with a sociology of material factors, such as political power and material production. These remarks on ontology will be clarified in the next chapter.

Anti-naturalism also holds that since constitutive rules provide the basis for the identity of actions, social science cannot evolve theories that contradict the objective meanings and therefore the constitutive rules of the society under study; because to do so changes the meaning and hence the criteria of identity of the actions in question. If we treat the actors' theories as potential scientific accounts (and part of the point of my critique of anti-naturalism is to uphold this possibility), then the problem of the relation between the actors' and observer's conceptualisations of actions can be posed as the general question of the relation between the meanings of two terms in different scientific theories which ostensibly refer to the same thing: can we give conditions under which it is reasonable to say that terms in different theories refer to the same thing, so that the theories can be taken as rivals?

The two terms need not have identical extensions for us reasonably to say that they are talking about the same things; this point undercuts Malcolm's argument (see section 3.3 and Putnam [1975, ch. 15] for a detailed critique of Malcolm on this point). To demand that the two terms must have identical senses, that is, the same systematic connections with other terms, is too strict. For they possess different senses simply in virtue of forming parts of different theories. The question of how many of a term's systematic connections must be incorporated into the term's meaning is one of the most important unresolved issues in current philosophy of science; it must do justice to the facts, on the one hand, that different scientific theories can be about the same domain and, on the other, that terms are not meaningful in isolation. For our purposes there are two relevant possible resolutions to this debate. A Feyerabendian incommensurability thesis might be adopted. In this case the actors' and observer's theories would be termed alternatives, not rivals. We would be able to give no sense to the notion that apparently similar terms in the two theories referred to the same things, that the actor and observer were talking about the same action. But the relativist implications of this position would thereby have been accepted as characteristic of all science, not just of social science. Or, some solution might be adopted that did justice to the systematic connections of terms' meanings without yielding self-contained, incommensurable theories. The problem of understanding how two theories can be compared as genuine rivals, even given contextual accounts of meaning, would have been solved for all science, and *ipso facto* for the case of the actors' versus the observer's theories.

The subject matter of social science is distinctive in that the observer's theories might be adopted by the actors under study, thus changing the reality which the observer is studying. In the process (*pace* Winch and Malcolm) the criterion for the employment of the actors' terms might be gradually altered to the point where the actors decide that there had been a shift in meaning. But this change does not support anti-naturalism. It is to do with the processes of change in society as a result of the impact of ideas. The reality which the observer had originally investigated would have changed. The fact that the mechanism of this change depends on the observer's study introduces no special philosophical problems. Indeed, the phenomenon of change through the impact of ideas might be the next topic of study for the social scientist.

Nothing I have said precludes the possibility that human activities can sustain a type of study entirely different from that represented by naturalistic social science. Hermeneutic methodologies present alternative models for social study. In such models, the student is generally seen as participant or negotiator, not as observer. The object in the first instance is to grasp and clarify the actors' subjective and objective meanings. Part of the further aim of radical hermeneutic methodologies is to alter the self-understandings of both the actor and the student through their dialogue. This aim generates distinctive methodological problems. An example is the ambiguous hermeneutic circle. It is ambiguous because the idea of the circularity of whole–part intelligibility can be applied in many different contexts, as I have already noted. It could be used in presenting an account of the meanings of scientific terms, given current holistic analyses of the relation between scientific theories and the meaning of scientific terms (see Hesse, 1972, p. 280). Under some interpretations, however, the notion of the hermeneutic circle is specific to a non-naturalistic social study. It is characteristic of non-naturalism if interpreted in the sense that understanding actors' meanings requires the student to bring his system of meanings to the object of study, while the student can fully grasp his own framework of meanings only in dialogue with the other. This sense underpins the idea that an aim of hermeneutics is to change the self-consciousness of both actor and student. In the situation of dialogue with an alien culture, the problem of the hermeneutic circle may be posed as that of the 'dialectic of translation' (see Needham, 1972, p. 171, and Winch, 1970, pp. 102 ff.).

Imagine someone ignorant of the social organisation of a modern British colliery going to a pit with the intention of learning about its social structure. Whatever model of knowledge he is operating with, the student starts by concentrating on certain facets of the structure. Language is clearly crucial: to learn who or what onsetters, tail-gates, back-rippers, gobs, etc. are reveals a lot about the pit. Learning the language merges into learning the social roles, the organisational structure and the underlying regularities associated with the pit; the two learning processes cannot always be sharply differentiated, though the latter is in general wider than the former. Any student will want to know how the pit looks from the point of view of typical and key workers: the face worker, the ripper, the transfer point attendant, the winder, the surface worker, the timekeeper, the weighman, the storekeeper, the deputies, the nurse, the surface superintendent, the engineers, the clerks, the secretaries, the control room operators, the Lodge Secretary and Committee, the personnel staff, the managers, etc. All these people give different accounts of the nature and workings of the pit. The idea of reconciling or combining them in a single account is ridiculous, especially if the student is sensitive to the various structures outside the colliery with which it is connected and to the changes which occur over time. Understanding a colliery from the point of view of its members in this way is a process common to students operating with all methodologies.

But the next question is: what kind of knowledge is the student aiming at? As an ideal, the student might be using the participant or the observer models. The participant tries to formulate in as complete a way as possible the self-understandings of the actors. The difficulty and importance of this task should not be underestimated, especially in a unit as complex as a colliery. The participant model can be further sub-divided in terms of whether the student pursues a self-effacing or an active course. This is not just a question of investigational strategies. The investigator who listens and records and the investigator who argues, criticises and welcomes criticism learn different things and arrive at different conclusions. Of course, I am drawing the contrast in stark terms. The mere facts that the student has a history and that he is typically a foreigner to the situation he studies mean that he cannot be ideally self-effacing; or, as Easthope puts it, we should not confuse 'the observation of events by participants with participant observation' (1974, p. 102). Yet both types of investigators, even if depicted in idealised terms, remain essentially within the orbit of the actors' self-interpretations. The person working with a naturalistic view of knowledge certainly notes the actors' views of the colliery. He does not rest there, however, not least because he becomes aware of the diversity of views which the various actors hold. He is much more concerned to suggest conclusions about factors and regularities in the running of the colliery which – usually for very good reasons – are of no interest to the colliery members.

The distinctions I have sketched are ideal-typical. A social study usually secretes various models of the student and of social knowledge. This is clear from the Chicago participant observation school of sociology, a school which was firmly committed to the participant non-naturalistic end of the spectrum, but which could not rid itself of all elements of the model of the naturalistic observer. The tension is succinctly summarised by Whyte in *Street Corner Society*:

I began as a nonparticipating observer. As I became accepted into the community, I found myself becoming almost a nonobserving participant. I got the feel of life in Cornerville, but that meant that I got to take for granted the same things that my Cornerville friends took for granted. I was immersed in it, but I could as yet make little sense out of it (p. 321).

Whyte's model of a student is a mixed one, as emerges from comments such as: that Doc began as a 'passive informant', but rapidly became a 'collaborator in the research' (p. 301), someone with whom he discussed what he was trying to do, what problems were proving puzzling and so on; that while he had been instructed not to argue with his subjects, he found that 'arguing on some matters was simply part of the social pattern' (p. 302), though he still avoided sensitive topics; that maintaining a degree of social distance, so long as he took a friendly interest in Cornerville people, was useful and expected, not least because different groups in Cornerville had different standards of behaviour; that nevertheless his language and topics of conversation were profoundly affected by the study; that he tried to avoid having any gross influence on the people, for example through accepting formal positions, because he wanted to study 'the situation as unaffected by [his] presence as possible' (p. 305); but that it was 'difficult to remain solely a passive observer' (p. 337), and at one stage he went to the extent of organising a demonstration. Whyte's account of his research veers between his inclination to give a personalised description of how he interacted with the various Cornerville inhabitants and his adherence to a naturalistic methodology in many ways unsuitable for a thoroughgoing philosophy of participant observation.

Ultimately, whether we engage in a naturalistic social science or a non-naturalistic hermeneutics depends on our interests in studying. The kind of interests which determine the two types of study have been elucidated by Habermas (1972). He differentiates a naturalistic social science, based on the interests of objective prediction and control, from hermeneutics, based on the interests of dialogue and clarification.[6] I likewise take Dunn to be saying that different social scientific methodologies are underlain by different values when he writes that our intention of pursuing one particular type of social study 'may even be a category within naturalistic ethics' (1978, p. 175). What forms our naturalistic or hermeneutic social studies take may also turn on our interests. Varieties of hermeneutics stem from such controversies as whether subjective or objective meanings are the focus of study, and whether the student is or is not committed to radically changing his and his subjects' self-understanding. Similarly, a facet of the move-

[6] Compare Strawson (1968) on the objective and participant attitudes.

ment from strong empiricism was the desire to reject a view which required science to deny the significance of all metaphysical, artistic, political and religious statements. I have tried to establish neither the impossibility of a non-naturalistic social study nor a preference for naturalistic social science, but only to salvage and explicate the very possibility of the latter.

3.4.d. Meaning and social science: conclusions

The social scientist must note the actors' subjective and objective meanings. For where they can be identified as existing independently of the actors' action they are potentially explanatory of that action, and because they involve a classification of actions that the social scientist may either accept or reject. In holding that meanings are potential explanations, I accept the compatibility in principle of explanations in terms of actors' meanings (e.g. the giving of reasons) and non-meaningful explanations. Typically, however, the social scientist suggests classifications and explanations of actions which cut across those given by the actors' subjective and objective meanings. He may interpret what the actor conceives to be a religious activity as a form of artistic or economic activity. With certain explananda, the decision whether to deny the actors' accounts may even be an essential step in the social scientist's theoretical work, as when the actors claim that in dancing they are making rain (see Pitkin, 1972, pp. 257–8). When the social scientist has produced alternative classifications of the actions in question, he evolves an explanatory theory of the actions (identified in terms of his classifications) which refers to social features that may not be meaningful in any sense to the actors under study. Thus, Taylor and Walton (1971, pp. 241–2) construct a three-fold typology of acts of industrial sabotage, and they suggest explanations for each type in terms of the structural features of the workplace in which the type most commonly occurs.

The compromise position adopted by many commentators, namely that the social scientist accepts the actors' classification of actions but then suggests his own explanations, is inherently unstable. Explanatory superstructure and classificatory base are part of a systematic theoretical whole. We cannot consider to be useful and reasonable the actors' classification of certain of their actions as ones of worshipping their totemic ancestors and then explain those actions, described by the actors' classifications, in terms of the need to assert social solidarity; classifying an action as one of worshipping totemic ancestors brings with it explanatory implications about why people are carrying out that action. Winch does not develop his claim that any non-native concepts which the observer uses in his account must be ultimately intelligible in the actors' terms. Indeed, Winch's own usage of concepts such as those of language, belief, etc., already transcend the actors' self-understanding (see Putnam's [1975, pp. 62–4] point in a different context that the concept of a rule of language, which is central to Winch's account, is a technical one derived from the theory of formalised languages).

The fact that even Winch's social study may have to use concepts and make assumptions which diverge from the actors' self-understanding does not depend just on an isolated analysis of some of Winch's concepts. Rather, it is a necessary feature of the anthropological situation. For the social scientist has to make assumptions even in trying to understand alien beliefs. Winch, happy to relativise truth to different social contexts, has no clear way of preventing a relativisation of meaning too, a relativisation which would stop the social scientist from even understanding the alien beliefs. Winch proposes two strategies for avoiding this disastrous incomprehensibility across social contexts. The first, in 'Understanding a Primitive Society', involves the undeveloped notion of a dialectic of translation around certain human constants (birth, death and sexual relations). The second, an implicit assumption of *The Idea of a Social Science*, portrays the anthropologist's statements as presuppositionless pictures of the alien meanings. This second strategy demonstrates a naivety about the learning of alien languages. For one thing at least is clear from the debate about radical translation. Fundamental presuppositions to the effect that the conceptual scheme of the alien actors does not differ in a radical ontological and epistemological way from that of the translator are necessary, if the translator is to have any chance of arriving at a determinate translation.[7]

Correlative with the observer's ability to classify and explain actions in his own terms is his ability to break down in his explanatory accounts the total social context within which the actors act. Certainly, in classifying and explaining a set of activities, we must note the social context in which they occur. But this requires careful analysis of the interconnections of the explanandum with other features in its environment and especially with features held to be structurally more basic. Producing this analysis fits the explanandum into several contexts of varying generality, not into a single total social context. Adherents of a radical contextualism are under the illusion, noted in section 1.2, of thinking that social understanding takes the form of absolutely complete knowledge of some entity – in this case, specific social contexts. We explain totemism by specific social structural features, not by

[7] Quine (1969, ch. II) provides the classical statement of the radical translation problem. Hollis (1970) and Hookway (1978) investigate its relevance to social science.

the total social context. Moreover, isolation of these specific social features is a necessary part of the advancement of general hypotheses. Writers who stress the notion of social context often show no more than that previous social scientific work fitted some social item into a general classification insensitively. Thus, stripped of its philosophical support, Winch's argument shows that anthropology would have done better to classify Zande magic as an instance of religion, not science. It might be held that there just are no cross-cultural constants in human organisation, that all social contexts are uniquely constituted. As a matter of fact, this seems especially implausible in the modern world (see Gellner [e.g. 1974a, p. 49] on the absence of self-contained forms of life in modern society). As a methodological point, this conclusion should be reached, if at all, after the failure of a lot more social scientific research. It cannot be sustained by philosophical arguments.

I have argued that there are six senses of meaning with which the philosophy of naturalistic social science should concern itself. (I) Social scientific terms have meaning by purporting to refer to things. (II) A social scientific term possesses meaning in virtue of its systematic connections with other terms in its theory. (III) Sets of statements embodying these systematic connections typically purport to refer to deterministic relations in the actual world. Elucidating the deterministic relations which govern a phenomenon – that is, giving the phenomenon's explanation – is often loosely characterised as giving the meaning of the phenomenon. (IV) Statements of relatively basic data in social science are meaningful in that they are at least partly constituted by the meanings of the other terms and sentences of the social scientific theory in which they play a part. (V) Actors employ subjective meanings in order either to classify or to explain their actions. (VI) There are certain objective meanings in the actors' society which can be used either to classify or to explain their actions.

I have argued that senses (I)–(IV) of meaning are concerned with the language of social scientific theory and that an identical analysis can be given of the languages of natural scientific theory. Senses (V) and (VI) are distinctive of social scientific objects. But where the observer does not simply refer to the actors' meanings as items in the causal universe, he can either accept them as satisfactory classifications and explanations of what he is studying or, more typically, reject them in favour of his own systematic theory. In arguing this, I have criticised the idea (which is one possible reading of Weber's methodology) that the social scientist can first understand (= classify) an action in the actors' terms and then explain it in his own terms, because it fails to note the holistic nature of scientific theory.

Finally, let me briefly state the implications of my argument for 'understanding' in social science. Here again various senses are at issue. (I) The prime aim of social science is to explain its various explananda by incorporating them into a systematic and successfully tested theory. Any theory which achieved this aim would provide explanatory understanding of those explananda. Explanatory understanding is a common aim and achievement of all science. We can speak with equal propriety of our explanatory understanding of the motions of the planetary and economic systems. I have argued that the actors' subjective and objective meanings may occasionally serve as explanations in a social scientific theory, but that this is a point about the distinctive subject matter, not about the methodology of social science.

(II) The classification of an object can be said to further understanding of that object. Again, this understanding is common to all science, though social science's distinctive subject matter means that the social scientist will sometimes accept the actor's classificatory understanding of his actions.

(III) The actors' subjective and objective meanings are likely to be social scientific explananda and may even be incorporated into the social scientist's theory, that is, into his classifications and explanations, and therefore into his understanding in senses (I) and (II). Hence, they must be understood by the social scientist. This sense of understanding cannot be reduced to (I) and (II), because it is prior to his proposals for explanatory and classificatory understanding. Access to the actors' classifications and explanations is given in the first instance by coming to understand the actors' language. As far as I know, there is no currently accepted complete account of what is involved in understanding a language. But there are two arguments which suggest that the centrality of this type of understanding to social science does not impugn its claim to scientific status. First, all science presupposes the understanding of language. The social scientist is peculiar in having to understand the actors', in addition to his own. Insofar as he treats the actors' theories as potential scientific accounts, his work does not differ from that of the natural scientist who learns the language of a rival scientific theory in order to develop his own. Secondly, and this elaborates the first point, once the social scientist has learnt the actors' language as a necessary part of his study, he can cease to use it when he comes to offer his explanatory understanding of the actions under study. Moreover, sensitivity to problems of radical translation supports my contention that the observer must ultimately be prepared to impose his conceptual framework on the objects and actors under study.

(IV) The social scientist may have experiential understanding of an action. That is, he has also performed that action or something like it (or something he thinks is like it) and therefore understands (or thinks he understands) the reasons why (some) people perform such actions. Or, (he thinks that) he has some character trait which (he thinks) is necessary for the performance of that action and therefore understands (or thinks he understands) the actor in question. Criteria for the objectivity of experiential understanding are impossible to state: if doubts were raised about the warrant for a student's claim to experiential understanding (if we invoked any of the sceptical contents of the brackets in the preceding two sentences), we would look to other types of evidence, reasoning and understanding. In any case, experiential understanding is irrelevant to many social scientific concerns. In general, experiential understanding is neither necessary nor sufficient for the provision of explanatory or classificatory understanding, though it may be of heuristic use.

3.5. TWO EXAMPLES

I will give two schematic accounts from the social scientific literature as examples of two themes I have argued. First, I will exemplify the thesis that the actors' meanings are to be treated as a possible, but typically not useful, account of the explanandum by means of studies in the sociology of religion and magic. Secondly, I will exemplify the thesis that the actors' meanings might form part of the explanatory accounts of social science by means of the Marxist theory of the role of class consciousness in the proletarian revolution.

3.5.a. Approaches in the sociology of religion and magic

The social scientific study of religious and magical beliefs and practices, especially non-Western ones, poses the problem of the relation between the observer's and actors' theories in its most clear-cut form. I will outline various approaches under two headings. (A) The observer accepts the actors' conceptualisations of their religious beliefs and actions, sees his job as elucidating those conceptions, and refuses to postulate explanations of the actors' beliefs and actions which contravene the actors' self-understandings. (B) The observer rejects the actors' self-understandings, typically holds that the actors' beliefs and accounts are false, and postulates his own classifications and explanations. This division of studies in the sociology of religion would be eccentric for any other purpose than showing the implications they have for the topic of meaning in social science. The division between (A) and (B) is also not sharp. In particular, few sociologists are entirely faithful to (*A*), which in itself is a measure of the degree to which Winch's methodology would lead to a revision in social study. Whatever their philosophical professions, most propose elements of a non-native account of religion. This is not surprising, given my argument that we could stop with actors' accounts, but that there are strong reasons why we should not do so. But enough sociologists of religion fall mainly into category (*A*) to make this a good example of the point that it is possible, but typically not useful, to accept at face value the actors' self-understanding.

In this sub-section, I ignore a whole series of issues concerned with how exactly we identify religious beliefs. With any religion, there are likely to be discrepancies between the official dogma, the beliefs of the professional guardians and the lay adherents' beliefs; between what is professed as belief and what is practised; and between the beliefs of the different versions of the religion. Further, there is the problem of decoding the belief that a religious image symbolises. (For these issues, see Holm, 1977, pp. 22–3 and 44–6.) But my analysis is quite general. No matter how we specify a set of religious beliefs, the points I am about to make are applicable.

(*A*) Those who argue that religious beliefs and practices are to be classified and explained in actors' terms pursue a basic strategy. They hold that religion forms a system so self-contained that no appeal to extraneous concepts can help in interpreting it. Generally, it is suggested, religion and magic are self-contained systems in respect of the nature of their objects, their underlying purposes, their internal relations, and the actions which sustain them. For example, the objects which religious and magical beliefs and practices seek to render intelligible are *sui generis*. Thus, Evans-Pritchard (1965, pp. 70–3) writes that Zande witchcraft tries to explain events which we dismiss as inexplicable accidents and coincidences; and Malinowski states that the Trobriander appeals to magic only when he has no other recourse, only 'whenever he has to recognise the impotence of his knowledge and of his rational technique' (1926, p. 34). With respect to the internal structure of religious and magical systems, Tambiah (1973) argues that magic uses a distinctive mode of analogical reasoning and Skorupski (1973) states that religion has a specific logical structure which depends on the centrality of paradox. Exponents of this approach suggest that religion and magic are to be compared, if at all, to activities such as drama, not to any system internally structured by criteria of the rationality or verisimilitude of beliefs. On such bases, it is held that definitions and interpretations of religious beliefs should aim to conform with the substantive beliefs of religious actors (see Spiro, 1968). Further, Evans-Pritchard (1967b, p. 121) argues that the anthropologist should eschew the search for causal explanations of religion in terms of non-religious factors and instead explicate how the actors under study conceive the nature of spiritual reality – a programme which he carries out for Nuer religious symbols (1967a, ch. V).

The results of such studies have often enhanced our understanding, especially our classificatory understanding and those types of explanatory understanding which are internal to actors' meanings. But it is doubtful whether the basic strategy of showing that religion is self-contained can support position (A), that religious items must be classified and explained in actors' terms. First, mere elucidation of religious beliefs (like elucidation of constitutive rules of meaning) tends to transcend actors' self-understanding. Secondly, insofar as the thesis of self-containment hopes to preclude a social scientific theory of religion by arguing that religion is a different enterprise to natural science (this is the conclusion which most such writers try to establish), it is wrong-headed. For there is no reason why there cannot be naturalistic social scientific theories of non-scientific systems. Moreover, the very fruitfulness of moving beyond actors' concepts, of taking approach (B), suggests the basic criterion under which approach (A) is to be rejected: its general inability to provide adequate explanatory understanding of religion. In any actual case, specific religious actions and beliefs might be sufficiently explained in terms of the actors' subjective and objective meanings. But remaining within the actors' religious framework means we could propose explanations only in terms of the actors' subjective and objective meanings. Such explanations, I have urged in this chapter, are at a low level of theoretical understanding and are often to be termed simply false.

(B) Most sociology of religion rejects the actors' self-understanding in order to postulate its own theory of religious beliefs and practices. In doing so, it typically conceptualises religion as like other areas of human activity and therefore as explicable in the same ways. Thus, it has been held that magical beliefs and practices: contain or express social conflict (Firth, 1959, Thomas, 1970, and Trevor-Roper, 1967); arise in forms of societies where there is a need for, but a lack of, clear role-definitions (Douglas, 1970); are rational attempts to achieve certain goals and explain certain events, but, unlike other means which actors use to those ends (e.g. medical or agricultural techniques), are based on beliefs which are not rationally tested (Jarvie and Agassi, 1970). Of religious systems, it has been held, for example, that they satisfy biological needs (Malinowski, 1926) and that they are determined by the authority relations in their concomitant kinship systems (Fortes, 1959).

It can be seen that there is room for wide theoretical diversity and disagreement within approach (*B*), within the approach which breaks with religious actors' self-understandings. Approach (*B*) encompasses, for example, the very different theories of millenarianism that treat it, on the one hand, as coded political protest and, on the other, as a collective psychosis. More specifically, it encompasses specific theoretical debates about, for instance, whether early nineteenth-century Methodism advanced when Radicalism was advancing or was retreating. (For such examples, see Thompson, 1977, pp. 51 ff. and 919 ff.) (*A*) and (*B*) are differentiated by fundamentally different views of social science's methodological and epistemological orientations towards actors' self-understandings, not by predilections for a specific theory of religion.

We cannot construct such social scientific explanations of religion on a prior acceptance of the religious actors' accounts of their activity. It is generally impossible to combine two such disparate conceptual frameworks within a single scientific theory. Moreover, the specific decision whether to accept the actors' accounts as true or false has to be made before the observer knows what type of explanation he is to give. The theorist who classifies religious actions as being at root economic, social or psychological and explains them correspondingly is committed to denying the classificatory and explanatory pretensions of the actors' accounts. Ultimately, the conflict between the actors' and observer's theories of religion is expressed in the observer's denial of existence to the most fundamental religious object, God. This ontological conflict occurs in the three most influential social scientific theories of religion: the Marxist, the Durkheimian and the Freudian, where God is interpreted as the disguised forms of, respectively, alienated humanity, the social totality and the parent-given Superego.[8]

I should add that there are two ways in which the sociology of religion might be committed to denying the religious actors' accounts of their religious beliefs and practices. I will call these the strong and weak senses in which the sociology of religion conflicts with religious accounts. The sociology of religion usually conflicts with religious accounts in the strong sense. Yet there are certainly views of religion which would render social science and religion incommensurable, rather than incompatible, thereby preventing social science and religion from being genuine rivals. On these views, I will argue, science and religion are in a situation of weak conflict.[9]

[8] See e.g. Marx (1844, p. 37), Engels (1882, p. 173), Durkheim (1971) and Freud (1949, p. 214).
[9] For what follows and especially for attempts to reconcile science and religion, see e.g.: Barbour (1968), Butterfield 'The Christian and Historical Study' in his (1951), Duhem (1954, first Appendix), Hick (1964), Hook (1962), Hudson (1968), Mitchell (1973), Phillips (1965), Wisdom (1957), and Wittgenstein (1967a).

The simplest way in which religion and science can be reconciled is to hold that science tells us about the natural order, beyond which there may or may not be a divine order. The natural realm is self-complete and the theist and atheist may both investigate it scientifically. Such investigations are held to have no logical bearing on the transcendental question of whether God exists.

Whether or not this thesis is plausible in general, it is not acceptable as an account of the scientific study of religion itself. As a matter of fact, most religious and magical systems claim that certain events occur because of supernatural intervention. Such claims usually involve the further belief that, were it not for the supernatural intervention, some event other than the one being explained would have happened. In consequence, there must have been a point of interaction in the natural world between the natural and supernatural forces. Religious statements thus at times suggest explanations of specific events in the natural world. These are also the points at which social scientific and religious systems are rivals in the strong and straightforward sense that each contains statements in contradiction with statements in the other. For the sociology of religion is committed to the general ontology of science, which – whatever was the case in the past – currently excludes the category of supernatural forces and *ipso facto* the possibility of divine intervention in the world. Science instead conceptualises the ultimate constituents of the universe as material in some sense. Hence, the sociology of religion must reject any statements by religious actors that purport to explain phenomena in terms of the existence and activities of supernatural forces or beings. In particular, it must reject any attempts to explain the phenomenon of religion itself in such terms. The atheistic import of Marx's, Durkheim's and Freud's theories of religion is to be understood thus, and indeed has been so understood by religious believers (see e.g. Lukes [1973, pp. 506–20] on religious reactions to Durkheim's theory). These points also set limits to the possible reconciliation of religious and social scientific theories of religion. Despite all the parallels which MacIntyre can draw in his *Marxism and Christianity* between the nature and content of Marxism and Christianity, MacIntyre cannot assimilate to Christianity the brute fact of Marx's commitment to the non-existence of God on the basis of his materialist ontology and consequent materialist paradigm of explanation.

Religious believers hold views on the nature of religion which would avoid this strong conflict between social science and religion. These views have been developed recently in the philosophical literature. They rest on the same sorts of bases as the non-naturalistic approach (*A*) to the sociology of religion. They differ from (*A*) in not embracing

111

the incorrect argument that because religious systems are not comparable with scientific systems there can be no naturalistic study of religion. On these views, religion serves different purposes from science's interest in cognitive prediction and control, purposes which can still regulate our lives in a fundamental way. These purposes might be to recommend a way of life and a set of moral principles, and to express certain attitudes and experiences, such as the non-cognitive ones of worshipping. Recent analyses in the philosophy of science are often used to suggest that religion has a structure whose form can be understood by reflection on the notions of a holistic scientific theory or paradigm, but whose content is *sui generis*. It is argued, for example, that the most important religious statements are highly theoretical ones not simply related to an experiential base. The sorts of factors which support the fundamental religious statements are *sui generis* (e.g. the experiences of love and awe), as are the sorts of factors which *prima facie* count against the basic religious claims (e.g. the phenomenon of pain). Within such religious systems, the mode of argumentation is also held to be distinctive. Many writers have emphasised the allegorical and paradoxical elements in religious argumentation. Wisdom (1957) parallels religious argument to legal debate and Mitchell (1973) calls it 'cumulative', comparing it to literary, historical and metaphysical discussions. Finally, it is argued, a distinctive religious reality governs the truth-value of statements made within the religious framework. There is no independent reality which can be used to test the basic framework principles of religion or to judge between the religious and scientific systems. In particular, the existence of God, as part of the basic religious framework, cannot be meaningfully doubted within the religious system. No writer is more consistent in his adherence to this type of theology than Phillips in *The Concept of Prayer*. For instance, Phillips holds that God is not an existent among existents, nor an agent among agents (He is neither a moral nor a natural agent); that religion is not concerned for the natural world to be one way, rather than another; and that, more specifically, genuinely religious prayers, even apparently petitionary ones, are not attempts to change the world, but expressions of dependence on and love and awe of God, no matter what happens in the world.

I do not know whether such views are satisfactory accounts of religion. They would have to answer the point that they seem to theorise a God withdrawn from nature and those areas of human existence not specifically religious, and hence an unsatisfactorily limited God. Similarly, they appear to conceptualise a God bounded by the contingencies of human usage of religious language. Yet central to religious belief has usually been the notion that God is at work in the world. Without doubt, they at best give an account of the sort of religious beliefs held by only the most intellectually sophisticated believers. But abstracting from these critical points, what should we say of the social scientific study of religious beliefs and practices, if we accept the view of religion I have just sketched? Not that a naturalistic sociology of religion is impossible, for this is to ignore the fact that religion, whatever else it is, is a phenomenon in the natural world. It also commits the fallacy I have already noted of holding that there cannot be naturalistic studies of non-naturalistic systems. Rather, a naturalistic social science of religion, first, considers the accounts of the existence of religious beliefs and actions to be found in these sophisticated theories of religion. Social science considers them because they are proposed accounts which might prove acceptable in its own terms. Secondly, it decides that the religious actors' beliefs cannot be accepted as satisfactory classifications or explanations for a social scientific theory. In consequence, the sociology of religion advances its own theories of religion. This sequence of consideration and rejection is how social science and even sophisticated theories of religion conflict. But I do not claim that this conflict is anything but weak. It is weak for two reasons: because there is no clear-cut contradiction between the two systems, as in the situation of strong conflict; and because the student could therefore hold a naturalistic social scientific theory of a religion and believe in that religion, if the religion incorporated the type of sophisticated theology I have outlined. Both these weaknesses might be summarised by saying that the religion and social science in question are not genuine rivals; though, as I have argued, the social science must establish this by rejecting the religion *qua* social science.

3.5.b. The Marxist theory of the role of consciousness in the proletarian revolution

Marx saw the proletariat as the historical agent which would transform capitalist into socialist society and as the epistemological agent which would first achieve collective insight into the real structure of society. To understand these ideas fully requires consideration of such basic features of Marxism as its philosophical anthropology, a philosophical anthropology which postulated the proletariat as the negative image of the positive ontology of human nature and which sustained its critical attitude to bourgeois ideology. My aim here is more limited. Taking this philosophical background for granted, I will elucidate the sociological hypotheses which Marx advanced concerning the role of proletarian consciousness in the proletarian revolution. I will show how the phenomenon of proletarian consciousness fits into Marx's explanatory framework sometimes as explanandum and sometimes as explanans. Marx's belief that the existence of proletarian consciousness would at times explain the course of the revolution required him to accept the accounts of certain actors, the proletariat in a revolutionary situation, as correct explanations of the situation at hand. But Marx was not committed to accepting actors' accounts *per se*, as is clear from his critical theory of bourgeois ideology.

In arguing that the existence of objectively correct proletarian consciousness was for Marx a necessary condition of the proletarian revolution, I take Marxism to be a naturalistic social science. As in my general discussion, I am not trying to show the impossibility of a non-naturalistic Marxism. I wish simply to exemplify how a naturalistic social science may treat actors' theories by means of the formal features of certain parts of Marxism, interpreted naturalistically, without judging whether Marxism can also be interpreted non-naturalistically. Non-naturalistic, idealist models of Marxism have indeed been advanced by, for example, Lukács, Korsch, Gramsci and the Frankfurt School. They hold that proletarian consciousness is not just a necessary condition of the revolution, but rather constitutes the revolution. I have argued that the thesis that meanings constitute actions can be reformulated in naturalistic terms as the thesis that meanings are a necessary condition of action. The views of some proponents of non-naturalistic Marxism can indeed be thus reformulated, given a qualification to the effect that the existence of correct proletarian consciousness is the *decisive* condition of the revolution. But tough-minded idealist Marxism is committed to the thesis that the arrival of proletarian consciousness is constitutive of, in the sense of is identical with, the revolution. Of this, I will just remark that it leaves completely unexplained how the phenomenon of a change of consciousness is identical with a change in social structure; in the Hegelian terms in which it is developed, the thesis is based on a mistaken reduction of objectification to alienation (see Marx, 1973a, 'Critique of the Hegelian Dialectic and Philosophy as a Whole', and Lukács, 1971, self-critical preface).

Marx sets out several sociological pre-conditions of the proletariat being able to effect the transformation to socialist society. First, the capitalist mode of production is a world-historical or universal one, and therefore necessitates the existence of the proletariat as a universal class (Marx and Engels, 1974, p. 56). Secondly, the historical occasion for the proletarian revolution of society is provided by the spiralling crises in the capitalist mode of production. These crises are rooted in the conflict between the social forces of production and the individualistic relations of production, a conflict which finds expression in such pathologies as over-production. Capitalist crises also result, and this is the third point, in a growing polarisation of the classes in

bourgeois society, as the intermediate strata are increasingly pro-
letarianised by the extension of the capitalist mode of production
(Marx and Engels, 1848, p. 36). Fourthly, the proletariat does not only
become larger and more cohesive, it also becomes more destitute
(Marx, 1847, pp. 90–3). As such, proletarian needs form the material
pre-condition of the revolution (Marx, 1844, p. 46).

These sociological conditions of the proletarian revolution also
determine the existence of the proletariat as a cohesive, self-conscious
class. They thus precede the very possibility of correct proletarian
consciousness playing a part in the development of the revolution. The
fact that Marx identifies non-conscious conditions for the existence of proletarian consciousness is an instance of his ontological
commitment to explain the ideal in terms of the material, and, at the
sociological level, phenomena of thought in terms of phenomena of
production (Marx and Engels, 1974, p. 47).

But Marx's general commitment to explaining phenomena of consciousness in terms of phenomena of production does not imply that
Marx postulated a simple one-way causal relation between the
material substratum and the conscious superstructure for all social
situations (Marx and Engels, 1974, p. 58). So far from there being a
simple causal relation between base and superstructure, the ideological elements of the superstructure can achieve relative autonomy
(Engels, 1890, pp. 687–8). The causal efficacy and the relative autonomy of ideas explain the importance which Marx and Engels attributed to ideas. It is correct and important – this is to re-emphasise the
ultimate determination by production – that for Marx and Engels the
significance of ideas is partly rooted in the fact that their emergence
and conflict indicate developments in the mode of production: as when
Engels argued that the emergence of a positive proletarian morality
demonstrates the outmodedness of capitalist production (Engels,
1884, p. 9). But the independent importance of ideas is understandable
in terms of Marx's commitment to man as a thinking and acting
creature who controls (or ought to control) his history consciously.
Thus, Engels wrote that correct theory was preferable for the Party to
success in recruitment (Engels, 1873, p. 675).

This is the framework which allows Marx to hold that, although
proletarian consciousness can be explained in terms of the kind of
conditions (not necessarily conceptualised by the actors in question) I
have elucidated, it can also form part of the explanation of the generation of the revolution. Specifically, correct proletarian consciousness
becomes an important historical factor as the result of two long-term
features of the development of capitalist production. First, the increasingly severe economic crises which beset capitalism, the developing

polarisation of the classes and pauperisation of the proletariat, which at first produce sporadic unconscious conflict between proletariat and bourgeoisie, in time reveal to the proletariat the true exploitative nature of the capitalist mode of production (Marx, 1973b, p. 107). Secondly, the positive aspects of capitalist development, in which, for example, the workplace unit becomes ever larger, provide the institutional basis on which the proletariat can conceptualise itself as a single social entity. That is, they provide the conditions under which the proletariat can become a class subjectively, a possibility not open to such classes as the peasantry (Marx, 1973b, p. 148, and 1852, p. 171). The consequences of the development of proletarian consciousness for the outcome of the revolution (and hence the way in which correct proletarian consciousness can enter into an explanatory account of the revolution) are given in many details. For example, the proletariat will increasingly have a clear strategy and make clear demands, thus avoiding the mistakes the Communards made due to their theoretical confusion (Engels, 1891, p. 255). In general, clear self-consciousness of aims and strategy is a decisive weapon for the proletariat, given that 'theory also becomes a material force as soon as it has gripped the masses' (Marx, 1844, p. 45). It is not a question of proletarian consciousness developing at a single instant, with the struggle before that instant being undirected and the struggle after that instant being completely determined by consciousness. The interconnections of objective conditions and proletarian consciousness will be complex in any specific case. But this is another way of making the basic point that for Marx proletarian consciousness is at times a feature to be explained, and at times a feature which explains.

Other writers, working under the influence of Marxism, have also held that proletarian accounts can be fitted into a theory of revolution. In *The Mass Strike*, for example, Rosa Luxemburg applies the Marxist theory of the role and development of proletarian consciousness in revolutionary situations to her study of the mass strikes in Russia between 1895 and 1905. She argues that a new stage in the objective conditions of class relations, one where the proletarian revolution is imminent, produced a new form of class struggle, the mass strike. What starts as an economic strike tends to become a political strike, which in turn produces the development of proletarian political organisation and the creation of a correct proletarian consciousness. Once created, proletarian consciousness is instrumental in creating other strikes. Here again, consciousness has a dual role: as something to be explained, and as something which can explain objects of study in its own terms.

When Marx holds that proletarian consciousness explains aspects of the revolution, he means not only that the existence of proletarian consciousness is a necessary causal factor in the production of the revolution. He also holds that proletarian conceptualisations and explanations of events are correct – that the actors' accounts are scientifically correct versions of certain aspects of the revolution. Just as the proletariat is the privileged agent of history in the coming of socialism, so too it is an epistemologically privileged subject. The proletariat does not possess a distinctive mode of appropriation which could form the basis for a new type of class rule, so its revolution will result in the abolition of all partial modes of appropriation (Marx and Engels, 1848, p. 45). With it, therefore, class rule will end, so proletarian emancipation equals human emancipation (Engels, 1885, p. 437). The proletariat has thus no need to pretend to represent a false general interest and so has no need for an ideological disguise similar to that of bourgeois ideology (Marx and Engels, 1974, p. 66). But precisely because its outlook is non-ideological, because it cannot be satisfied with the ideological social theories which have existed hitherto, the proletariat requires a radically new theory (Engels, 1887, p. 243). This new theory is scientific socialism or historical materialism. Its gradual emergence corresponds with the gradual development of the proletariat to full self-consciousness. The first consciousness of the proletariat is utopian, based as it is in an immature proletariat and bourgeois productive mode. It lacks an understanding of class, revolutionary activism, history, capitalism and the materialist basis of ideas (Marx and Engels, 1848, p. 60, and Engels, 1975, pp. 28 and 305). With the further progress of capitalism and class struggle, the proletariat emerges as a self-conscious class for itself, the possessor, that is, of a scientific theory of its actions.

4

〰〰〰

Values and social science

4.1. VALUES

By evaluative statements, I mean statements about how the world ought to be. They are perhaps best construed as statements of how the utterer desires the world to be, though in a sense which does not include purely personal desires. This conception of values appears in discussions of values in social science in two different contexts. First, in the notion of values in use, values are held partly to determine actions. It is in this sense, for example, that it might be argued that social science is value-laden because it has implications for what we do. Secondly, we might suggest that values enter social science by generating assumptions that the world is (or is not) as it is desired to be. In section 4.3, I will argue that, of the two appeals to the conception of values in social science, the second poses the interesting problem for social science. The whole of the subsequent chapter will therefore be directed to drawing out its implications.

There are a number of reasons why we can discuss the relationship between values and social science without taking a prior stance on the question of the ontological or epistemological status of values.

(A) An analysis of the relation between evaluative and non-evaluative elements of a social scientific theory is possible, no matter which side we take in the debate on the fact–value distinction. Social science has usually assumed the correctness of one side of this debate. It has assumed the radical heterogeneity of fact and value. It has held that moral statements have neither an objective subject matter nor, in consequence, a determinate truth-status. Indeed, commitment to a rigid fact–value separation is often considered to be a defining feature of naturalistic social science, as by Kolakowski in *Positivist Philosophy* (ch. 1). This assumption of fact–value heterogeneity yields an intentional account of values whereby, for example, what people believe to be just, not what is just, might have causal force in a social situation. On this assumption, our question is the relationship between the social

118

scientist's value commitments (however they are generated, whether by individual choice or through group membership, for example) and his perception and theory of social reality. This relationship is typically held to be a non-logical one, with the values which help to generate the social scientist's statements having no bearing on the meaning or truth-status of those statements. But there is a growing opinion, which I am about to support, that the relation is logical.

On the other hand, suppose we were to produce an ethical argument to the effect that evaluative statements have a determinate truth-status. Suppose, that is, we were to break down the fact–value distinction on this point. Imagine further us to hold that no social scientific statement is either entirely evaluative or entirely factual. We could still ask, even on these suppositions, whether and to what extent social scientific statements are relatively evaluative and relatively factual. In pursuing this investigation, we might postulate an ideal of a purely factual social scientific statement. Even if we did not believe such statements to exist, we could consider the extent to which actual social scientific statements diverge from the ideal. This inquiry would be similar to our ability to use the analytic–synthetic distinction in a relative sense as an instrument of analysis, even if we accept recent criticisms of the absolute tenability of the distinction. In the case of values, what determines the degree to which a social scientific statement is relatively evaluative tends to be similar to what determines the degree of analyticity in the relative analytic–synthetic distinction, namely distance from the empirical base; this remark will become clearer in what follows.

So, on the above argument, relations between evaluative and non-evaluative statements or elements of a social scientific theory can be studied, however we see the ultimate nature of values.

(B) There is a sense in which the views I am about to present have no direct implications for the abstract fact–value distinction. Certainly, they have implications for the tenability of the fact–value distinction within the context of social science. This must be so for any argument which holds that social science is value-laden, but is not a purely ideological discipline. For if a social scientific theory is composed of both empirical and normative elements in such a way that the two cannot be separated from one another within the structure of a social scientific theory, then normative and empirical arguments become relevant to one another within that particular theory of the social world. But the relevance for the fact–value distinction remains firmly within the context of a social scientific theory. By this I mean that I will elucidate specific ways in which values play a role in social scientific theories, which are yet empirical, and hence specific ways in which distinctions between the evaluative and the informative become unclear and even unimportant in social science. But I present no general argument against the fact–value distinction. Thus, even granted my thesis that values are part of the foundations of social scientific theory, it is still in principle possible to use a particular social scientific theory T which is based on values V_1 to act on the world in the service of a different set of values V_2. The social scientist who proposes T is unlikely to do so, however, unless he is morally schizophrenic. It is probable that the development of either a unique social scientific theory or a very sound social scientific theory by a society would lead members of that society to adopt the basic values of that theory as values in use governing their actions; but this is not a logical point.

(C) In any case, while essaying a prior resolution of the status of values within ethical theory, we would need to consider on this meta-level the type of argument I am shortly to make for the level of social scientific theory. For the adoption of a particular theory of values, whether of their heterogeneity or their non-heterogeneity, is itself not value-neutral. As Montefiore argues in 'Fact, Value and Ideology', commitment to individualism and anti-authoritarianism typically underlies the doctrine of the heterogeneity of facts and values. Even to envisage a choice between ethical theories prejudices the issue in favour of an individualist–heterogeneous ethics.

I use the notion of factual statements in two senses which are sufficiently disparate to avoid confusion between the two. First, there is the sense which opposes factual to theoretical statements. Within the context of a scientific theory (which is the only context I am here concerned with), factual statements are, as I noted in the Introduction, lower level statements, with little systematic import for other statements in the theory, closer to the observational constraint and hence more likely to be revised in the face of recalcitrant experience. Given recent critiques of the theory–fact distinction, we can hold only that some statements are more factual in this sense than others, and even this only within the context of particular scientific theories.

Secondly, there is the sense which opposes factual to evaluative statements. I include as factual statements in this second sense (but clearly not in the first sense) the more theoretical statements of a social scientific theory, as well as metaphysical statements which I hold to be part of the abstract foundations of a scientific theory. Metaphysical statements are factual in that they are not definitional, nor meaningless, nor simply procedural or instrumental. They do not take the form of procedural statements. For if asked to justify why we operate as though space and time are such-and-such, we fall back on the claim that that is how the world is. So, they are factual in the sense of purporting to be informative, about the world. Further, metaphysical statements are factual in that they generate scientific theories. That is, they are presupposed by specific theories, perhaps through providing the ontology of those theories. On this basis, whether a scientific theory is successful is relevant to the criticism of the metaphysics that generated the theory, though there may also be distinctive philosophical criteria that a metaphysical statement must satisfy.

How this bears on the problem of values in social science will become clear in what follows. But the basic argument is that social science also has its metaphysical foundations. Social science's metaphysical foundations are value-laden. The social scientific theories they generate are, therefore, both value-laden and informative, in the same way that metaphysically structured natural scientific theories are informative. By the idea that a social scientific theory is value-laden, I subsume two connected features of a social scientific theory. First, conformity with one's values is an additional criterion of theory choice in social science. Secondly, the meaning of the concepts entering both the relatively theoretical and the relatively factual statements of a social scientific theory is in consequence partly determined by the values at the basis of the theory in question.

4.2. THE EMPIRICIST ANALYSIS OF VALUES AND SOCIAL SCIENCE

The following ways in which values might intrude into social science have been recognised by empiricist philosophy of social science.[1]

(a) Social science is committed to the value of the scientific enterprise and the value of scientific truth. This commitment may have moral implications. For example, genuinely to believe in the value of scientific truth may entail belief in the political autonomy of science and of the scientist. The form that scientific truth takes might also be partly determined at a meta-level by values. This idea has recurred in this book, in, for example, the point that the choice between a study based on the notions of the observer, prediction and control and one based on the notions of the participant and dialogue might be partly determined by values. It is not an idea I wish to discuss in detail, however, not least because it gives no basis for distinguishing between natural science and a naturalistic social science.

(b) Moral questions are involved in the ways in which social scientific results are used. A variant on this position holds that the moral usage to which social scientific results must be put is in a sense transparent.

[1] See e.g.: Nagel (1961, ch. 13, sect. V), Dahrendorf (1968, ch. 1), Passmore (1953), Popper (1961), Albert (1964) and Skinner (1973).

This variant is espoused by many radical non-Marxist social scientists. They believe that to show the world as it is, to bring out the facts of inequality and oppression, implies or encourages criticisms of received professional and everyday social theories and of the existing social structure, and shows how social ills can be cured (see e.g. Bottomore, 1969, p. 15).

(c) Social science includes the study of values. Social scientists from entirely different traditions have even asserted that social science's main aim is to study values (see e.g. Goldmann, 1973, pp. 27ff., and Harrod, 1971, p. 104).

(d) Attempts to view social science as a value-free analysis of means towards given ends, which was one strand of Weber's (1949 and 1957) methodology, forget that values also attach to means and that means can be construed as ends. Thus, Durkheim (1964, ch. 3) asks how we are to decide between the swiftest, most economical, surest or simplest means.

(e) Social scientific statements may be biased in a simple and negative way. Bias is to be differentiated from a more sophisticated and positive type of entry of values into social science, which I elucidate later. The basic index of bias within a theory is that claims are made which are neither supported by nor part of the foundations of the theory. They are unsupported by either more fundamental statements of the theory or the evidence for that theory. The claims in question are in the interest of the person or group propagating them. So, a statement is judged biased in relation to the theory within which the statement is presented. For example, bias may take the form of disguising the unempirical nature of purportedly empirical statements. Bias may also result from the overextension of a valid result, such as the extension of the claim that the normative basis of order is important to the claim that it is the only basis of order, when that latter claim cannot be supported by the theory of order at issue.

(f) Social scientists select what they study and what they ignore on the basis of their values, a view which also forms part of Weber's position. This thesis became a commonplace of the attacks on what until recently were the received orientations and theories in social science. They were accused, for example, of studying only the currently existing social systems and the forces which made for consensus and stability, while ignoring those forces which furthered conflict and change. Social scientists who believe that the value selection of problems is inevitable, however, may use this thesis more positively. Thus, Wright Mills (1973) believes that the values of reason and freedom determined the foci of classical social theory, and that modern sociology ought to select its problems on the basis of these values. For example, it ought to study those social forces which are tending to increase or decrease reason and freedom.

(g) Values determine the identification of facts, in the sense that terms are applied and phenomena are individuated partly on the basis of values. An interesting general example is the contention that the primordial sorting of facts into different social scientific disciplines is evaluatively determined (see Edel, 1964, pp. 225–6). A more specific example comes from American social scientific theories of social pathology. One of the background assumptions against which the pathological is identified is that the norms of rural middle class people are the generally accepted norms of American society. Deviation from these norms is the crucial index of the pathological (see Wright Mills, 1963, pp. 539–42).

(h) Values determine what a social scientist considers to be good evidence and sound method. For example, liberal theorists of political power (that is, of actions which contravene a person's interests) are committed to the belief that a person's interests are identical with his conscious preferences. On this basis, they concentrate on the observable behaviour of those over whom power is supposedly being exercised. A different conception of human interests would yield different foci for the study of exercises of power and hence perhaps also a methodology attuned to studying things other than observable behaviour (see Lukes, 1974).

(i) Values might determine what a social scientist states in his explanations in particular and in his conclusions in general. For example, anthropologists studying recent cultural changes among American Indians concluded that they were due to assimilation by the dominant European culture and to positive acceptance of that culture by the Indians. What the American anthropologists missed – an understandable omission on the part of representatives of the dominant culture – is that many of these cultural changes were the result of strong resistance by the Indians to assimilation by the European culture (see Clemmer, 1972).

Faced with this list, empiricist philosophy of social science makes certain standard moves in order to avoid the dangers of infiltration by values.

(I) First, it uses the fact–value distinction to good effect. It points out that most of the above points are ambiguous between the claim that values may enter social science in the ways elucidated and the claim that they must so enter. The latter is, of course, a much stronger claim than the former, and it is undeniable that many writers have thought they were establishing the necessity of the value permeation of social science by establishing its possibility.

Defenders of the value freedom of social science argue further that, in general, the above points presuppose the distinction between facts and values. For example, the radical version of point (*b*) is a conjunction of the belief that it is possible to state how the world objectively is and the hypothesis that facts about poverty, etc., confirm certain left-wing positions. For any specific case, it is held, analysis of the value permeation of social science provides a basis for the removal of the values. This argument is particularly effective against points (*e*) and (*f*). With respect to point (*e*) concerning bias, the recognition of the writer's prejudices – for example, in the type of blame/praise moral judgments which are likely to infect history – is held to enable their removal, with a consequent gain for scientific understanding (see Butterfield, 1951, pp. 101ff.). Even studies of the systematic biases which operate in social science can be welcomed as weapons in the fight for objectivity. Phillips (1973, chs. 1–4) gives evidence that subjects' behaviours in social scientific investigations are largely determined by such factors as their conceptions of what is socially desirable and of what the investigator's opinions are. But he gives no reason why his findings should not be incorporated into the design of better social scientific studies. As an answer to the critical version of (*f*), defenders of value freedom argue that the very statement that functionalism has ignored change or conflict points in the direction of a more complete social scientific theory.

In *The Structure of Science*, Nagel elaborates this basic first strategy in his distinction between 'characterising' and 'appraising' value judgments, a distinction which is mainly directed against point (*g*). Although, say, 'liberal democracy' can be used appraisingly, it can also be used value-neutrally in a scientific theory. In this latter usage, the required judgment is only that a predicate applies. It is *'an estimate* of the degree to which some commonly recognised (and more or less clearly defined) type of action, object, or institution is embodied in a given instance' (p. 492). A characterising value judgment does not presuppose an appraising value judgment, though the converse relation holds. It is further argued that any genuinely informative claims about a society will not be affected by the fact, if it is a fact, that our judgment of the supposed necessary and sufficient conditions for the characterising application of a term is determined by our values (see Runciman, 1972a, p. 58). This argument seems to me dubious. Why it is dubious will become clear when I set out a holistic philosophy of social science and when I criticise Runciman's theory of descriptions.

(II) Secondly, an attempt is made to neutralise the threat of value-infiltration by pointing out that, with the exception of (*c*), the whole list is also true of natural science. Point (*c*), it is correctly stated, concerns

124

merely the specific subject matter of social science; there is no reason why there should not be a value-free study of values.

(III) Most of points (*a*)-(*i*) are held to deal with 'extra-scientific' practice, where 'science' is restricted to the validation or invalidation of statements. In the specific case of *pre*-validation practice, the distinction between the psychology of discovery and the logic of validation (which was implicitly central to Weber's response) is invoked. This argument is used liberally against the most basic points (*f*)-(*i*). Social science is thereby excused the task of rationally analysing the values which structure social scientific work, even if, as Wright Mills claimed, there is a single set of values at the heart of the classical sociological tradition. Only the hypotheses which a scientist's values prompt are to be submitted to social scientific validation.

(IV) Finally, those who do not trust scientific validation to dispose of the particular prevalence of value permeation in social science often call for the explicit statement of our values. Myrdal writes that the 'only way in which we can strive for "objectivity" in theoretical analysis is to expose the valuations to full light, make them conscious, specific, and explicit, and permit them to determine the theoretical research' (1970, pp. 55–6). But even Nagel calls this advice 'a counsel of perfection' (1961, p. 489). On its own, the advice is pointlessly utopian because many of the values which permeate a piece of research are invisible to the researchers. They are only apparent either in retrospect (how else could we explain the 'end-of-ideology' fiasco?) or by deliberately distancing ourselves from the perspectives which inform the research (American anthropologists can pass a resolution condemning 'scientific racism' as an expression of 'felt truth', while to them any 'issue that departs from present ethos or that reveals an unresolved split appears as politicisation' [Hymes, 1972, p. 51]). I argued in chapter one that social science could benefit from certain ideal methodological prescriptions. I do not support a similar position for value freedom in social science because, besides being impossible, value freedom is also undesirable, as I hope to show.

4.3. A HOLISTIC PHILOSOPHY OF SOCIAL SCIENCE[2]

These responses to the threat of value permeation cannot be defeated decisively on the ground of the value question alone. Rather, we must criticise the empiricist philosophy of science on which they are based. This criticism has, of course, recently been made. But before consider-

---

[2] The whole of this chapter, but especially the opening paragraphs of this section, have been influenced by conversations with Mary Hesse. Her essay 'Theory and Value in the Social Sciences' (1978) sets out her position.

ing the discontinuities of the empiricist and post-empiricist philosophies of science and hence analysing the new approach to the value problem in social science facilitated by post-empiricist philosophy of science, it is well to be clear about the continuities. Post-empiricist philosophy of science stands in the empirical tradition. So, it is not surprising that it accepts certain elements of empiricism's response to the threat from values. Specifically, points (*a*)–(*e*) of the original list are also rejected as extra-scientific by post-empiricist philosophy of science. It would take a much deeper epistemological shift than that from empiricism to post-empiricism in order to render plausible, for example, point (*b*), that the fact that values govern the usage made of social scientific results may reflect on the validity of those results. Point (*b*) assumes the first notion of values which I noted in section 4.1, namely values in use determining actions, a notion which is not the fundamental one for social scientific methodology.

But let us concentrate on the crucial points (*f*)–(*i*). The empiricist response here is one of divide and rule. It lists the ways in which values might enter isolated segments of a social scientific theory and then juxtaposes one segment against another, so as to restore objectivity to the whole. For example, the 'objectivity' of facts is used to correct the 'subjective' value determinants of theory. Now the characteristic of post-empiricist philosophy of science which is important here is precisely its holism. Insofar as we accept the main tenets of post-empiricist models of science, we cannot pursue the segmentation of a scientific theory, a segmentation which is necessary for the empiricist strategy in relation to the value question in social science.

Two propositions of post-empiricist philosophy of science are crucial to my analysis of values and social science. First, theoretical and factual statements and concepts cannot be radically separated; that is, facts are theory-laden. Secondly, what theory we accept is underdetermined by the world. These two propositions are crucial because both are necessary for us to argue that every element of a social scientific theory is value-laden. The underdetermination thesis allows us to suggest that the room left for social scientific theory construction by the social world might be at least partly filled by value commitments. These value commitments act as an extra criterion of theory choice. This suggestion would not of itself necessitate the conclusion that the relatively empirical facts of social scientific theories are value-laden. For there might be gaps between the value permeation of the theory and the theory permeation of the facts. For example, particular theories of class or democracy or inflation might confirm particular evaluations. In that case, the evaluation could serve as an extra criterion of theory acceptability. But, the empiricist might argue, this does not mean that the facts used in support of the theory are value-laden. The value levels of the theory might have no bearing on the statement of facts within the theory. To the extent that we accept that theoretical and factual statements cannot be radically separated, however, this empiricist defence becomes untenable. For from the thesis of the theory-ladenness of facts, we can argue that the concepts used in the relatively factual statements of a scientific theory have their meanings at least partly determined by their relations with all the concepts of a theory. Insofar as some of these high level concepts are evaluative, then the meanings of the relatively factual concepts and therefore how these concepts are applied to reality will also be partly value-determined.

This argument seeks to show the relation between the evaluative and cognitive elements of a theory to be internal or logical, not just an external matter of specific values causing a certain social scientist to suggest a specific theory. It begins with the idea that values act as a criterion of theory acceptability. The entry-points for values are at the relatively abstract levels of a social scientific theory. But they cannot be isolated there. For a scientific theory forms a unity, in which distinctions such as those between fact/description and theory/explanation are relative and shifting. Moreover, even if an absolute theory–description distinction were plausible for each theory separately, it is doubtful whether we could abstract a value-free descriptive level which would be common to various social scientific theories; because, for example, Marxism and functionalism disagree on precisely what constitutes a full description of a phenomenon.

The significance of this argument will become clearer when I apply it to examples in both social science and the methodology of social science, and also when I consider its implications for naturalism. First, I will give a short example of how it can be used to elucidate social scientific work. I deliberately chose a highly empirical social scientific example. At the end of *Family and Kinship in East London*, which I discussed in section 1.3, Young and Willmott reveal that they value considerations of 'community spirit' more highly than those of the physical standards of housing. In the light of this value commitment, we understand why Young and Willmott choose to explain as they do the central puzzle of the slum-dwellers being less happy once they had moved to the new housing estates. Young and Willmott explain this fact by the hypothesis that the slums possessed more community spirit than the housing estates. Other accounts are plausible: for example, that people prefer to stay in the area in which they were brought up, that the people on the estates felt that they had less control of their environment than when they lived in the slums, that – as the subjects

127

themselves suggested – people suffer from the discrepancy of the standards of behaviour, governing such factors as the appearance of oneself, one's children and home, which are expected in different types of housing. But why Young and Willmott choose their explanation is at least partly explained by their commitment to integrated communities. Moreover, the manner in which they conceive and value integrated communities determines not only the explanations they advance. It also affects the descriptive statements they make, because the meanings of the concepts used in these lower level statements are partly determined by their evaluations. For instance, Young and Willmott describe Bethnal Green as closely integrated on the grounds of data such as that 55% of married women with mothers alive had seen their mothers in the previous twenty-four hours (p. 48). Yet they also discover that the majority of people (while acquainted with many non-relatives in the area) neither visited, nor were visited by, non-relatives (p. 108). Some theorists, valuing different elements in the notion of an integrated community, would not apply such a term to a community characterised by so little non-relative contact. It would seem, therefore, that Young and Willmott's usage of terms such as 'community spirit' – a usage which would determine the types of community we would investigate if we wanted to test their theory – reflects a positive evaluation of kinship over non-kinship ties for the establishment of an integrated community.

4.4. EXAMPLES OF A HOLISTIC PHILOSOPHY OF VALUES AND SOCIAL SCIENCE

Some excellent methodological studies of the role of values in social science have already been carried out. None of these studies puts forward precisely the same holistic philosophy of values and social science which I advocate. Nor have they drawn the implications for naturalism which I do. However, they are much more sensitive than empiricism to the fundamental sense in which social science is permeated by values. They have taken off from programmatic assertions such as that normative theories tend to contain an implicit theory of social reality (e.g. Geertz, 1964, p. 64) and that philosophical theories often favour certain social and political theories against others (e.g. Partridge, 1968, p. 34). Recently, such insights have been developed systematically.

Taylor's 'Neutrality in Political Science' is an already classic analysis of the logical links between the evaluative and theoretical bases of a political scientific theory. Taylor says that a political scientific theory typically provides a theoretical framework which defines certain crucial dimensions of variation whereby political phenomena can be explained. But, he continues, the provision of such a framework also typically falls to normative political philosophy. Thus, the two types of political theory (the 'scientific' and 'normative') are not detachable in the simple manner which empiricism maintains. Particular political philosophies sustain particular political scientific work (e.g. a Rousseauist egalitarian is not impressed by the claims to universal validity of elite theories) and vice versa (e.g. to modern conflict theorists who take class conflict as a perpetual dimension of variation, Marx's commitment to the end of class conflict becomes vacuous). So, normative statements have specific implications for non-normative statements and vice versa. The point is not just that, on the basis of particular political scientific theories, particular writers value differently certain phenomena. It is rather that with certain political scientific theories, given their lack of recognition of certain dimensions of variation, particular normative theories lose possible referentiality and therefore become untenable; equally, explanatory variables in social science are deemed either fundamental or derivative, depending on what evaluative beliefs we hold. In Taylor's words: 'a given dimension of variation will usually determine for itself how we are to judge of good and bad, because of its relation to obvious human wants and needs' (p. 40). For example, Lipset's statement that democracy is the good society in operation is the result, not the premise, of his political scientific theory. For Lipset's dimensions of variation are such that the alternatives to democracy are despotism or primitive oligarchy. It would be very strange for us to prefer either of the latter two without qualification. To prefer either of the two with qualification is, by the very fact of qualification, to alter Lipset's original political scientific framework. This alteration would involve either overriding the values being appealed to (e.g. aesthetic values are preferable to political ones) or undermining the dimensions of variation (e.g. by arguing that occasional outbursts of public violence are necessary for the maintenance of peace). Nor could we hold a different view of human nature to Lipset and thereby draw different conclusions from his political scientific theory. For 'if one adopted a quite different view of human need, one would upset the framework' (p. 41). Lipset's theory, for example, presupposes that people do not become unhappy if granted too much freedom, thus excluding the likelihood of preferring despotism or oligarchy to democracy. But if we held a radically different theory to Lipset of what people are (i.e. concerning their needs, purposes, interests, etc.), we would be committed to the expectation that people would act differently and hence to a different framework for any science of political behaviour.

129

Gunther and Reshaur's 'Science and Values in Political "Science" '
presents an equally illuminating analysis. They look at the various
types of valuations which might enter into different elements and
levels of a social scientific theory. They argue that if we explain, say,
the activity of a person contributing funds to a political party on the
basis of marginal utility theory, we assume the following types of
values. (i) We choose 'a particular value utility for explaining the
behaviour of some men in a political situation', so that 'Political Funds
Contributing Man has been transformed into Utility Measuring Man.
He has become someone with values and these values motivate his
actions'. (ii) We accept the valuational theory in which utility theory is
itself embedded. This value theory presupposes, for example, 'that
free competition provides maximum utility', 'an *egoistical* theory of the
good' and an 'essentially non-developmental model of Man', since it
assumes that the individual's preferences have not changed between
the times that his preferences are measured. (iii) We accept, at a still
higher level, the 'ontological assumptions' on which 'the theory of
utility is based': for example, (*a*) the liberal, individualist concept of
man as a consumer of utilities – i.e. market-place man, (*b*) instrumental
rationality, and (*c*) that basic needs are satisfied prior to engaging in
political activities, so 'political action is best understood as a means to
the fulfillment of needs rather than as a good in itself' (pp. 116–17). On
this basis, Gunther and Reshaur state that the 'picture of the political'
which emerges from utility theory would be understood by an actor
who assumes 'a tacit contractual relationship between himself and
society'. It would 'appear distorted or meaningless to an actor in tribal
society' (p. 117) – or, we might add, in feudal or socialist society.

Gunther and Reshaur further produce a useful analytic model of the
kinds of values involved at different levels of political scientific theory:

LEVEL 1: Statements of observable regularity. Gunther and Reshaur hold
these to be non-explanatory, non-theoretical and non-scientific.

LEVEL 2: Statements of the values which actors give to things. In their
extended example, the political actor values things according to the
expectations of marginal utility theory. Here 'we must be aware that the
choice of these interpretative values may be arbitrary'.

LEVEL 3: 'the *ground* for valuing things is set in a more abstract and ideal
context': for example, against the background of *laissez faire* freedom.

LEVEL 4: Ontology: for example, the evaluative 'implications of interpreting our empirical generalisation as part of the ontological presumption
which underlies *laissez faire* freedom, namely, Utility Man or Market-
Place Man'.

LEVEL 5: At the highest level, theories of cognition or 'world hypotheses':
for example, a static empiricist notion of cognition, with the knower

130

detached from what he knows, as against a dialectical one, based on a concept of *praxis*, with the knower changing himself and his object during the process of cognition.

There is a role for values additional to the ones which Gunther and Reshaur stress, at least if we accept their account of the levels of a social scientific theory (many writers now doubt the existence of level 1). Namely, level 1, the pre-theoretical observation statements, and level 2, the lowest level explanatory statements, have to be connected. In the Young and Willmott study which I used in section 4.3, the pre-theoretical regularities are patterns of contact between people. We would have to decide which of these represented ties of friendship and family. These decisions are typically shaped by our morality, for instance, by what we consider to be a relation of friendship. Further, we would have to decide the type and extent of contact which needs to be present before we term a community closely integrated. This, as I have already argued, is likely to be determined by what values we hold concerning such things as the family.

Gunther and Reshaur's basic hypothesis is that concentration on different levels of theory 'may alter one's interpretation of a particular empirical generalisation' because of the different kinds of values involved at different theoretical levels. Their implicit methodological position is the one I am adopting. Namely, evaluative and empirical propositions may be distinguished to an extent methodologically within the structure of a given social scientific theory, because the role of values becomes more important and transparent the higher the level of theory considered. But such analytic distinctions do not imply that values can be removed from social scientific work.

Finally, Stretton argues in *The Political Sciences* that value judgments are essential in social science, because they determine which explanations are advanced and where these explanations are brought to a halt. Values govern the theory and explanations advanced often through the 'by-products' of the explicitly given explanations; that is, the implicit causal associations of the explanans are being valued. Thus, a Marxist explanation of the First World War would look beyond the precipitating factor of bad diplomacy to the ultimate cause in the structure of capitalism. The Marxist believes that associated with capitalism as effects (but not necessarily as relevant causes of the First World War) are such factors as private property, class differentiation, privilege, conspicuous waste, worker exploitation and repressive government. The Marxist values these associated effects negatively, and two consequences flow from his negative evaluations. First, he also opposes capitalism. Secondly, he seeks to associate capitalism with a universally disliked event, the First World War, by holding capitalism to be its cause.

An alternative explanation of the First World War might be that diplomatic mistakes alone caused its outbreak. Such an explanation might be politically conservative or it might be 'apolitical'. It would be politically conservative if the theorist implicitly substituted for the Marxist causal framework one which, also based in capitalism, has such (positively valued) features associated with it in virtue of being effects of capitalism as private property, class differentiation, the rewards of merit, high culture, labour at market price, productive efficiency, rationalisation, mass-production and liberal government. This framework would not be invoked in the explanation of the First World War by the conservative, because it would be deemed irrelevant. Given that he values its elements positively, however, it would determine his decision to stop his explanation at 'bad diplomacy'. For he does not wish those things he values positively to be associated with the outbreak of a despised war. The 'bad diplomacy' explanation might also be 'apolitical'. Or, rather, it might be proposed by a writer who thought his only concern was with the facts and the value-free explanation of the same. For, as Stretton argues, the implicit value position of such apoliticism is clear: 'If war could be sufficiently explained by some avoidable mistakes of government or diplomacy, then we could satisfy the universal desire to rid society of war while preserving intact the remainder of society's more controversial fabric' (p. 57).

4.5. THE CRITICAL FORCE OF A HOLISTIC PHILOSOPHY OF VALUES AND SOCIAL SCIENCE

In order to see the critical force of the position I have advanced, I will use it to show the incompleteness of two variants of non-holistic philosophy of social science. The views I will criticise contain a sophisticated response to the problem of values and social science. Yet they are defective in virtue of the fact that they try to isolate values in a single area of scientific theory on the basis of an unintegrated philosophy of social science.

In *The Political System*, Easton characterises his views as a reaction against previous political science with its 'conviction that complete freedom from value premises was possible' (p. 224). Easton argues 'the impossibility for political research ever to free itself from involvement with values' (p. 223), on the grounds that political research is oriented morally towards human needs, that facts and values are invariably intertwined in any discussion of politics, and that values provide the matrix for the selection and formulation of the research problems and for the selection and interpretation of data. But Easton is unable to comprehend the pervasiveness of the value permeation of social scientific theory for the following reasons. He remains committed to the absolute heterogeneity in principle within the structure of a social scientific theory of facts and values. The factual aspect of a proposition refers to reality. The evaluative aspect expresses the writer's emotions. Consequently, Easton maintains that the likelihood of facts and values being intertwined in a piece of social scientific theory does not impinge in any way on the question of the scientific validity of that research. Validity is determined by whether the factual aspects of a proposition correspond to reality. As a means of minimising the merely pernicious effects of unstated values on our social scientific research, Easton advocates self-conscious creative moral speculation. Social scientists should engage or take interest in 'a long process of moral inquiry'. This requires 'creative insight' and is 'the study of strict political (value) theory'. Such study is needed because 'we are not unambiguously aware of our ultimate preferences, of their general ranking or hierarchical arrangement' (p. 229). Easton's advice is within the bounds of an empiricist philosophy of the role of values in social science. Given his position on values, Easton considers the normative political philosophy which enters a social scientific theory to be determined only by the theorist's emotional preferences. For Easton, normative theory stands in an intellectual vacuum, undetermined by any conceptions the theorist might hold about social and political reality. Admittedly, our values partly determine what scientific theories we hold, but we are free to bring any values we wish to our scientific work. It is precisely the point of the move to a holistic methodology to show how this logical segregation of the evaluative and factual elements of a social scientific theory is impossible.

Runciman presupposes a similarly unintegrated model of scientific theory in his ingenious philosophy of the role of values in social science.[3] Runciman argues that social and natural science differ in a way unrelated either to explanation or to evaluation. They differ in the differential roles of 'description'. Disputes about description in social science are about neither facts nor values, though they can be termed ideological. A social scientific explanation can be accepted by the social scientific community, yet there can still be debate about 'the terms in which the experience of the people observed should be framed' (1973, p. 31). The point is that the social scientist, unlike the natural scientist, has to suggest descriptions 'as appropriate to the meaning which the experiences he describes had to the participants themselves' (1973,

---

[3] See Runciman (1972a, ch. VI, 1972b, and 1973).

p. 29). Social science has to suggest what the experiences are *like*. For example, are these non-western practices and beliefs like magic, religion or science? Are these beliefs like prejudices, a moral philosophy or a science? The observer has a certain 'discretion' in his choice of descriptions for the double reason that different descriptions can be equally factually adequate and that different descriptions may be incommensurable, rather than contradictory. How the observer exercises this discretion may be partly determined by the values he holds.

In supporting the possibility of different descriptions in different social scientific theories, Runciman ignores the point that how an item is described cannot be divorced from how it is explained and evaluated within a theory. The problem of labelling in social science ramifies throughout the whole structure of a social scientific theory. The descriptions we use set limits to the systematic explanations we can invoke and vice versa. Could two social scientists, one of whom describes Britain as a liberal democracy and the other of whom describes it as a capitalist state, put forward the same explanations and the same evaluations of British political processes? Disputes about description are basically disputes about classification, about what objects in the world the theory recognises. These disputes occur at all levels of a social scientific theory. How they are resolved sets limits to subsequent explanations and evaluations we make within the theory, just as fresh descriptions within the theory are partly determined by any prior explanations and evaluations accepted by the theory. As to the 'discretion' which social scientists use in their formulation of descriptions, the point of this chapter is to argue that it is partly determined by the values at the basis of the theory.

I do not need to dispute Runciman's analysis of describing in general. Runciman writes: 'it would be odd to claim that either logic or science can settle the argument between us if you disagree with my description of the walk we both took yesterday afternoon as much as I disagree with yours' (1972b, p. 377). I need not deny this contention. Nor need I quarrel with Runciman's points that judgments of appositeness, rather than of truth or falsity, are those by which we evaluate descriptions, and that this does not imply that descriptions are merely subjective and hence equally plausible. Nevertheless, my more limited point remains. It is misleading to talk of the discretion in the formulation of descriptions of phenomena exercised by a social scientist who is also offering a theory of those phenomena – unless, of course, we also talk about discretion in the choice of the theory itself. A social scientific theory necessarily includes descriptions of the phenomena in question. These descriptions cannot be detached from the theorist's explanations or evaluations, so that the theorist might take one line in his descriptions and another either in his explanations or evaluations. It is implausible to suggest that a theorist might describe the police in Britain as 'the main element in the repressive state apparatus' and then theorise about them as 'the enforcers of law and order'.

Disputes about how we describe the British political system or about the application of the term 'democracy' are, in the first instance, theoretical ones. Since these theoretical disputes are determined by decisions about which features of a political system constitute a democracy (e.g. rule by the people) and by either positive or negative evaluations of the actual political systems we decide are democracies, the disputes are also evaluative. They are not primarily factual disputes. In saying this, I disagree with Skinner (1973) who argues that the sole entry-points for values into a social scientific theory occur because terms such as 'democracy' are ideologically contestable and conventionally commendatory. He repeatedly states that it is an 'empirical' matter whether a theorist's concept of democracy embodies the conditions necessary and sufficient for being able to say that a political system is genuinely a democracy, that is, genuinely involves 'rule by the people'. A claim on a theorist's part that his concept of democracy embodies these conditions could not, however, be settled by empirical means. It is to be settled, if at all, by the 'ideological' debate on the nature of 'democracy' and 'rule by the people'. At the same time, I do not deny that empirical considerations are central to theories of democracy. In 4.6.b, I will try to show how empirical considerations are relevant to theories composed of these theoretical-cum-evaluative terms.

Gallie's 'Essentially Contested Concepts' develops the idea of the evaluative nature of theoretical social concepts, though with respect to political philosophy, rather than social science. He argues that political concepts such as that of democracy are essentially contested. That is, if I use 'democracy' to refer to Britain, it is essentially open to someone to dispute the criteria on whose bases I use the concept and to put forward a rival interpretation of the same concept. The idea that rival political theories involve different interpretations of shared common concepts is plausible even for the most abstract political concepts. Thus, MacCallum (1972) argues that there is *one* concept of freedom and that it is a triadic relation, comprising the freedom *of* x, *from* y, *to* do/become z. Hence, 'positive' and 'negative' theorists of freedom are disagreeing about one of two things: either the differing emphases to be placed on the term variables of the concept of freedom; or the ranges of the term variables, that is 'for example about what persons are, and about what can count as an obstacle to or an interference with the freedom of persons so conceived' (p. 181). Such disputes are the very stuff of deciding to use one theoretical framework rather than another for the purpose of scientific study, as I will argue further in the next section. In any case, Gallie's thesis is certainly plausible for the more limited terms which would enter into the lower levels of a social scientific theory (e.g. 'class', 'democracy', 'rule', 'conflict', 'neurosis'). For with them it is reasonable to suggest that they recognise a common exemplar; for example, all theories of class might accept miners as paradigmatic of the working class. Sharing a common exemplar is for Gallie a condition of correctly being able to say that we are dealing with rival interpretations of the same concept, rather than with different concepts.

Finally, two points which correspond with some of the central features of my analysis of meaning should be noted. First, in chapter three I criticised the compromise methodological view that we should accept actors' theories at the level of classification and then impose our own theories at the level of explanation. Analogously, I now criticise the compromise methodological position that normative elements of a social scientific theory can be isolated in one area of the theory. Both criticisms are based on the idea that a scientific theory is too unitary to allow the suggested segmentations.

Secondly, the result obtained in the previous chapter, namely that there is no good reason why the observer's theory should replicate the actors' theory, carries over into the problem of values. There is no good reason why the values on which a social scientific theory is based should be the same as the values of the actors that the theory is about. Some writers have urged not only that actions are constituted by actors' meanings, but also that these meanings are always or predominantly moral (see e.g. Louch, 1972, and Bernstein, 1976). Even if it were true that the constitutive actors' meanings are always moral, it would not follow that the observer has to accept the actors' morality in constructing his social theory; just as the weaker claim that the actors' meanings (whatever their nature) constitute their actions does not establish that the observer's theory has to be based on the actors' meanings. This view is also effective against positions less rooted in the kind of ideas I criticised in chapter three. For example, Myrdal in *Objectivity in Social Research* holds that the values at the basis of a social scientific study should be the values of the society under study. Thus, he took the values of the American constitution for the basis of his study of the American dilemma of racial discrimination. This procedure gives us some sort of a decision-procedure for the choice of values for a social scientific study, even if a doubtfully determinate one for the study of a complex society. It is not necessarily a decision-procedure defensible on rational or empirical grounds, however. On the contrary, Myrdal leaves himself open to the risk of uncritically accepting the prevailing ideology of the society under study.

4.6. NATURALISM AND A VALUE-LADEN SOCIAL SCIENCE

It is important that I state the steps in my argument clearly. My argument is in essence a very simple one. But exigencies of exposition have separated the various steps from one another. So, at the risk of being too schematic, I will summarise in barest outline the relationship of the various points I make in sections 4.3 and 4.6.

The idea that social study must be evaluative depends on three premises. (1) The statements of social theory are underdetermined by the social world. (2) Values act as an extra criterion of theory choice in social study. (3) The significance of valuations for social study, from the point of view of both truth-judgments and meaning-relations, cannot be segregated in any specific area of social theory, because of the holistic nature of theory. I set out these three premises in section 4.3. They are all based in ideas from post-empiricist philosophy of science which I sketched in the Introduction. Premise (2) also requires an additional argument to show why values are peculiarly relevant to social study; I attempt to supply this additional argument in 4.6.a.

Granted that social study must be evaluative, we are then presented with the problem of naturalism. Does the value permeation of social study imply that it can be modelled on political philosophy or moral theory, but not on natural science? In relation to the value issue, social science might be classified in three ways: (i) as a value-free science; (ii) as a study which is value-laden and yet scientific; and (iii) as a purely normative study without significant empirical content. Options (ii) and (iii) are on a continuum, in that both types of study can assimilate facts to some extent. A purely normative study, such as traditional political philosophy, uses facts for illustrative, persuasive and confirmatory purposes. Orientation to facts in these ways, however, is not sufficient for the study to be a science. A science is primarily interested in depicting how the world is; it therefore must assimilate facts critically and systematically. I have argued against option (i). In this section, *I will give two grounds for thinking (ii) a possible option.*

(*A*) A value-laden social study can reproduce the form of natural scientific study. That is, it can be formally analogous to natural science. The roots of this idea lie in premises (1)–(3) of the argument that social study must be evaluative. For I analyse the entry and role of values in social science by means of categories and ideas from the post-empiricist analysis of natural science. As it stands, however, the analysis is too formal. In 4.6.a, I therefore attempt to isolate the role and primary locus of values in social theory. I surmise that values are peculiarly relevant to the choice of social theory's basic metaphysics. This allows me to draw another, less formal analogy between natural and social science. For, I argue, natural science has metaphysical assumptions, to which the evaluatively determined metaphysical assumptions of social science are analogous. This argument, then, fills out the more abstract argument of section 4.3 by showing how a relatively theoretical element of a social scientific theory (its metaphysics) is value-laden.

Several items typically compose a social ontology, the core of a social metaphysics. History, society, social relations and human nature are some of the more obvious ones. *In order to exemplify my position*, in 4.6.a I take human nature as a typical constituent of social ontology and study its role in social theory in relation to values. I cannot stress too strongly that this is an *example* for my formal analysis. My argument does not depend on the view that views on human nature are to be found in all social theories.

(*B*) Someone might correctly note of (*A*) that I have not done enough to show that a value-laden social study can be scientific. All I have shown is that a value-laden social study can reproduce the forms – that is, can be formally analogous to – natural science. I noted in 3.5.a that a sophisticated theology can be constructed on the basis of formal analogies with post-empiricist philosophy of science; yet the very purpose of this theology is to argue that the religious cognitive system of which it is giving an account is completely unlike empirical science.

I need to argue further that a value-laden social study is not merely formally analogous to science, but can also pursue the *point* of science, namely knowledge of the world. I try to do this in 4.6.b. That is, a value-laden social study can be empirical; it can be used to investigate and tell us things about the social world. It is subject to rational and empirical constraint.

Someone might still say that the mere fact that social study is based on values prevents it from being a science. Two things might be meant by this. First, an implication of my analysis is that social science should not, morally or cognitively, work with a single theory. So the objection might be that a study cannot be scientific if it works with more than one theory. I deal with this point in chapter five. Secondly, the objection might simply be that the *mere* fact that social study is based on values prevents it from being a science. I am at a loss to reply to this. I will have tried to show that a value-laden social study can replicate the structure and pursue the point of science; it can be organised along the lines of scientific theory and it can provide us with systematic empirical knowledge. If anyone says that, *even so*, because of its relations to values, social study cannot be scientific, I suspect he is legislating about words. He is making a purely verbal point, which, like all purely verbal points, is unenlightening.

Showing how social science can be both value-laden and scientific is a project which has never been carried through. Empiricists have usually held that by arguing that social study cannot be value-free, we are thereby arguing that it cannot be scientific. That is, options (i) and (iii) exhaust the possibilities. Even traditions which might welcome the idea of a social study that is both moral and scientific have been unenterprising in their attempts to construct a philosophy of such a study. For example, Marxists have typically conceptualised Marxism either as a science or as a morality, hence accepting empiricist epistemological categories. Even Marxists who have wished to present Marxism as both morality and science have usually considered the Marxist science and the Marxist morality (the latter understood, for example, in a neo-Kantian way) to be simply complementary, not unified. More commonly, of course, to speak of the value relevance of social science is to make one of two limited claims: either that values are causal factors in the generation of social scientific hypotheses, the values being irrelevant to understanding or criticising the hypotheses they generate; or that social knowledge can frequently, even if inconclusively, be used in the assessment of moral and political positions (for the latter, see Weber, 1957, and Edel, 1961).

Emphasising the novelty of the idea that social science is value-laden and yet scientific is less important than stressing the power of a social science understood on these lines; though, strictly, to stress its power is to advocate the naturalistic methodology I have presented, while my concerns are to argue its possibility and to analyse its nature, not to advocate its adoption. But, briefly, the social science I depict unites moral and empirical elements and therefore recognises both moral and empirical arguments as relevant to its theories. It thereby avoids, on the one hand, the moral superficiality of a value-free social science (were that possible) and, on the other, the irrelevance to an understanding of social reality of a normative study without empirical content.

4.6.a. Values and the metaphysics of social science

The part played by values in social science can be understood via an analysis of the role depicted for metaphysics in natural science. The argument that natural science has metaphysical foundations must ultimately rest on the history of science. Burtt writes in *The Metaphysical Foundations of Modern Physical Science*, for example, that Newton gave 'new meanings to the old terms space, time and motion'. In these aspects of his work 'Newton was constituting himself a philosopher rather than a scientist as we now distinguish them . . . These metaphysical notions were carried wherever his scientific influence penetrated' (p. 20). Abstracting from these historical claims, let us take the thesis of the metaphysical basis of science for granted and ask what role metaphysical elements play in a scientific theory.[4]

Metaphysical elements are depicted as providing overall conceptual schemes or research programmes for a scientific theory. Included in total conceptual schemes are statements in favour of the ultimate existence of certain types of entity. That is, a metaphysics includes an ontology. This ontology typically sustains a preferred model of explanation (e.g. the mechanical one), in the sense that it determines which type of things can be satisfactorily referred to in the explanatory statements of a theory.

The role of the metaphysics in a physical theory is to provide a direction for the development of that theory. A metaphysics 'sketches possible explanations' (Agassi, 1964, p. 204). Scientific statements prompted by a metaphysics show that it is a potentiality fruitful research programme. Agassi exemplifies this with Newton's metaphysics, which 'asserts that the universe consists of atoms with their associated conservative central forces' and was instantiated by the theory of gravity. This instance 'illustrates the potentiality of his metaphysics and thus constitutes a challenge to construct instances of that metaphysics which are satisfactory explanations of all known physical phenomena' (p. 204).

Metaphysical statements are not assessed directly in an empirical manner. They are too global to be strictly testable. We could not, for instance, settle the debate about the existence of human freedom by trading instances and counter-instances. An implication of this point is that scientific theories are not deduced from metaphysical premises; metaphysical statements do not function as axioms for scientific theories in any strict sense. If the contrary were true, the metaphysics would be indirectly refutable by scientific evidence, which it is not. The relation is looser. Agassi talks of scientific theories being 'interpreted' in terms of metaphysical elements. A metaphysics suggests views about the basic entities of a scientific theory. It thereby sets limits to the meanings of the concepts referring to those entities in the theory; and, derivatively, to the meanings of all the other concepts in the theory.

[4] See Agassi (1964), Popper (1972, chs. 2 and 8) and the contributions to Pears (1970), especially those of Williams and Buchdahl; Collingwood (1969) on metaphysics as absolute presuppositions; and Körner (1970) on the basic elements of a conceptual framework and their relations to metaphysics.

Yet metaphysical statements are said to be true in some sense which is not reducible to analytic truth. Metaphysical statements, then, are said to be true in neither a purely empirical nor a purely formal sense. They often claim a distinctive sort of self-evidence, leading to the diction that they are known, not just believed. This self-evidence seems prior to all possible empirical knowledge, which is what we would expect if they have to be adopted before their derivative scientific programmes can be carried through.

But a metaphysics is not invulnerable to criticisms in its role as a heuristic for scientific research; metaphysical systems are not equally good at that job. Above all, a metaphysics must be fruitful. Not all are: if it is the case that the only sciences developed in the Soviet Union which differ from the sciences developed in the West have proven defective in a Lysenko-like way, then that would provide a telling criticism of Soviet metaphysics. Positively, a metaphysics is valued if it can be interpreted in such a way that it leads to more successful scientific theories in a domain than can be generated by other metaphysics. Negatively, a metaphysics loses face if its scientific theory in a certain area is rejected in favour of a theory interpreted in terms of a different metaphysics, remembering always that the relation between metaphysics and derived theory is less direct than one of deduction.

Social science has its metaphysics too. Most social scientific theories operate with assumptions concerning the philosophies of history, of society and of human nature, for example. In *The Political Element in the Development of Economic Theory*, Myrdal analyses the two metaphysical bases of classical economic theory, namely the philosophy of natural law and utilitarianism, for instance. The view that social science has metaphysical foundations does not imply, as Bottomore takes it to imply in *Marxist Sociology*, that 'the construction and development of sociological theories has depended upon, or does depend upon, the prior elaboration of, and continual reference to, a total world view' (p. 66). Lower level social scientific work can proceed satisfactorily without explicit reference to the metaphysics which underlies it. A social scientific theory's metaphysical foundation is most likely to be revealed by work which is conventionally undertaken by philosophical or historical reconstruction, not by contemporary social science; though this is not to concede, which would be false, that the development of a social scientific theory might not be helped by philosophical scrutiny of its foundations.

If pressed to generalise, I would say that an object which, under divergent interpretations, typically forms part of the ontology of social science is human nature; just as views about space, time and matter are typically to be found at the foundation of a physical theory. Considerations of human nature entered my account of Taylor's and Gunther and Reshaur's analysis of the value foundations of social science in section 4.4. A particular theory of human nature is also probably an implicit element of the philosophical bases of economics which Myrdal elucidated; because utilitarianism treats individual pleasures and pains as the basis of the measurement of social welfare, assumes that all people are equal in the social calculus and presupposes a harmony of interests in its calculations (see Myrdal, 1955, p. 43, and 1970, p. 87). Differences in philosophies of human nature have been fundamental to the numerous different forms which the various human sciences have taken.[5] A social scientific theory will be developed in terms of which features of people it sees as basic (e.g. people in conflict) and which as derivative (e.g. people in harmony).

This view is easiest to grasp in the case of psychology, where how human nature is to be conceptualised is clearly the most important ontological decision which a psychological theory must make. Dagenais in *Models of Man* (chs. I–III) has set out some of the choices which a psychology faces in constituting its core concept of human nature. These include: taking behaviour or consciousness to be the more fundamental; breaking people down into elements or trying to study them as a whole in some sense; seeing them as similar or dissimilar to animals or physical objects; a commitment to physiological reductionism or psychological emergentism; and methodological predilections for experimentation or observation (including introspective and phenomenological observation), and for causal or teleological analysis. The image of people which is formed by taking the first series of options in this set of dichotomies is of passive creatures, whose behaviour is uniform, controllable and predictable. The second series of options reveals creatures who are active, free and who can radically alter their patterns of behaviour. Behaviourist psychology has tended to take the first options. Different interpretations of the second options (together with occasional commitment to some of the first options) have yielded a kaleidoscope of psychological theories, including functionalist, introspectivist, *Gestalt*, phenomenological, existentialist and developmental psychologies. Freud was sufficiently ambiguous in his concept of human nature for different psychoanalytical schools (with very different theories and practices) to be created on the bases of divergent theories of human nature, about, for example, whether there are universal and immutable human needs.

Divergent models of human nature also provide the point of depar-

---

[5] See Dagenais (1972), Hollis (1975) and Quinton (1975).

ture for different social scientific theories. At the level of sociological schools, we have Marxist sociology where people's real nature is to be consciously productive, phenomenological sociology where people are meaning-giving creatures, and structuralist theories where people are the point of intersection of the forces of a number of structured systems. The effect which such differences have within a single social science is indicated by Taylor, Walton and Young in *The New Criminology*. They analyse some of the distinctive features of positivist criminology in terms of its theory of human nature. For example, positivist criminology typically holds an individualistic theory of the formation of personality, often commits itself to both free will and determinism (e.g. in the view that the normal majority is free and the criminal minority determined) and occasionally adopts the notion of certain universal human sentiments as the means for an objective definition of crime. Against such a theory of human nature, Taylor, Walton and Young propose that people are free, changing and meaning-creating beings, both producer and product of themselves and of society.

The role of a theory of human nature in an individual study can be exemplified by Durkheim's *Suicide*, where such a theory is vital despite Durkheim's best intentions. Durkheim's argument, which I discussed in sections 1.3 and 2.3, can be summarily reconstructed as follows. First, he shows that suicide rates vary uniformly with some other factor (e.g. religion, occupation, familial status, social crises). Secondly, he explains this variation in terms of a theoretical term which is defined by him (e.g. egoism, a lack of social cohesion; anomie, a lack of social regulation). Finally, he has to explain why this is an explanation. That is, he has to show why, say, a lack of social cohesion should be a cause of suicide. It is at this third stage that Durkheim's theory of personality enters. For, as Lukes (1973, p. 215) has noted, Durkheim's theory of suicide has force only if we presuppose a theory of individual psychological health. Thus, in effect Durkheim is committed to four basic psychological propositions, corresponding to the four suicidogenic currents. For example, corresponding to the anomic current, we have the belief that people's desires must be regulated, lest they outstrip any possibility of satisfaction. In their turn, these four propositions derive from Durkheim's fundamental dualist theory of human nature, in which people's pre-social instincts and passions struggle against their socially given morality and conscience.

Durkheim's dualistic view of human nature is pervasive to his project in *Suicide*, entering even into the explanation of such relatively low level findings as that the cross-societal correlations between the suicide and divorce rates are systematically discrepant on a sexual basis.

That is, in societies with low divorce rates, whereas fewer husbands commit suicide than unmarried men, more wives commit suicide than unmarried women; while in societies with high divorce rates, the converse relations hold. Durkheim explains this discrepancy by means of assumptions about the different sexual natures of men and women. Durkheim's dualism is also central to his sociology of knowledge. Here, the dualist opposition is between two types of psychic functioning: in the individual mind, where there is 'only a continuous flow of representations which are lost one in another, and when distinctions begin to appear they are quite fragmentary' (Durkheim and Mauss, 1963, p. 7), and, in the social mind, which uses relatively fixed and universal concepts that transcend and constrain the empirical experience of any single individual (see Durkheim and Mauss, 1963, pp. 7–8, and Durkheim, 1971, pp. 10–20). Durkheim fuses the instinct–morality dualism of *Suicide* and the sensation–concept dualism of his sociology of knowledge; he claims that the structural parallel of social morality with social concepts allows us to understand the authority possessed by the latter, which is the very authority of society. The obligation to think in terms of our society's concepts is analogous to moral obligation because no communication between human beings would be possible if they did not accept the given conceptual structure (see Durkheim, 1971, pp. 17–18).

In what sense is the philosophical basis of social science distinctively moral? Why do moral judgments serve as an extra criterion of theory choice in social, but not in natural science? To answer these questions we must state a fact of the first importance. Namely, we just do take moral and political attitudes to the kinds of issues which enter the philosophical foundations of social science. Take the theory of human nature as a typical constituent of social scientific metaphysics. I claim that we just do take positive and negative moral attitudes towards such statements as that people are creatively productive, that people are essentially equal, that people are divided between their biological instincts and their social soul, indeed that people have a fixed nature at all. Views on other likely components of social ontology, such as history and society, are also morally determined. While the fact of the peculiar moral sensitivity of the basic social scientific entities is in essence a simple one, its status is not so transparent. Strictly, it is a contingent fact. It is contingent in that there is no *a priori* reason for concluding that we must take moral attitudes towards the basic social scientific issues. It is also contingent in that people might have been such that they did not adopt moral positions on these issues. However, to say that this fact is contingent is almost as misleading as to deny that it is contingent. For it is barely imaginable that people might not have found these issues to be of moral significance; this is an index of the fundamental nature of the fact in question. At the risk of raising philosophical corpses perhaps best left buried, I am driven to say that the fact that we find the concerns of social science morally relevant is a synthetic *a priori* truth. Put another way, the fact that its objects are morally relevant is a knowledge-constitutive fact about social theory; just as, according to the metaphysics of human nature I am proposing as part of the epistemology of social science, our moral interest in social theory's objects is central to what is involved in being a person. Whatever this fact's status, however, another fact of the same status is equally significant. Namely, people no longer think morally about the basic entities of physical science (e.g. matter, space, time), though we once did. This difference between natural and social science has profound implications for the conduct of social science.

Before turning to some of these implications, I want to try to avoid a possible misunderstanding of what I have just said. I have suggested neither that there is some absolutely determinate relation between a morality and a social metaphysics nor that any social theorist has believed there to be such a determinate relation. Let us again take human nature as representing an item from social scientific ontology.[6] It is clear, for example, that straightforward inferences from statements of human nature to a morality are implausible. That people are distinctively rational does not support the notion that the most rational person is the best person. Moralities generated from our distinctive characteristics would in any case often be repellent. For some of our arguably distinctive features are by no means spotless from a moral point of view; our rationality, for example, has realised itself as much in creating as in alleviating suffering. Further, moral evaluation typically operates in the very choice of essentially human characteristics, in the decision to term people peculiarly rational or free, rather than peculiarly prone to kill for fun or despoil the environment (see Williams, 1972, pp. 72ff.).

But I do not need to hold that there is some strict logical relation between a writer's morality and his theory of human nature. The links between the elements of a social scientific theory – including those between the underlying morality and the metaphysics, and between the metaphysics and the relatively factual statements – are not fully deductive. Were this not the case, the metaphysics would be empirically testable, albeit in an indirect way. All I need maintain is that what morality the social scientist holds tends to determine his theory of human nature and vice versa. Thus, what we consider to be a possible

[6] For the relation of human nature theories to morality, see Quinton (1975), Williams (1972, pp. 72ff.) and Winch (1972, pp. 74ff.).

145

content of morality is partly determined by our view of human nature. People (and hence how we conceptualise people) enter moral principles, in that moral principles are about the character and actions of people, and especially about their actions in their effects on other people. How we identify, explain and justify moral choices and codes are all partly determined, in their respective ways, by how we conceive human nature, what needs and interests, for example, we take to be essentially human. In a secular age, the terminal points in moral debate and commitment tend to be our theory of what it is to be human. Moreover, as I noted in the previous paragraph, the lines of argument run not only from our theory of human nature to our morality, but also in the reverse direction. What theory of human nature we hold is partly determined by our morality. For instance, Durkheim's political conservatism probably determined his postulation of his individualistic Hobbesian man. His moral and political beliefs supplemented the criteria of theory acceptance, a supplement necessitated by the under-determination of theory by empirical constraints. The fact that his political beliefs underpinned his views on human nature, which in turn structured his whole theory, means that the whole theory is structured by Durkheim's political beliefs. These beliefs are confirmed whenever we use the theoretical framework they determine; whenever, for example, we accept the cogency of Durkheim's explanations of phenomena which depend on his theory of human nature.

As a way of summarising this sub-section, I will give a final example. It is similar to the one from Durkheim which I have just discussed. But I will deviate from the Durkheimian example somewhat in order to underline the artificial nature of the case I am considering. This example is the kind of token example familiar from the philosophical literature. It is a gross oversimplification of any actual social scientific theory and, for that reason, may be misleading. However, it illustrates a few of the points I have tried to make.

A theory of democracy might take the following form:

   (i) values (e.g. conservative) → a view of human nature (e.g. Hobbesian);

   (ii) a view of human nature → a view of society (e.g. necessarily hierarchical);

   (iii) a view of society → a view of democracy (e.g. only representative possible);

   (iv) a view of democracy → empirical judgments (e.g. Britain is a democracy).

A theorist's conservative values (concerning the desirability of social institutions being stable, for example) supports a view of human nature (that people must be conditioned by society to suppress their

146

more selfish and anarchistic wants), which in turn supports a view of society (that society is necessarily hierarchical), which in turn yields an interpretation of democracy (that only representative – not participatory – democracy is possible), which in turn produces judgments at a relatively empirical level (that Britain is a democracy).

The arrows do not symbolise deductive relationships. The left-hand side statements are neither necessary nor sufficient for the right-hand side statements. Rather, the arrows indicate that the left-hand side statements are grounds or supports for the right-hand side statements. Strictly, the arrows should run in both directions. For our views of democracy are as equally likely to sustain our views of society, and our views of human nature are as equally likely to underpin our politics, as vice versa. I have shown the arrows in only one direction to emphasise that, for the purposes of analysis, and at any single instant and for any given set of explanatory concerns, a theory can be frozen to reveal a relatively formal layered structure. If these statements are brought together in one theory, then the meanings of the concepts in the statements will be mutually dependent. The meanings of 'human nature', 'society' and 'democracy' will determine one another. Moreover, since the meaning of 'human nature' is in part fixed by certain political preferences, these political preferences infuse the interpretations of the other terms in the theory.

4.6.b. Rational and empirical constraints on a value-laden social science

If a social scientific theory is value-laden, we have to ask whether it is at the same time criticisable; in particular, whether it is subject to empirical constraint.

First, I will show how social scientific theory can be criticised in non-empirical ways. To do so, we should take seriously the idea that social science is structured by philosophical concerns. This idea runs against the conventional wisdom that philosophy and social science are independent. The doctrine of independence is shared, from the basis of very different conceptions of philosophy, by Durkheim (1964) and Ryan (1970b); it led in the 1950s to the belief that a mature political science had put an end to political philosophy.

Rather, I have argued, the framework of a social scientific theory is structured by both philosophical and moral considerations. Insofar as metaphysical and moral beliefs are rationally criticisable, therefore, such criticisms are relevant to our analyses of the foundations of social scientific theory. A set of moral or metaphysical beliefs can clearly be scrutinised for inner consistency. In the case of values, this scrutiny may involve the direct assessment of our evaluative commitments and assumptions. Or, we may ask the indirect question whether the realisation of any of our values would require conditions or would produce results incompatible with our morality (see Weber, 1957, pp. 147–52). In the case of metaphysical beliefs, besides the straightforward requirement of the consistency of our set of beliefs, the most cogent critical test is whether or not they solve the problems they purport to solve. Of one set of metaphysical beliefs and one group of problems, we can ask: does the set solve the problems? Does it solve them better than another metaphysics? Is the solution simple? Is it fruitful? Does it contradict other metaphysical views needed for solving other problems? (see Popper, 1972, p. 199). These questions are particularly relevant if we are considering a metaphysics in the context of its power to generate scientific theories, where the issue of the fruitfulness of the metaphysics is crucial.

As an example of the direct criticism of a morality underlying a social scientific theory, take Marxism. If Kamenka's argument in *The Ethical Foundations of Marxism* that Marx's morality involved the perception of conflict as both an essential cause and sign of evil is correct, and if Kamenka is also correct in the view that conflict has a positive place in all social development, then he has shown a flaw in the whole of Marxist social science and not just in an abstract Marxist moral philosophy; Hawthorn's critical point that Marx wished 'the abolition of anything that we understand as human beings, finite, particular, separate people' (1976, p. 64) is equally relevant to the whole of Marxist social science. Similarly, a philosophical critique of the notion of human interests would bear directly on a comparison of the three approaches to power which Lukes analyses (see section 4.2, point (h)).

The thesis of the moral and philosophical underpinning of social science has a second implication, not so much to do with the possibility of rational criticism, but with how natural and social science are likely to differ in the light of the distinctively moral nature of social science. Just as it is a contingent fact of the first importance that people take moral attitudes to the kind of issues to be found at the root of social science, so it is an important contingent fact that people adopt *different* moral attitudes on such points. Hence, the social scientific study of an area is likely to develop in terms of the postulation and study of a number of different theories, based on different moral and philosophical assumptions. Many sociologists have recently espoused the idea of the value permeation of social science in the belief that it gives them a means to criticise the conservative implications of functionalism and to postulate a uniquely correct value basis for social science. This putative uniquely correct value basis conforms with – *mirabile dictu* – the commitments of many of the new generation of sociologists, namely radical left-wing ones. But the argument that social science is value-laden is, in fact, neutral between different possible value bases. More than that, it positively welcomes value diversity. For the values underlying different theories may direct each of them to a comprehensive analysis of some area of social reality. Functionalism may indeed tell us more about the forces making for stability in society than Marxism. Hence, the project, occasionally mooted, of finding a single philosophy for the study of society is intellectually misguided.

The reason for theoretical plurality in social science deriving from its distinctive moral relevance is additional to the *a priori* point about the underdetermination of theory by the world, and to the pragmatic point that criteria of theory choice (such as correspondence with the world, simplicity and consistency) are unlikely in the foreseeable future to yield unanimity in theory choice. The *a priori* underdetermination point also applies to natural science. The pragmatic point clearly does not. One reason why criteria of theory choice do not produce unanimity in social scientific theory selection is that social theories are underlain by different values. For even given that the moral foundations of a theory can be debated rationally, the debate is not likely to be sufficiently determinate to arrive at the conclusion that only one moral underpinning is plausible.

Someone might detect a tension in the claims I have made about the underdetermination thesis and the role of values at the foundation of social theory. For my account of values in social science was premised on the idea that they are required in order to mitigate the underdetermination of social theory by the social world. Yet now I claim that theoretical plurality in social science is sustained by its distinctive need to take note of values. The point, however, is that we are concerned with two different types of theoretical plurality. The underdetermination thesis is an *a priori* idea; it states that the relationship of theory to the world is not sufficiently determinate to rule out any of in principle an *infinite* number of theories about the world. In natural science, as a matter of fact, the various criteria of theory choice (truth, simplicity, consistency, etc.) typically rule out all but one theory in a domain at any one time. Due to the immaturity of social science and the practical complexities of its subject matter, these criteria are by no means so determinate in social science. It is at this point that the distinctive value relevance of social science aids theory choice. A social theorist's value commitments are crucial in his decision as to which theories he will work with. But so long as different social scientists remain committed to different values, there will not be a unique theory in a social scientific domain.

A pessimistic note must be sounded here, however. The two contingent facts which are fundamental in understanding the role of values in social science – that people adopt moral attitudes to the sorts of issues which appear at the bases of social science, and that they adopt different attitudes on such issues – possess different degrees of likely universality. I have claimed that it is barely possible to imagine people who do not adopt moral attitudes on such issues as whether man is at root rational or aggressive or creative or selfish or altruistic or equal, and whether society is basically in a state of rest or of change. It is all too possible to imagine people who take exactly the same moral attitudes on these issues. They would not have ceased to make moral assumptions in their theory of society. They would simply have ceased to think about these assumptions. They would thus satisfy the idealisation with which I opened chapter one in the respect of moral uniformity. Further, if what I have just said about the heuristic importance of value diversity is correct, the social science of such people would be deficient as compared to the social science of people who allow value diversity. It is in this context of charting the progress of an empirical sociology which has apparently been established on the basis of a monolithic value unity that a study of post-1956 Soviet sociology might prove so useful to the philosophy of social science.

Finally, I will turn to the empirical constraints on a value-laden social scientific theory. I have argued only that the metaphysics of a social scientific theory is partly determined by values. This leaves open the possibility that the metaphysics is also partly determined by how the world is in its most general forms, given that metaphysical statements are neither meaningless nor analytic. As such, however, the point is too abstract, because only an omniscient being would be in a position directly to confirm or reject a metaphysical statement. What we must show is how the notion of scientific confirmation and refutation is applicable to holistic, value-laden social scientific theories. In doing so, we support not just the point that such theories are empirical. We support the idea that they are able to replicate the full internal structure of scientific theories (relatively empirical and relatively theoretical levels, predictions, explanations, etc.) whose applicability to social science I defended directly in chapter one.

I will approach the question of the empirical nature of holistic, value-laden theories in two stages. It should be noted, first, that the principle of refutability within a single scientific theory is easy to state. A theory need contain only the concept of negation in addition to its own distinctive theoretical concepts for it to be possible to make contradictory statements within a single theoretical scheme. In judging between these conflicting statements, observational evidence is more likely to be decisive the lower the level of the statements within the theory. When a statement continues to be adhered to within a theory despite clear observational evidence against it, the statement may be biased in the negative sense I noted in section 4.2 point (*e*).

The argument of internal refutability applies whatever the nature of the theoretical system – even if it contains evaluative terms such as 'democracy' or 'exploitation', provided their basis in empirical application is indicated. Indicating the empirical reference of an evaluative and theoretical term such as 'exploitation' might be a complicated business. But that it is complicated does not mean it is impossible.

Giving empirical content to the notion of an exploited group might run somewhat as follows. An exploited group consists of people who are destitute; their destitution results from specific social arrangements; and the arrangements in question benefit a definite social group at the expense of the destitute group and are changeable. It then becomes an empirical question whether there are exploited groups in contemporary Britain, so long as the defining terms of 'exploited group' can themselves be rendered empirical and precise – but these are problems for substantive social science. Similarly, it is an empirical question whether Britain is a 'democracy' under a particular definition of that term, even if the definition is theoretical and evaluative; though the theoretical and evaluative nature of the term means that theoretical and evaluative considerations could also be brought to bear on the definition of 'democracy' and on any theory in which it is embodied. Certainly, the empirical interpretation of exploitation is more than purely descriptive. It involves implicit reference to the social mechanisms whereby the exploited group is made destitute and the exploiting group is benefited. But this is to be expected in the light of one of this book's pervasive themes, namely that scientific theories do not rest on absolutely pure observation languages.

It is much more difficult to conceptualise the possibility of empirical debate, refutation and change across theories. The constraint of consistency is essentially intra-theoretical, as is the idea that theories might be compared in respect of their fruitfulness in dealing with old problems and suggesting new ones. For we have to show how two statements in different theories can be about the same thing, before we can even raise the questions of whether they are in contradiction with one another or of which solves a supposedly identical problem more adequately. Ideally, we should be able to give an account of the possibility of empirical debate across theories. I will return to this issue in the Conclusion, where I will briefly suggest that it is critical for post-empiricist philosophy of science. In the meantime, to rest with an understanding of how empirical debate is possible within value-laden social scientific theories is not worthless. For as a matter of fact social science has advanced by the internal development of its theories, not by fruitful cross-theoretical debate. Moreover, this problem – dialogue across theories – is not unique to an account of social science. Together with its associated issues of the nature of refutation and meaning in science, it is the major currently unresolved question in the philosophy of any science.

4.7. AN EXAMPLE: THE PHILOSOPHICAL PRESUPPOSITIONS OF MANNHEIM'S SOCIOLOGY

Moral, philosophical, theoretical and empirical elements were fused together as a unity in Mannheim's thought. To justify this claim, I must show three things. First, philosophical concerns were basic to Mannheim's sociology. Secondly, the philosophical views he held were partly determined by his fundamental political beliefs. Thirdly, his philosophical conclusions partly determined the types of study he carried out in theoretical and empirical social science. The fact that the problems and direction of his theoretical and empirical work were set by his philosophical beliefs establishes his claim to be a social scientist, and not just a philosopher.

Mannheim was pre-occupied throughout his life with certain key problems, which he resolved in different ways and with different emphases at different times. Most of these key problems were philosophical. Some were directly concerned with human nature, an entity, I have claimed, typically part of the ontology of social science. The different positions which Mannheim took on his key problems were partly determined by his changing moral and political convictions. To establish this claim in detail would involve historical analysis not possible within the bounds of this book. We would have to note, for example, how Mannheim's ideas evolved in relation to what he considered to be the main problems of his time. He was consistently concerned with what he thought were the crises of the age, whether the loss of faith in thought and value, the problem of massification, or the need to go beyond a *laissez faire* society while avoiding totalitarianism. I will make the more abstract point that the attitudes he took on his key philosophical issues were appropriate to his basic political orientation, which might be designated 'reformist conservatism'. I give the following as a profile of his fundamental philosophical positions. As a sum, they distance him from liberalism and socialism, and also from reactionary conservatism, hence justifying the appellation 'reformist conservatism'. Mannheim was concerned with synthesis to the point of making compromise an epistemological and moral category. He was aware of and to an extent desirous of change, but mitigated its possible abruptness by emphasising continuity across history, ultimately postulating an eternal realm of values and of human nature. Despite his methodological anti-individualism, he wished to emphasise the primacy of the individual, the realm of the undetermined, the reality of freedom and the power of thought. His idealism, in particular, resulted in the rediscovery of religion and a naivety on his part concerning the nature of social power. Insofar as it is possible to correlate changes in his political and philosophical beliefs, they were both in the direction of a growing conservatism. Mannheim ended, in Floud's suggestive phrase, as 'a utopian of the right' (1969, p. 204). I will try to exemplify the effects of his drift rightwards on his philosophical options when I discuss his views on the relationship between thought and action.

I cannot analyse here the full range of Mannheim's philosophical presuppositions. I will concentrate on just two areas of his thought. My main purpose in doing so is to exemplify the argument of this chapter. A subsidiary purpose is to illustrate the usefulness of the concepts and ideas I have invoked in this chapter for the history of social science. The philosophical and moral foundations of many social scientific theories have been neglected. There are notable exceptions, such as Marxism, but much work remains to be done in the philosophical history of social science. In Mannheim's case, his views are difficult to understand as a whole because of his notorious eclecticism. They appear to be blatantly in tension with one another not only across his whole corpus, but even within single works. The tensions at the heart of his thought can be explained by the sort of philosophical analysis I am about to present. For it exemplifies how his views on a set of constant philosophical problems changed in line with his moral and political beliefs.

4.7.a. Mannheim on society and the individual

Mannheim is consistent in his beliefs about the relationship between society and the individual. He is, to use Lukes's (1972) distinctions, a methodological anti-individualist and an ontological individualist.

As a methodological anti-individualist, Mannheim holds that it is both possible and often necessary to advance explanations of social and individual phenomena that do not refer to individuals alone. In *Ideology and Utopia*, Mannheim makes it clear that this anti-individualism is central to his sociology of knowledge. Paralleling the supra-individual natures of thought and language, he writes that 'it is incorrect to explain the totality of an outlook only with reference to its genesis in the mind of the individual' (p. 2).

Mannheim's methodological anti-individualism is instantiated in his theoretical and empirical works in sociology in ways too numerous to detail exhaustively. For example, in 'The Problem of Generations', Mannheim argues that the ultimate vehicle and seat of any new strand of thought is a collectivity, such as a generation or a class; and his later work is full of statements of the need for a supra-individual approach to the study of valuations and education. But let us look at the role of Mannheim's methodological anti-individualism in the formulation of two of his most important theoretical theses in more detail. First, in his movement from the 'particular' to the 'total' conception of ideology, it is precisely Mannheim's contention that the former is limited by its individualism. The particular conception of ideology restricts its attention to segments of the thought systems of specific individuals. It explains their lies, distortions and concealments in terms of a psychology of interests. The total conception, in contrast, adopts a 'more formal functional analysis' (1972, p. 51). It relates the structure of total outlooks to that of their social carriers. The superiority of the total conception rests in the fact that it allows us to grasp the structure of a group world-view, an object which is not even open to the particular conception. Secondly, in the theory of different modes of meaning offered in 'On the Interpretation of *Weltanschauung*', Mannheim is careful to distinguish the basic mode of meaning, 'objective meaning', from individualistic intentional meaning. Objective meaning is characteristic of all cultural products. It can be understood in terms of the relevant contextual system of the object in question, without knowing the intentions of the object's producer. At that time, Mannheim did not see all such contextual systems as social systems; he thought, for example, that there were non-social aesthetic systems. But he was already committed to the necessity of invoking social context in the understanding of the objective meanings of certain of the actions of individuals. Thus, with respect to the objective meaning of his friend giving money to a beggar, we need 'to know the objective social configuration by virtue of which there are beggars and people with superfluous cash' (1921–2, p. 45).

Mannheim's methodological anti-individualism further dictates his attitude to psychology. Mannheim by no means ignored or belittled the role of psychology in social science, as many commentators have claimed. In *Ideology and Utopia*, he emphasised the importance of a psychology of thought for the development of the sociology of knowledge. Indeed, in 'Structural Analysis of Epistemology' Mannheim characterised psychology as a presuppositional science for epistemology before he had even asserted the significance of the social; that is, psychology is one of the studies which constitute epistemology, with different epistemologies being based on different psychologies. In later works, Mannheim thought psychology important for an understanding of the plasticity of human nature. He devoted the first two chapters of *Systematic Sociology* to a description of people's 'psychic equipment', trying to integrate behaviourist and psychoanalytic concepts and perspectives in his theory of the basic social processes. But, given his methodological anti-individualism, Mannheim was bound to argue that psychology could offer only a limited perspective. In the case of a psychoanalytic theory of education, for example, he wrote that psychoanalysis yields only a partial understanding of the pupil–teacher relationship; it needs to be supplemented by sociological analysis.

Although they have escaped most commentators, the individualistic elements of Mannheim's thought have not gone entirely unnoticed. In *Prisms*, Adorno criticises Mannheim's theory of the intelligentsia for ignoring the social determination of individualistic phenomena. To call Mannheim an ontological individualist needs a word of explanation, however. For Mannheim did not argue any of the points which Lukes holds to be characteristic of ontological individualism. That is, Mannheim did *not* argue that social entities cannot be observed, that individual phenomena are easier to understand than social phenomena, that facts about individuals are not contingent upon facts about non-individualistic social entities, or that statements about social phenomena can be neither true nor false. Mannheim maintained a clear realism with respect to the social: 'Our previous insistence that the individual is the primary locus of reality need not make us forget the fact that human relations, however complex, are also real' (1956, pp. 68–9). This realism renders unlikely a commitment to any of the just stated indices of ontological individualism.

In what sense, then, was Mannheim an ontological individualist? The clue we need is in the last quotation where Mannheim wrote that 'the individual is the primary locus of reality'. Mannheim's ontological individualism emerges in two stages. First, he held that we need to posit the reality of the individual no matter where sociological analysis leads us. This need is grounded in our authentic experience of the world. Thus, the early Mannheim – having raised the possibility of the dissolution of the subject into structural configurations of meaning – writes:

Understanding of another self must start with configurations of meaning. It cannot, however, end with it . . . The existential postulate of a real other self is grounded in an act of immediate intuition: When I look into the eyes of a person, I see not only the colour of his eyes but also the being of his soul (1921–2, pp. 59–60).

The later Mannheim maintains this ontological commitment in terms of Mead's distinction between the 'me' and the 'I'. The 'me' is built out of experience and provides the basis for social roles. The 'I', in contrast, is 'actor or initiator, the agent of change'. It incorporates 'the uniqueness and coherence and waywardness of choice' (Mannheim and Stewart, 1969, p. 93). Secondly, Mannheim argued that we need not only to posit the individual ontologically, but also to posit him or her as a deeper level of reality than the social: 'ultimate reality (or existence on the level of ontology) attaches only to the individual and only he constitutes the ultimate unity of social action' (1956, p. 53).

This individualistic presupposition structures certain of Mannheim's hypotheses in theoretical and empirical sociology, where he studies the conditions necessary for the emergence and knowledge of individuals. The disputable nature of these hypotheses shows that Mannheim's commitment is not just truistic (see Lukes, 1972, p. 77). I will give two brief examples. First, Mannheim's notion of the basic reality of the individual is reflected in his sketch of the sociology of privacy. Mannheim believed that privacy is a basic means of individualisation. Far from being ubiquitous, the widespread desire for and possibility of privacy is largely distinctive of recent society. Secondly, we can mention Mannheim's sociology of distance. Mannheim discusses various forms of social distance and then notes pre-social, existential distance which is the distance or lack of it between 'purely personal' selves: 'these two kinds of distance are usually confused. The social mask and the personal, existential character usually act simultaneously. The democratising process, as a rule, tends to diminish social distance and uncover the purely existential relationships between men' (1967, p. 54).

4.7.b. Mannheim on thought and action

At the most abstract level, the social philosopher might hold three positions concerning the causal relation of thought and action. (i) Action determines thought. (ii) Thought and action form a unity in some sense. (iii) Thought determines action. Mannheim held all three positions at different times in his life, and he did so in the order in which I have listed them.

(i) At the beginning of *Ideology and Utopia*, Mannheim adopts as the framework for the sociology of knowledge the general thesis that the structure of a group's thought is determined by how the group as a whole acts upon its surrounding reality. Two strands of this thesis should be emphasised. First, in line with his methodological anti-individualism, Mannheim holds that it is group action which determines thought. Secondly, action is held to determine all elements of the thought of the group in question: for example, the emergence of problems, the forms, content, development and validity of ideas, and the most detailed perceptions and conceptions.

The assertion of the determination of cognitive perspectives by group activities provides the possibility of Mannheim's theoretical and empirical work in the sociology of knowledge. More than this, the sociology of knowledge emerges with the attainment of the total and general conceptions of ideology: that is, when the totality of a group's thought and the thought of all groups are seen as existentially determined. Mannheim does not follow Marx in making classes the basic group-vehicle of thought (*pace* Bottomore, 1956). Mannheim identifies many different social bases of thought, including the epoch, the nation, generations, roles derived from a variety of social institutions and classes. Even more varied are the objects which Mannheim submits to analysis by the sociology of knowledge. The thought objects range from the sociology of epistemology to the sociology of the concept of the English gentleman.

But with the thesis of the determination of thought by action we find a correlative theme which provides the basis for Mannheim's move to a more idealistic thesis. Namely, Mannheim sees thought not only as determined by action, but also as action made self-conscious. For example, in 'Conservative Thought' Mannheim depicts nineteenth-century conservatism as a raising to consciousness of two modes of activity which had existed previously, but at a non-reflective level: feudal survivals and the universal pre-theoretical characteristic of traditionalism. Similarly, 'Historicism' terms historicism the modern *Weltanschauung* because it has raised the central problems of modern life to self-consciousness. How this theme provides an entry for idealism is clear. A way of arguing towards the causal predominance of thought over action is to give thought the strategic role of determining the nature of the action context which is to be changed.

Such, then, is Mannheim's first position on the relation of thought and action: action determines thought. Were I concerned to criticise Mannheim's philosophical presuppositions here, I would suggest that as an abstract thesis it is wooden and implausible, though it certainly generated useful research on Mannheim's part. But leaving aside criticism, I will outline the other positions Mannheim took on this key problem.

(ii) Mannheim also espoused the notion of the unity of thought and action. This theme is not dominant in Mannheim's work, however. It can best be regarded as a transitional phase between his adherence to (i) and (iii). Although elements of a unity thesis can be found in his early work, it is most consistently expressed in *Essays on the Sociology of Culture*, written in the early 1930s. There, Mannheim asks:

How was it possible to doubt the social character of the mind and to ignore the mental involvements of social behaviour? To cogitate an abstract intellect without concrete persons who act in given social situations is as absurd as to assume the opposite, a society without such functions as communication, ideation and evaluation (p. 34).

The very nature of the unified thinking-and-acting object means that sociology must ultimately unite the sociology of structured groups and the sociology of ideas, which are to be treated as no more than expedient abstractions. In consequence, Mannheim refused to countenance all questions about the relations of determination between thought and action, because the two elements can be separated only for the convenience of analysis, not ontologically. Hence, the sociology of the mind studies, not the determination of intellectual processes, but the social character of those intellectual expressions whose action context is not transparent.

This theme is not developed by Mannheim. But the way in which it is suggested prevents it from having a heuristic role in sociological research. A philosophical postulate of the unity of thinking and being would only be of use to the study of actual social conditions if it specified, first, the kind of circumstances under which thought and action are relatively united and relatively disunited, and, secondly, what interaction between thought and action looks like and under what conditions it occurs. Mannheim does not elucidate this thesis so as to make it empirically useful. Indeed, he rules out *a priori* the possibility of interaction between thought and action.

(iii) I have suggested that Mannheim's thesis that thought is action raised to self-consciousness provides a path to an idealism which holds that thought determines action. For it gives thought the strategic role in action of identifying what has to be changed. Specifically, Mannheim charges the sociology of knowledge with becoming aware of the action determinants of thought and thereby neutralising their influence. In 'American Sociology', he criticises American sociology precisely for having ignored the sociology of knowledge and therefore for having no basis for controlling the extra-theoretical determinants of its own thought.

But Mannheim goes beyond the argument that thought can partly determine action by being conscious of what has to be changed. He holds further that being aware of our action context provides us in some way with knowledge of the course that action must follow. Thought then comes to set the goal of action. Mannheim repeatedly asserts or implies that knowledge of the present social situation dictates what has to be done. Specifically, Mannheim sees the basic fact of the modern social situation as that we live in a changing society. He adds: 'If sudden changes occur, it is impossible to find the right way of action without reference to the meaning of change' (1950, p. 63). Pursuing this link between the meaning of present social change and the 'right way of action', Mannheim asks: 'What are the characteristic, pervasive aims of the present time which seem to stem from a long history of striving and clarification and in the other direction seem to point to a future to which most people would wish to commit themselves?' (Mannheim and Stewart, 1969, p. 45). He answers that the desire to move to a democratic and co-operative social order is 'the characteristic pervasive aim of the present time'. It is implied that the very fact that these values have a long history and a contemporary social basis justifies them. Similarly, the fact that one element of the modern crisis of valuations arises from the declining importance of primary social groups (such as the family) and hence of their values, 'calls for' the translation of primary values into a wider context; the primary value of family love should be translated into the social value of citizenly respect, for example (Mannheim and Stewart, 1969, p. 121).

Rooting the power of thought and ideas in knowledge of the social structure, however, gives way inexorably in Mannheim to an idealism *tout court*. The basic assumption of Mannheim's later work is the ability of planning, thought and value choices to shape the already existing structures of social action. Thus, Mannheim holds that technological factors can be manipulated according to culturally agreed human ends; he argues that the tendency to class struggle in present society can be avoided by planned reforms; he urges the importance of decisions concerning educational aims; and he accepts the eternal value of Christian ideals. Mannheim evolves a theory of personality to provide the subject for his new ethical idealism. He calls the desired person one who will fulfil the qualities of 'democratic personalism': the individual should be socially responsible, but should be able to stand above his society and culture when the need arises.

In this latter theory, the idealist and individualist strands of Mannheim's thought merge. They also come together in Mannheim's analysis of freedom. Freedom, as Remmling notes, assumed 'decisive proportions for a thinker who combines the conviction that planning is inevitable with the belief that undemocratic, authoritarian planning is a disaster' (1975, p. 102). Both his commitment to the pre-social individual as a basic ontological category and his final belief in the efficacy of chosen ideals seemed to Mannheim to necessitate a free subject of some sort, by which he meant a subject outside the causal universe. That Mannheim reasoned thus shows that he adopted the philosophical position, unstated and undefended by him, which at the very least is controversial (see section 1.4), that people and actions are not free insofar as they are predictable. This assumption is instantiated in his notion of 'planning for freedom', which involves the deliberate creation in social life of areas where individuals and groups are free or relatively free from external interference.

I have noted the major positive element in Mannheim's concept of freedom. Freedom is attained by becoming aware of the unconscious determinants of our thought and action and thereby neutralising them. In this context, freedom is conceptualised as choice within the limits set (i.e. among the alternatives determined) by the given socio-historical context. For example, an artist is free to develop the Baroque within the structural limits set by that artistic style as it has developed up to his time. Thus did Mannheim seek to mediate between his methodological anti-individualism, which was bound to extend the range of what is determined in human thought and action, and his commitment to the individual and the power of thought. At the institutional level, the programme of 'planning for freedom' will use the increasing social self-consciousness of the modern age as an instrument for the removal of unconscious determinants.

Mannheim's increasing stress on the power of thought determined not only what he studied in theoretical and empirical social science, but also what he ignored. Specifically, his idealism led to a basic naivety on the question of power. Social change is effected by the dissemination of ideas among people of goodwill. The realities of power, struggle and entrenched social groups do not disturb the pages of Mannheim's work. In short, he lacked a sociology of politics.

5

~~~~~~

Paradigms and social science

5.1. PARADIGMS

One possible reaction to the position advanced in chapter four is to argue that if social science is likely to encompass diverse theories and if this diversity rests on the distinctive value relevance of social science, then social study cannot be modelled on natural science. My argument that social science is structured by evaluative considerations certainly introduces a distinction between knowledge of the human and non-human worlds. But this distinction, though resting on the question of values, can no longer be posed in terms of a division between the expression of non-cognitive moral attitudes and positive knowledge. For social science's evaluative foundations sustain the development of empirical social scientific theories. To justify this last statement, I could only repeat what I have said in chapter four. However, the point that if social science operates and should operate with a diversity of theories, it cannot be modelled on natural science, deserves separate discussion.

A way of focusing this discussion is to refer to Kuhn's work. I must again disclaim any interest in exegesis for its own sake, not least because the literature on Kuhn is now vast. I will ignore many of Kuhn's central ideas and of the criticisms which can be directed against his views. I am primarily concerned with using Kuhn's analysis as a tool to talk about the issue I raised in the last paragraph. Yet I would be disingenuous if I failed to admit the appropriateness of reference to Kuhn at this point. For Kuhn first popularised, where he did not originate, the central tenets of the post-empiricist philosophy of science which I have been assuming throughout. Many social scientists, in particular, came to these ideas through Kuhn's work. Indeed, a substantial debate about the status of social science in Kuhnian terms has arisen, on which I will draw.

A further way of understanding Kuhn's importance in post-empiricist philosophy of science is to note that his work differs less from other recent analyses of science than is often supposed. For example, his work and Lakatos's advanced Popperianism agree: the need for a sociological and historical analysis of the scientific community as a means of isolating the actual methods and evaluations used by scientists; that the unit of ultimate scientific choice is very holistic ('paradigm', 'research programme'); that elements of a scientific paradigm/research programme are internally unfalsifiable and are rejected only by moving to another research tradition; that the characteristics of Lakatos's 'degenerating research programme' are those of Kuhn's 'paradigm in crisis'; and that Lakatos is committed to the rationality or the irrationality of science to the same degree as Kuhn (see Kuhn, 1971, pp. 137–9, and 1972b, p. 238). One of the few differences between the two is that Lakatos encourages competing theories, whereas Kuhn discourages alternative theories in periods of normal science. Kuhn sets up the fact of a discipline being in the sway of a stable and dominant paradigm (which I will call an 'exclusive' paradigm) as the criterion demarcating the boundary of fully scientific studies. It is on this crucial issue that the present chapter focuses.

I do not advocate the ultimate acceptability of Kuhn's work. A subsidiary intention of this chapter is to show that Kuhn's analysis of social science is mistaken; and, therefore, to advocate that we bury the whole issue of paradigms and social science, which has generated as much confusion as light. Moreover, the massive amount of attention which his writings received revealed certain fundamental flaws. The key concept of paradigm was shown to be vague. Kuhn's (1970, Postscript) clarificatory analysis of 'paradigm' into the 'sociological' and 'exemplary' senses remains inadequate in the face of Masterman's (1972) elucidation of twenty-one different senses of paradigm in *The Structure of Scientific Revolutions*. This conceptual ambiguity has bedevilled attempts to apply Kuhnian themes to social science. For it is easy to understand 'paradigm' either so loosely that it is uninformative to say that social science possesses paradigms or so strictly that it is merely pedantic to deny the existence of paradigms in social science.

Since I am not attempting an exegesis of Kuhn's work, but am rather using his writings to develop certain themes central to this book, I omit an exercise in Kuhnian textual analysis. As a working definition, I identify 'paradigm' with what I have called the metaphysics of a scientific theory (that is, including its ontology), together with the central theoretical statements and concepts of the theory; the sociological and concrete exemplar elements of Kuhn's original notion are less important for my purpose. My rough, working definition makes the notion of paradigm equivalent to the central concepts and ideas of a scientific theory. It would be wrong to include what I have called methodological elements within this notion. For methodology – the principles of scientific reasoning and validation – is not specific to any particular paradigm. Indeed, if we are to have principles which at least in part determine choices between paradigms, then these will be drawn from general scientific methodology.

More interesting than these terminological issues are the substantive criticisms which have been made of Kuhn's account of scientific activity, in relation to both how science is and how it ought to be. This chapter concentrates on Kuhn's claim that there must be an exclusive paradigm in a discipline if it is to be a mature science. I will suggest, especially in the case study of Soviet sociology in section 5.5, that it is harmful from a scientific point of view for a social science to be dominated by an exclusive paradigm. However, I wish to establish this point within the framework advanced in this book, rather than as a critical point against Kuhn, because to prove it within Kuhn's own assumptions and concepts would require a much fuller analysis of his work than I give here.

5.2 THE STATUS OF SOCIAL SCIENCE IN KUHNIAN TERMS

Kuhn is committed to the same hierarchical ordering of the sciences as empiricists have traditionally espoused. In Kuhn's case, however, as Martins puts it: 'the basic distinction is between mature, consensual, paradigmatic science on the one hand, and immature, natural-historical, paradigm-lacking sciences on the other' (1972, p. 28). Kuhn on balance tends to assign social science to the immature side of this dichotomy. Indeed, he says that social science's very concern with the issue of whether it is fully scientific is an index of its scientific immaturity. He remarks that 'it remains an open question what parts of social science have yet acquired. . . paradigms at all' (1970, p. 15). This bald statement is amplified by the belief that 'this century appears to be characterised by the emergence of a first consensus in parts of a few of the social sciences' (1963a, p. 347). In at least one place, he specifies economics as having reached scientific maturity (see 1972b, p. 254).

An interesting terminological change occurs in Kuhn's thought on pre-scientific studies, a change which signals a shift in his views on these matters. In his early work, Kuhn talked of 'pre-paradigm' studies. While in his later writings, the corresponding notion was that of 'immature' sciences. The abandonment of the notion of the pre-paradigm period was occasioned by Kuhn's acknowledgement that paradigms can be delineated in most areas of study, even when those areas are composed of the competing schools which Kuhn holds to be characteristic of immature sciences. This change undoubtedly has implications for the nature of research in immature sciences (taking 'immature sciences' in Kuhn's sense).

For what is the import of calling social science a pre-paradigmatic or immature science? In the first instance, because Kuhn tells us more about mature than immature sciences, it helps to understand what social science is not. A paradigm in a mature science is a fundamental, open-ended achievement, which is accepted by the members of the scientific community to the exclusion of all other paradigmatic rivals. As such, it both encourages and constricts research undertaken within that science. Research is encouraged, because the paradigm directs scientific attention to highly specialised problems and because the paradigm requires clarification, articulation and extension. Research is constricted, because any issues that fall outside the paradigmatic boundary become unsayable for the science so long as the paradigm holds sway. The paradigm determines the range of solvable puzzles, the limits of their admissible solutions and the methods that can be used to arrive at these solutions; therefore, it lays down – here Kuhn would appeal to some to the assumptions about the meaning of scientific terms, which I have used in this book – the set of possible facts.

Kuhn calls the process of research encouraged within a mature science's exclusive paradigm 'normal science'. So sure is Kuhn that normal science is distinctive of a mature science that he even offers it as a demarcation criterion of science. Normal science is the thorough investigation of the possibilities of understanding nature secreted within the paradigm; it articulates and extends the paradigm. Normal science aims to study the problems or 'puzzles' laid bare by the paradigm and to fit all phenomena into the paradigm's categories, not to falsify the paradigm. While normal science thus restricts vision, in compensation it allows scientists to pursue detailed research, 'to investigate some part of nature in a detail and depth that would otherwise be unimaginable' (1970, p. 24). Such esoteric work 'is undertaken only by those who feel that the model they have chosen is entirely secure'; for this reason 'there is nothing quite like it in the arts, and the parallels in the social sciences are at best partial' (1963b, p. 86) Within the paradigm's boundaries, normal science is cumulative, for the solutions are virtually given with the problems and reaching these solutions tests only the scientist's patience and technical competence. This steady amassing of esoteric knowledge within a paradigmatic framework is one key element in the notion of scientific progress and distinguishes the developmental pattern of a mature science from those of other studies.

Working within a paradigm provides clear criteria not only for successful outcomes of normal scientific research, but also for failures: 'because the test . . . carried settled criteria of solution, it proves both more severe and harder to evade than the tests available within a tradition whose normal mode is critical discourse rather than puzzle solving' (1972a, p. 7). Nevertheless, Kuhn thinks that a scientific community at first ignores a paradigm's anomalies (and paradigms are usually faced with anomalous results), especially if the paradigm is sustaining successful normal scientific research. The paradigm is doubted only when the anomalies become too central or too numerous. *Ad hoc* articulations of the paradigm are the first reaction to the crisis. If these prove unsuccessful, then the science leaves the certainties of normal science for the stimulating, but insecure period of revolutionary or extraordinary science, where there are several competing paradigm candidates.

This brief sketch was meant to suggest some of the characteristics which social science cannot possess, if it is an immature or pre-paradigmatic science in Kuhn's sense. It must lack the uncontroversial, esoteric, progressive research programme which normal science provides.

Moving to a positive understanding of social science within Kuhn's methodology, we see that how we describe social science depends on whether sciences without an exclusive paradigm are pre-paradigmatic or immature. At times in his early work, Kuhn accepts the apparent implications of the idea of a pre-paradigmatic study. He depicts a study which has no guidelines for research, a study where all facts seem equally relevant, so that 'early fact-gathering is a far more nearly random activity' and 'is usually restricted to the wealth of data that lie ready to hand' (1970, p. 15). Whether or not any cognitive activity falls under such a description, it is clear that most immature sciences and all social sciences do not. Indeed, this suggestion that immature research consists of random fact-gathering was one of the first which Kuhn later abandoned.

Instead, we are given a distinctive immature stage of scientific research, without normal science, which is not 'pre-paradigmatic'. In this version, it is acknowledged that 'each of the schools whose competition characterises the earlier period is guided by something much like a paradigm' (1970, p. ix). The immature stage is now marked by a plurality of paradigms, with each paradigm investigating the area of reality that seems best to confirm its principles, not by an absence of paradigms, with a jumble of disoriented data. The exclusiveness of the paradigm in the mature discipline remains sufficiently important to distinguish fundamentally between those disciplines which possess one paradigm and those which possess many. The decisive factor is still the exclusive paradigm's ability to sustain normal science. In contrast, the non-exclusive paradigm eschews esoteric normal science for constant engagement in debate with its competitors over fundamentals (e.g. ontology, and the delineation of problems and their possible solutions).

At first sight, it is tempting to parallel research undertaken in immature disciplines with that which occurs in periods of revolutionary science, when an exclusive paradigm has entered a critical period. In both, a number of competing paradigms engage in fundamental debate, a debate whose resolution is underdetermined by empirical considerations. Kuhn even writes that 'a typical effect of crisis' is that research increasingly resembles 'that conducted under the competing schools of the pre-paradigm period' (1970, p. 72).

This parallel is at best superficial, however. To say this is not just to make the exegetic point that the notion of revolutionary science makes sense in Kuhn's methodology only as a stage produced by one period of normal science and leading to another. It is also to argue that there are basic differences between immature and revolutionary research which, if ignored, would obscure our understanding of immature sciences. Most crucial is the fact that periods of revolutionary science are short, while a discipline can harbour competing paradigms for centuries before one of them becomes exclusive. Consequently, competing paradigms in revolutionary science are bound to concentrate on only the fundamental aspects of the paradigm candidates and the anomalies that originally prompted the crisis. On the other hand, competing paradigms in immature research – while they may also engage in fundamental debate – have the time and resources to develop research programmes similar to the normal science that is sustained by an exclusive paradigm.

In important respects, then, the type of research that is carried out in the paradigms of an immature science is more like normal science than revolutionary science. For the paradigm of an immature science defines its own concepts, problems, and limits of solution. It generates a research programme, which concentrates on problems central to the paradigm, and progress is registered in understanding these problems. Finally, over the course of its work it tends to throw up anomalies which it finds difficult to give an account of, as in, for example, the Marxist problem of explaining the failure of revolution in the West or the functionalist difficulty in explaining the zero-sum aspects of power. True, much of its time will be devoted to fundamental debate, but this fact by itself begins to look less significant. The idea of comparison between paradigms, and therefore progress within the immature discipline as a whole, is also problematic. But the issue here is the familiar one of trying to devise an extra-theoretical standard for self-contained, holistic theories. It applies equally on Kuhn's premises to the chronological succession of exclusive paradigms in mature science, as his critics have never tired of stating.

The fact that a study has several competing paradigms, then, does not of itself preclude it from being scientific in the relevant respects. Interesting in this context is the later Kuhn's less dogmatic reference to 'the relative scarcity [not the absence] of competing schools in the developed sciences' (1970, p. 209). But, as I have said, this chapter is not a critical study of Kuhn, so I will not press further this point that Kuhn's methodology, in its ban on paradigm candidates during normal science, seems too rigid an account even of natural science.

A further question which ought to be posed about social science's status in Kuhnian terms is whether there is any basis in Kuhn's thought for declaring social science *necessarily* immature.

It is obvious that there are differences in the relations between social science and its subject matter and between natural science and its subject matter. These differences were central to chapters two and three, and were briefly mentioned in section 1.2. As Gouldner puts it in *The Coming Crisis of Western Sociology*: 'social theory may . . . change as a consequence of changes in the infrastructure in which it is anchored' (p. 397). By changes in the infrastructure forcing changes in social theory, we might mean either of two points. First, changes in the views of the actors under study force changes in social theory. Secondly, changes in concomitant social events force such changes. But whichever interpretation is adopted, the claim is that social theory is likely to change as some element in its social context changes. Hence, there is unlikely ever to be an exclusive paradigm in social science, at least not a relatively stable one.

Kuhn stresses that attention to the sociology of science is essential to an understanding of why scientific beliefs are held and how they change. For example, the sociological identification of the scientific community will yield greater precision in our decisions as to which work is normal and which revolutionary. However, the sociology in question here is, to use the conventional internal–external distinction, an internal sociology of science. It encompasses, for example, Mulkay's investigation of resistance to scientific change because of the scientific community's commitment to paradigm-generated norms in *The Social Process of Innovation*. Kuhn's invocation of the sociology of science does not extend to an external sociology which might explain the cognitive contents of the paradigm by means of concomitant social factors. Kuhn specifically states that the latter sociological work is relevant only to immature sciences:

Early in the development of a new field . . . social needs and values are a major determinant of the problems on which its practitioners concentrate . . . The new fields which emerged in the seventeenth century and a number of the modern social sciences provide examples . . . The later evolution of a technical speciality is significantly different . . . The problems on which such [specialities] work are no longer presented by the external society but by an internal challenge to increase the scope and precision of the fit between existing theory and nature (1968, pp. 80–1).

With mature sciences, Kuhn argues, external considerations are of relevance only to an account of aspects such as: the timing of scientific change; how much effort is channelled into the scientific enterprise in general; and the areas in which anomalies arise and therefore where development occurs, through, for example, encouraging specific patterns of speciality cross-fertilisation or concentration on certain problems.

The force of these points for a philosophical characterisation of social science can be disputed in several ways. First, we might, as many recent philosophers and historians of science have done, criticise the idea that external sociology cannot in part explain the contents of natural science. Secondly, as I noted in section 1.2, that social scientific accounts change with society in itself means no more than that social science takes note of its data, a relation precisely isomorphic with the one between natural science and its data.

Thirdly, even if we accepted that the contents of social science are peculiarly likely to be affected by changes in the surrounding society, we might still argue that social science can develop research programmes sufficiently esoteric and progressive for the Kuhnian notion of normal science to be applicable to them. Certainly, if Marxism is to remain progressive and empirical, it must assimilate the facts of the failure of proletarian revolution in the West, the survival of religion in the Soviet Union and the changes in the structure of Western capitalism, for example. But one reason why Marxism should study these issues is that, in its own terms, they are *prima facie* anomalous for some of the central tenets of the Marxist paradigm. The Marxist response is likely to be couched in the esoteric terms of the Marxist paradigm; and if the response was successful, we would conclude that the paradigm had been articulated and extended in the best normal scientific manner. Given that the world underdetermines theory, the same set of institutions or of institutional changes can be theorised in different ways; moreover, as we saw in chapter one, it is a function of theory to

168

decide which superficially different data are to be deemed relevantly different data. Only a naive empiricism of a kind that Kuhn could not espouse supports the idea that social development uniquely determines social scientific change. Any change in social scientific paradigms will, rather, be strongly mediated by the existing state of the paradigm.

Fourthly, even if it were necessary for social scientific theories to change when actors' theories change, the question at issue would not have been answered. For those wishing to argue that social science is necessarily immature would then have to show that actors' theories are necessarily immature. The whole idea of social science mirroring developments in actors' theories has in any case shown to be one-sided by my interactionist account of the social science–common sense relation.

A more substantial, though ultimately not logically decisive, argument for the conclusion that social science is necessarily immature in Kuhnian terms can be constructed by considering the relation of social science to values. Here, I need do no more than indicate the position I developed in chapter four. If values act as an extra criterion of theory choice in social science, if moral statements are themselves underdetermined by rational and empirical considerations, and if there is in any case a strong tendency for people to adopt different moral views, then it is likely that social science will encompass a diversity of theories in any of its domains. But this tendency for people to adopt different moral stances is a contingent fact about the world, however basic. There is nothing logically absurd about the idea of a society with a monolithic morality which could act as the underpinning of an exclusive social scientific paradigm. In section 5.5, I will suggest that Soviet sociology at least approximates to such a paradigm.

Finally, we might briefly consider what implications would flow for a Kuhnian characterisation of social science if anti-naturalism were correct. Kuhn's philosophy could serve as a model for a philosophy of non-naturalistic social study, just as philosophers of religion have recently used analyses of science as models for the development of theories of religion. The danger in this approach, of course, is that Kuhn's already vague concepts will be rendered vaguer. In particular, the notion of a paradigm becomes much less interesting if it is detached from that of normal science. Comparing art and science, Kuhn writes that in both there are periods of rapid change when one tradition supplants another, and that in both there are periods dominated by traditions consisting of values, techniques and models. But 'that much', Kuhn continues, 'can probably be said about the development of any human enterprise'. The recognition of these gross similarities can be only a first step to the study of 'a number of revealing differences in developmental fine-structure' (1969, pp. 409–10). Luckily, I am spared the need to judge whether it would be fruitful to apply Kuhnian categories to non-naturalistic studies. For the basic argument of this book is that social science can be naturalistic.

5.3. EXCLUSIVE PARADIGMS AND SOCIAL SCIENCE

A lively debate arose in several social sciences in the decade after the publication of *The Structure of Scientific Revolutions* about how social science was to be characterised in Kuhnian terms. This debate, which has died away with the passing of the vogue for Kuhn's work, was in many ways unsatisfactory. It was primarily disappointing for a reason already indicated: the vagueness of the notion of paradigm allowed writers to be meaning different things when they claimed that social science did or did not possess paradigms or exclusive paradigms. In particular, many people forgot that an exclusive paradigm must have the allegiance of almost all the practitioners in its field and must eschew fundamental controversy in its pursuit of esoteric paradigm articulation. Yet the debate does provide a short cut into the issue of whether social study is a mature science in Kuhnian terms; in this section I will consider several of the contributions to the debate.

Most boldly of all, Wolin in 'Paradigms and Political Theories' claims that traditional political philosophy is 'a special form of paradigm-inspired research' (p. 139). Wolin argues that traditional political theorists have been self-consciously concerned to distinguish their assumptions of what is significant for political study, of what are the best methods for political study and of what kinds of answers can be given to certain basic questions, from the corresponding assumptions of previous political theorists. Wolin holds further that there has been continuity within paradigms in political theory, usually as a result of the work of hordes of forgotten commentators who extended the Master's works into areas not originally intended for them: in Wolin's example, the Aristotelian political paradigm was articulated by the medieval debate about church–state relations. In political theory, Wolin adds, the attempt to enforce paradigmatic conformity is not typically directed at other political philosophers. Only rarely, as with the French Encyclopedists, is there a school in political philosophy. Rather, the drive towards an exclusive paradigm is directed into attempts to convert the mass of the people to the political theory in question, often via a conversion of the society's ruling forces (the *philosophes* and the Enlightened Despots, for example).

Ryan (1970b) supports this contention that there have been paradigms in political theory. He exemplifies the argument in terms of social contract theory: 'both as a matter of logic and a matter of history, the social contract played a paradigmatic role in social thought' (pp. 82–3). He argues that the social contract theory has explanatory potential (e.g. the actions of the American republic's founders are understandable from a contractual viewpoint) and that the social contract literature is full of the kind of puzzles characteristic of normal science: e.g., did the origin of society or only of political organisation depend upon the contract? Is the theory refuted if the ruled do not consider their relations to the ruler to be contractual?

Wolin and Ryan show at most only that there have been competing paradigms in political theory, within each of which progressive work is possible. They describe precisely the situation that exists in an immature field; and, as we have seen, Kuhnian methodology cannot exclude progress in immature disciplines. Political theory would have reached maturity in Kuhn's sense only if a single paradigm were accepted by nearly all political theorists. But Ryan's 'puzzles' are the sort of high level theoretical disputes that have to be resolved before an exclusive paradigm can emerge, not the rigidly delineated, technical problems that are thrown up by normal science. Furthermore, a full analysis of Wolin's and Ryan's arguments would have to confront the issue raised in the last section. Namely, granted that traditional political theory is pre-scientific, how compelling is the extension of the language of paradigms into non-naturalistic studies?

In the middle of the 1960s, Wolin also argued that a 'behavioural' paradigm based on Easton's work was beginning to emerge in political science. Subsequent events have shown this thesis to be false, as Easton himself tacitly acknowledged in the epilogue to the second edition of *The Political System*, where he tried somewhat desperately to draw the sting from the basic criticisms that had been levelled against his views. However, more systematic attempts than Wolin's have been made to locate paradigms within political science.

We can combine Truman's (1965) and Almond's (1966) only slightly differing views to produce the following account of American political science. There was an exclusive paradigm in political science from the nineteenth century until about the Second World War. This paradigm proved to be increasingly anomalous, finally broke down, and was followed by a short period of chaotic, revolutionary discussion, before the eventual emergence of another exclusive paradigm.

The original paradigm had the following characteristics: (1) 'an unconcern with political systems as such', so that the paradigm worked with an implicit view of the elements, needs and boundaries of the political system (Truman, p. 866); (2) a generally implicit conception of political change which was blandly optimistic and reformist, including the assumption of an untroubled evolution of all constitutions towards an Anglo-American style liberal democracy, based on a mixed constitution and checks and balances; (3) a neglect of explicit theory and a consequent crude empiricist view of science; and (4) a parochial preoccupation with the U.S.A. which stunted the development of comparative studies and method. Almond stresses that this paradigm sustained a normal science based on the mixed constitution classification. Thus, various polities were analysed in terms of how they combined the legislature, executive and judiciary. Furthermore, the paradigm was underpinned by a simple moral approval of the view of change propagated in (2), given that separation of powers with checks and balances was held to promote and maintain 'a stable social order, combining justice with liberty and equality' (p. 872).

This paradigm broke down, Truman and Almond claim, in the face of twentieth-century political developments which were anomalous to characteristics (2) and (4). The most obvious of these anomalous experiences were: before the Second World War, the Bolshevik Revolution, the conduct of the First World War, the rise of fascism in Europe, the general instabilities of the 1930s, and the bankruptcy of the Third Republic in 1940, followed after the Second World War by the Cold War and the break-up of the colonial structure.

Truman and Almond stress, however, that this early paradigm was not as monolithic as might first appear. As Almond puts it: 'in the latter part of the nineteenth century, as professional university-based political science began to develop, almost with its first breath so to speak, questions were raised as to the validity of the theory in its whole and in its parts' (p. 873). For example, the legislature–executive–judiciary categorisation was rejected in favour of a distinction between politics and administration; or a fundamental role was found for elements, such as political parties or interest groups, which could not be accommodated within the original paradigm; or, again, there was much detailed, *ad hoc* questioning of the paradigm, with, for instance, the judiciary being shown to be law-makers and the executive to have judicial functions, detailed investigations which produced 'strained formulations' such as 'quasi-legislative' and 'quasi-judicial' (Almond, p. 875). It is clear, then, that this paradigm did not dominate its field as would be expected of an exclusive paradigm in a mature science. Truman writes that it was 'a product diverse both in quality and intent' (p. 875).

Similar diversity can be detected in the purported new exclusive paradigm, which is supposedly based on a systems approach. Certain of this new paradigm's stated characteristics belong to the level of formal methodology which should be present in any scientific paradigm: for example, a commitment to statistical and comparative methods, to a rigorous analysis of variables, and to an interest in explicit theory. Where the theoretical content of this putative exclusive paradigm is specified, it is clear that there is no homogeneity. Truman states that belief in explicit theory involves a commitment to *diverse* theories, and Almond's brief articulation of the supposed basic paradigmatic concept of political system encompasses a functionalist theory and an input–output model of the political decision process.

Palermo (1971) straightforwardly extends Kuhn's work to psychology. He argues 'that experimental psychology has had two paradigms already, with the appropriate scientific revolution between them' (p. 138). The first revolution led to the emergence of Wundt's introspective paradigm as a revolutionary break with the pre-scientific paradigm of the British associationists. Wundt's paradigm was characterised by its introspective method and by its consequential limitation of permitted subject matter to the conscious experience of adults. A critical period for introspective psychology arose due to three major factors: 'the unreliability of the introspective method; the interest in animals and the resultant necessity to anthropomorphise about animal consciousness in order to maintain the old paradigm; and the interest in the extension of psychological principles to practical application' (p. 140). The first period of revolutionary science in psychology, Palermo claims, involved an attempt to 'patch up the old paradigm' (p. 142) through the functionalist psychological theory of James, Dewey and Angell. *Gestalt* theory was another psychological paradigm candidate produced by the period of revolutionary science, but it failed to secure majority allegiance, and behaviourism emerged as psychology's new paradigm.

The behaviourist paradigm consisted of the following main aspects: (1) a concentration on learning theory, with Pavlovian classical conditioning at its core; (2) a commitment to study animal behaviour first in its own right, but more importantly as providing the elements from which more complex behaviour could be constructed; (3) an anti-emergence stance, whereby rat-results can be transferred to the study of humans; (4) lack of interest in physiology, because (5) the organism is seen as a passive receiver of stimuli, rather than an innate patterner of its environment; and (6) an anti-introspective methodology. The zenith of behaviourist normal science was in the 1940s and 1950s, when 'data were collected at fever pitch . . . [and] all played the game of psychology by essentially the same ground rules' (p. 144).

But Palermo's account crumbles if subjected to detailed scrutiny, in the same way as the apparently neat normal science–revolution–normal science sequence detected in political science proved unacceptable. Thus, Briskman (1972) argues that a psychological theory has never lacked external competitors or internal conflict. Even if we ignore Freudian and interactionist approaches, there has been a great deal of basic controversy under the umbrella of behaviourism. Leading practitioners such as Tolman, Guthrie and Hull, for example, have not been able to agree on fundamental questions in learning theory: for example, '(1) What does the behaving organism actually learn? and (2) By what basic mechanism does this organism learn what it learns?' (p. 91).

To the question whether sociology has ever operated with an exclusive paradigm, a brusquer answer might be thought sufficient. Of course a discipline that includes various forms of functionalist, Marxist, structuralist and ethnomethodological theories (to mention but a few of the more visible ones), each of which disagree on almost all the points characteristic of immature disagreement (e.g. the starting-points for discussion, ideals of explanation, the nature of the subject matter, what count as solutions, and the constituents of sociological ontology) and a discipline which has conspicuously not forgotten its founding fathers, is clearly not a mature scientific discipline in Kuhn's sense. Even historians of sociology, such as Hawthorn (1976), who purport to discover a basic unity of subject matter in sociology (in Hawthorn's case: the relation of human nature to society and nature, and ways of mediating between anarchy and reaction) invariably emphasise the great diversity of theoretical positions that have been adopted on this common subject matter.

Yet Douglas (1970) can say of functionalism in the near-related field of anthropology:

The anthropologists who let the homeostatic model govern their teaching and thinking, in spite of its many drawbacks, were accepting a scientific paradigm in much the same way as the natural scientists described by Kuhn . . . Kuhn supposes that the method of teaching in the physical sciences is more likely to produce a rigid 'mental set' than that in the social sciences. But everything that he says about the use of paradigms in scientific thinking has strong relevance for British anthropology following the Second World War (p. xxii).

In particular, Douglas claims that the functionalist paradigm, with its 'long years of microscopic attention to detail in social relations' (p. xxiv), produced two specific benefits which are typical of normal scientific progress: a realistic understanding of the role of conflict in all social systems and of the way in which thought systems relate to social structure.

The picture of functionalism derived from Gouldner's (1972) work is, however, interestingly different. Gouldner argues that in the nineteenth century sociology split into Academic and Marxist sociology. In the latter half of this century, Academic sociology in the U.S.A. was equivalent to Parsonian functionalism. Both Academic and Marxist sociology are now entering a crisis period, as is witnessed by the generation of several alternative paradigms within Academic sociology and by the convergence of strands within Academic and Marxist sociology. There is a crucial point about Academic sociology, however, which prevents us from interpreting it straightforwardly as an exclusive paradigm passing into crisis. Academic sociology or functionalism has engaged in a continuous, even if sometimes 'subterranean' (p. 157), theoretical/philosophical debate with Marxism. Hence, it has never held full control of the field of sociological theory and philosophy. Moreover, at least one of Douglas's examples of the success of functionalist normal science – awareness of the importance of conflict – is more usually seen as one of functionalism's theoretical silences, a lacuna which was forced on classical functionalism's attention by its 'subterranean' debate with paradigm competitors, including Marxism. Once again the attempt to read an exclusive paradigm into a social science collapses with even cursory attention to the history of social science.

Perhaps Kuhn's own work in the history of science can be represented as work within a mature paradigm or the establishment of a mature paradigm. Kuhn says that the new history of science is distinguished primarily by its orientation: 'Only in this century have historians of science gradually learned to see their subject matter as something different from a chronology of accumulating positive achievement in a technical speciality defined by hindsight '(1968, p. 75). This new history of science has a number of sources, including work on the history of philosophy which revealed the existence of different problems at different times, Duhem's pioneering work on medieval physics, attempts to write general histories of science leading to the realisation of the existence of changing disciplinary boundaries, and sociological and Marxist programmes for an external history of science. The basic orientation and the confluence of determining factors are, indeed, the kinds of elements that would define an exclusive paradigm for normal science.

But even adherents of the new history of science put different stresses on its different aspects. So any purported detection of an exclusive paradigm in the history of science becomes unreasonable. Such disagreements are especially prevalent over the relation of internal and external factors. Moreover, there are still many practitioners of the old history of science studying the progressive eradication of error and revelation of truth. Indeed, as Bernstein (1976, pp. 97–8) points out, social scientists are prone to the absurdity of using a Whig history of science in the service of a Kuhnian philosophy of science: we have emerged from error and confusion to the exclusive scientific paradigm of functionalism, for example. This historical myopia also leads many historians of social science to underestimate the degree of intra-theoretical consensus before the nineteenth century.

The most interesting historical work on social science in Kuhnian terms has been done on economics. Little agreement has been reached on how to apply Kuhn's concepts. For example, Bronbenbrenner (1971) sees at least three major revolutions in economics; Coats (1969) writes that 'economics may be regarded as more "uniformitarian" than the natural sciences, for despite persistent and often penetrating criticism by a stream of heterodox writers (e.g. socialists, evolutionists, institutionalists) it has been dominated throughout its history by a single paradigm – the theory of economic equilibrium via the market mechanism' (p. 292); and Haggett and Chorley (1970) see a more recent attainment of maturity by economics, given that 'the early debates over the nature of economics have been replaced by rather stable – but largely invisible – rules as to what problems and methods economic science should cultivate' (p. 27). It is arguable that this difference results from the vagueness of the concept of paradigm: for example, depending on whether one interprets a revolution, first, as a change in the basic metaphysics and, secondly, as a change in the central concrete exemplar, one might see neo-classical marginal utility theory, first, as fundamentally continuous with classical theory and, secondly, as a revolution.

Orthodox history of economics[1] tends to detect three paradigms (the classical, neo-classical and Keynesian), with one counter-paradigm (the Marxist). The three paradigms have arguably distinctive problems. Thus, simplifying greatly, classical economics is concerned with the causes and consequences of growth over a long period; neo-classical economics with the short-run allocative properties of a market, and especially with relative prices and economic fluctuations; and Keynesian economics with unemployment and inflation. These different problems yielded different interpretations of superficially the same concepts. For example, demand in classical economics was understood as the quantities of goods needed for a particular purpose and a commodity's price was largely determined by the labour input to that commodity. Neo-classical economics, in contrast, shifted the emphasis onto consumer preferences, which in classical thought had been considered largely static and therefore analytically unimportant:

[1] Barber (1970) and Robinson (1968) are representative examples.

consumer preferences were equated with demand, which (with supply) was a fundamental determinant of price. This change had many
consequences, one of which, for example, was a change in the concept
of productive labour. In classical economics, with its labour theory of
value, labour working directly on material objects was virtually the
only kind of productive labour; whereas in neo-classical economics,
any good which satisfied consumer preferences, which yielded utility
when consumed, was considered the result of productive labour, even
if that good were a non-material service.

From his attempt to apply Kuhn's analysis to economics, Bronbenbrenner concludes that Kuhn cannot account for the basic fact of
continuity, or what might be better termed 'eternal recurrence', in
economic theory. Kuhn implies that a paradigm, once displaced, is
abandoned completely, whereas in economics concepts, problems and
solutions of discarded theories are likely to persist or recur: for
example, 'currently fashionable incomes-policy proposals are based
on elements of the medieval *justum pretium*' (p. 137). Similarly, it might
be argued, recent work on the economics of developing countries is
based on classical economic analyses of the relations between an
industrial sector and a traditional subsistence sector at the point when
large-scale industrialisation is beginning (Barber, 1970, pp. 108–10);
just as Keynes re-introduced the moral problem of the justification of
inequalities in distribution which had lain dormant in mainstream
economics since neo-classical economics had committed itself to
automatic growth through *laissez faire* mechanisms (Robinson, 1968, p.
72).

On this basis, Bronbenbrenner develops a 'dialectical' model of
economic advance. Many antitheses are proposed against the dominant thesis when the latter is in a period of crisis. A synthesis emerges
out of the ensuing conflict and this synthesis provides the basis for a
new period of normal science. Some of the revolutionary antitheses are
absorbed into the synthesis. Others survive, if at all, 'hibernating in a
kind of intellectual underworld, and remain antithetical until the next
revolution . . . The old "thesis" often survives too, with relatively,
slight modifications, like the eighteenth century mercantilism in
contemporary trade-policy discussions' (p. 141).

Bronbenbrenner argues that this model allows for tradition and
continuous accretion in economic theory. Another interpretation of his
argument, however, is that it parallels the account which has emerged
from all the brief studies we have made of social science in Kuhnian
terms in this section. While there have been periods in social science
during which one paradigm has drawn the attention of most practitioners in the field, alternative theories have always been present. In

177

consequence, social science has continuously engaged in fundamental debate. As I argued in section 5.2, this does not prevent these diverse social scientific paradigms pursuing progressive normal scientific research. Indeed, Kuhn presumably values social science as a contribution to knowledge, because he often appeals to Piaget's work, *Gestalt* psychology and an internal sociology of science in justification of parts of his methodology.

5.4. METHODOLOGICAL PRESCRIPTIONS FOR SOCIOLOGY

Kuhn's methodology sustains methodological prescriptions. His work 'has consequences for the way in which scientists should behave if their enterprise is to succeed' (1970, p. 207). But these prescriptions, unlike those generated by empiricism, are in part determined by Kuhn's history of science. Kuhn's view of the relations of history and philosophy of science is basic to his enterprise. It is a view, incidentally, which I have assumed in this book, though I would dissent from his implicit judgment that the history of social science does not provide examples of successful social scientific theories as the basis for a prescriptive methodology of social science. This disagreement turns, ultimately, on my contention that there is no logical objection to pursuing a naturalistic social science.

An argument for his methodology, Kuhn believes, is that successful science in the past has exhibited the structure described by his methodology. Hence, Kuhn concludes, if we wish to continue to build a progressive science, we should act as we now understand past successful science to have developed. The relation between history and philosophy of science in Kuhn's final account is circular, therefore. For history reveals good science to have violated empiricist views of sound scientific practice. Kuhn then constructs a methodology which renders that development rational. And this methodology, in turn, comes to play a part in the identification of successful science. Yet this circularity is non-vicious, Kuhn contends. Both history and philosophy have their own internal constraints which act as limitations on the degree that either can be moulded by the other: history must ultimately be true to its data, including the data of plausible historical change, and philosophy has internal logical constraints. Lakatos's philosophical history, in contrast, has no place for an independent historical element and 'the philosopher can learn from it about scientific method only what he puts in' (1971, p. 141).

Despite this ability to derive prescriptions from his work, Kuhn writes that he provides 'no therapy to assist the transformation of a proto-science to a science' (1972b, p. 245). Nor does he think such a therapy possible. Given that he bases prescriptions on history and that he thinks social science is immature, the reason for his refusal to legislate for social science is clear. Since immature studies lack the secure pattern of progress to be found in exclusive paradigms, we cannot be confident in our identification of past great social scientific work as a basis for the making of prescriptions. Only after transition to maturity, Kuhn writes, 'does progress become an obvious characteristic of a field. And only then do those prescriptions of mine which my critics decry come into play' (1972b, p. 245).

The irony of the philosopher being prepared to prescribe for natural science, but not for social science, appears to miss Kuhn. For the philosopher's prescriptions for natural science are in the main ignored, because of natural science's complacency about its past and probable future success, while philosophy of social science often has a deal of effect on substantive sociological conduct. Thus, Kuhn shies away from normative methodology precisely where it appears needed.

Prima facie, then, a programme such as Harré and Secord's (1972) self-conscious introduction and articulation of a new paradigm in social psychology seems reasonable. So, taking sociology as an example, can we derive methodological prescriptions from a Kuhnian reading of sociology? I follow Martins (1972) and Urry (1973) in delineating a set of possible reactions.

Establish an exclusive sociological paradigm as soon as possible! This reaction usually assumes that functionalism is the paradigm to be established. Just as social scientists often mix a pre-Kuhnian history of social science with a Kuhnian philosophy of social science, so support for an exclusive functionalist paradigm is often equivalent to the advocation of formalisation, quantification, the exclusion of philosophical controversy, etc., so that 'Kuhnianism in social science is beginning to act as a functional equivalent and substitute for philosophical positivism' (Martins, p. 53).

This reaction is misconceived if sociology is in fact firmly in the immature stage, in which case we should develop individually the various paradigm candidates. Since we cannot know whether an exclusive sociological paradigm will emerge out of any of the existing paradigms, out of a synthesis of them or out of some future paradigm, 'the "sin" of eclecticism is really no sin' (Martins, p. 53).

Develop a revolution in sociology as soon as possible, because we have been too long in the grip of a functionalist orthodoxy which is now crisis-ridden! This reaction is based on two assumptions. The second becomes operative only if the first applies, but the first appears highly dubious if we read the history of sociology in Kuhnian terms.

Namely, (i) sociology has had a period of normal science based on an exclusive paradigm; and (ii) the exclusive paradigm has reached a stage of crisis.

Continue developing the various sociological paradigms! This reaction presupposes that sociology will remain in a Kuhnian immature phase for the immediate future. While my argument from the role of values in social science, developed in the last section, supports this presupposition, I see no justification for it from within Kuhn's methodology.

We fail to derive determinate methodological prescriptions from Kuhn for sociology, because Kuhn's categories are retrospective ones, primarily intended for the historical observer, not the scientific actor. On the one hand, many crises are resolved within normal science, so the scientist experiencing the crisis does not know whether it is a normal or a revolutionary one. On the other hand, whereas normal science does not seek fundamental innovation, the scientist, not knowing when revolution will come, must be oriented toward the permanent possibility of revolution. Working in an immature science, the scientist does not know whether his subject is to remain in this state for centuries or is about to throw up an exclusive paradigm. Without this knowledge, thinking in Kuhnian terms cannot rationally help to guide his research strategy.

Using Kuhn's work was intended to facilitate an analysis of the issue of theoretical diversity in social science. Central to Kuhn's account is the idea that any field which displays a number of different theories cannot be scientific in the full sense. But do we want to adopt Kuhn's views on this point? I have already suggested that progressive research work little different from normal science is possible within a paradigm, even if there are a number of other paradigms in the same domain. I will now study the disadvantages that would accrue to social science if it did operate with an exclusive paradigm by examining a concrete example.

5.5. AN EXAMPLE: SOVIET SOCIOLOGY

In chapter four I argued that it is both unreasonable and unfruitful to expect or to aim for the emergence of an exclusive social scientific theory, because moral considerations structure social scientific theories. In this chapter I have shown, first, that on Kuhn's methodology a discipline cannot be a mature science unless it is governed by an exclusive paradigm, and, secondly, that the history of the various social sciences strongly suggests that there never has been an exclusive paradigm in social science. Anyone who accepted my argument in chapter four and Kuhn's demarcation of science must conclude that social science cannot be scientific. As a way of understanding what would be involved if a social science were to accept an exclusive paradigm, I will set out a philosophical analysis of Soviet sociology. The point of this example is twofold.

First, I will argue that Soviet sociology is based on an exclusive paradigm which sustains progressive theoretical and empirical research. In Kuhnian terms, therefore, we should consider Soviet sociology to be more suited for rapid advance than Western sociology. The Kuhnian might reply that Soviet sociology, though in a sense based on an exclusive paradigm, is not properly mature, because there were no good intellectual reasons why Soviet sociology should form an exclusive paradigm in the Soviet Union and because there was no typical immature stage of multi-paradigmatic controversy. But it is not clear that the Kuhnian has a right to such a judgment, because, as I showed in the last section, it is impossible to derive a decision procedure from Kuhn's work for when or how an exclusive paradigm should be established in an immature discipline.

Yet despite the exclusive nature of the Soviet sociological paradigm, we remain uninclined to think that theoretical or empirical knowledge would benefit if Soviet sociology were the exclusive paradigm in world sociology, as well as in the Soviet Union. To demur thus is not because Soviet sociology is unscientific. Soviet sociology has a structure that could sustain theoretical and empirical generalisations, which in turn could be used as bases for explanations and predictions. That is, it is scientific in the sense portrayed in chapter one, since it can replicate key elements of scientific methodology. Moreover, it is scientific in that it can encompass progressive theoretical and empirical research, despite being highly self-conscious of its philosophical foundations and of rival Western social scientific theories. Here we see again, as we did in considering the possibilities of progressive research work in a multi-paradigmatic discipline, how a demarcation of science in terms of an exclusive paradigm sustaining normal science is too narrow. Rather, to shun Soviet sociology's exclusive paradigm is rational because it can be shown that other social scientific theories, sustaining their own progressive theoretical and empirical research, can study areas of Soviet reality that are not open to Soviet sociology.

Secondly, this example will again illustrate the relations between the moral, metaphysical, theoretical and empirical layers which I argued in chapter four to be characteristic of a social scientific theory.

I suspect that a philosophical analysis of Soviet social and natural science would exemplify another of chapter four's points: namely, that while moral considerations are logically relevant to social science, they are irrelevant to natural science. To attempt a philosophy of Soviet natural science would require a massive digression. But the lines this digression would have to pursue are as follows. It would study, first, the relation between dialectical materialism and Soviet natural science, because Soviet writers claim that dialectical materialism is of equal importance for social and natural science. A strong case could be made for the view that Soviet acceptance of dialectical materialism is value-determined, because there are natural affinities between an activist, revolutionary political creed and elements of dialectical materialism, such as its materialism and anti-reductionism. However, what is much more doubtful is whether the fact that Soviet natural science is officially committed to dialectical materialism has any rational bearing on the conduct of natural science in the Soviet Union. As Graham says of the relations between dialectical materialism and two *prima facie* politically sensitive sciences, biology and cybernetics: 'There is nothing in the formal framework of dialectical materialism about the inheritance of acquired characteristics, intraspecific competition, or the phasic development of plants. By the same token, there is nothing in dialectical materialism which inherently contradicts or affirms cybernetics' (1967, p. 101). Dialectical materialism purports to be an account of the structure and methods common to all sciences, a methodology as I have used that term. It cannot, therefore, decide between theoretical and empirical options in particular sciences. That function is partly fulfilled, however, by the morally determined layer of historical materialism in Soviet social science; in my previous terminology, historical materialism is the metaphysics of Soviet social science. But there is no equivalent within Soviet natural science of historical materialism in Soviet social science. While I now ignore Soviet natural science, I will return to the formal levels of Soviet sociology.

Before proceeding further, I will state some qualifications to my study. So basic are these qualifications that I could not object if someone were to say that my study is of 'Soviet sociology', rather than of Soviet sociology. First, my ignorance of Russian has forced me to rely primarily on Western commentaries on Soviet sociology.[2] Particularly before the mid-1960s, these tended to be of a quite remarkably poor quality. When they tried to disguise the sheer crudity of their attacks on Soviet sociology, they talked about Soviet sociology being, for

[2] The main sources used in this section were: Brodersen (1967), Brown (1974), Feuer (1967), Fischer (1967a, 1967b, 1967c), Gellner (1974b), de George (1966, 1967), Graham (1967, 1971), Hollander (1967), Holloway (1974), Judy (1973), Labedz (1958, 1967), Lane (1970, 1971), Laserson (1971), Mikulak (1964), Osipov and Yochuk (1967), Powell and Shoup (1970), Simirenko (1967a, 1967b, 1967c), Theen (1971), Weinberg (1974), Wiatr (1964) and Znaniecki (1971).

values, I will say a few words on the history of Soviet sociology. Empirical Soviet sociology originated in 1956 at the Twentieth Party Congress which, in rejecting Stalinism, not only allowed once more the minimum controversy that is necessary for any social scientific discipline, but also recognised the need for empirical sociological research. In the 1920s, when controversial intellectual work was still possible, there had been a lively debate between Deborin and Bukharin about such issues as the status of dialectical and historical materialism, the role of will in history and the relation of the base to the superstructure. But this debate had not been linked systematically to empirical work. The decade after 1956 saw Soviet sociology's struggle for legitimation and institutionalisation. The struggle for legitimation involved commitment to 'the ideological and theoretical position of Soviet Marxism' (Simirenko, 1967b, p. 20), situating itself with respect to dialectical and historical materialism and criticising bourgeois sociology. The struggle for institutionalisation aimed at achieving all the paraphernalia of an academic discipline: its own university departments, degrees, research institutions, conferences, journals and conventional intellectual boundaries. The decisive events of its early history often resulted from its political context. Thus, for example, the Third Party Programme, adopted in 1961, recognised that consciousness lags behind changes in the base, and demanded the production of a new Soviet person and the encouragement of communist consciousness and morality. This call was met in the 1960s by unprecedented Soviet philosophical work on ideology and especially on ethics, work which, in turn, led to a dramatic increase in sociological work on subjective and ideological factors: see, for example, Aptekman's (1967) research on religious ideology and his policy proposal for the development of atheistic Soviet rituals. At the Twenty-Third Party Congress in 1966 sociology was finally explicitly recognised as an independent and legitimate discipline.

To give a full account of Soviet sociology, we would have to address ourselves to five distinct intellectual levels: Soviet values, dialectical materialism, historical materialism, sociological generalisations some of which would be predicated of all societies and others of specific societies, and empirical statements and research methods. These distinctions are relative and shifting, and it would often be impossible to assign individual statements and concepts to a particular level with certainty. However, they serve an analytical purpose, and their first use is to allow us to agree the irrelevance of dialectical materialism to our concerns. As I have suggested, dialectical materialism is part of what I have called methodology. It is a general philosophy of the contents, nature and structure of science. In particular, it espouses a realist epistemology, a materialist ontology and certain views on the necessary forms of scientific laws. As a general philosophy of science, it is unable to serve as a basis for relevant distinctions to be made either between natural science and naturalistic social science or between individual theories within a science.

Soviet sociology can usefully be regarded as consisting of the four levels: Soviet values, historical materialism, sociological generalisations and empirical statements. It grew from a nucleus of Soviet political values and historical materialism. Indeed, its first theoretical problem was to situate sociology within historical materialism: does sociology simply equal historical materialism or can they be distinguished? The consensus seems to be, though there is still debate on the subject, that historical materialism provides the framework statements and concepts for the lower level sociological work. Several Western writers have claimed to detect a distancing of Soviet sociology from its origins deep in Soviet philosophy. I will dispute this claim when I show that the permissible problems for Soviet sociology are determined by historical materialism. Analysis of the relation between historical materialism and the more empirical layers will also allow me to show that Soviet sociology is dominated by an exclusive paradigm which sets its exemplars and its possible problems, concepts and statements. This unity in Soviet sociological theory demonstrates the superficiality of the piecemeal paralleling of Soviet and functionalist concepts, a pastime beloved of many Western commentators.

A reason for the choice of historical materialism as the metaphysics for Soviet sociology and for the refusal to countenance rival theories is the internal relations between historical materialism and the officially accepted Soviet values. There may, of course, also be non-intellectual reasons for the choice of the specific Soviet sociological paradigm; just as there are non-intellectual factors helping to determine choice in Western social science. I do not know whether Soviet sociologists genuinely adhere to the values. All we need note is that they appeal to them in support of the Soviet paradigm and that acceptance of the values is in fact a ground for conceptualising social reality in terms of historical materialist categories.

The very establishment of sociology had to be justified in political and philosophical terms. Those who defended Soviet sociology in its infancy argued that it exemplified the Soviet beliefs in: the unity of theory and practice, which was interpreted to mean that sociology would be of practical benefit to society in the process of building communism; and the unity of value and fact, in that sociology was based on a commitment to Soviet values. Moreover, the ultimate judge in issues of historical materialism was always the Party and Soviet sociology developed initially by means of fierce attacks on Western sociology: these two facets illustrated Soviet commitments to, respectively, an institutional locus for judgments of truth and the distinctiveness of the Soviet system.

More important than Soviet values conditioning the very possibility of Soviet sociology is the point that they also act as criteria of acceptability for the basic theoretical framework of Soviet sociology. It is by reference to Soviet values that we understand why historical materialism was adopted as the paradigmatic framework for Soviet sociology. As Brodersen puts it, Soviet sociology:

conceptualises the dominant Soviet ideas of man and society, of power and history, of capitalism and socialism, of international relations and the world conflict. In other words, it sets the framework in which the rulers and the ruled interpret the political universe and define their own actions within that universe (1967, pp. 255–6).

Many of the main features of Soviet historical materialism are clearly derived from classical Marxism. The ideas that the nature of the mode of production is the most fundamental fact about a society, that the ideological superstructure is in the last instance an effect of the productive base, that classes (defined in terms of property relations) are the most important social groupings, that there is a relatively set pattern of historical development of social forms, that the urban proletariat is the class which is the dynamic behind the achievement of the final social forms of socialism and communism, and that communism does not exist while there are certain structural divisions in society (e.g. town versus country, intellectual versus manual labour), are all to be found in Marx's work and in Soviet historical materialism. Some of the values at the basis of these ideas are also shared by both: a commitment to ending the grosser forms of inequality in types of work, distribution of property and styles of life which have characterised all hitherto existing societies, and the general beliefs in communism and collectivism, for example.

Some of Soviet historical materialism's other features are, however, at least arguably departures from classical Marxism. Three basic theses ought to be noted in this context: first, the progressive weakening of the base–superstructure model, encompassing the notions that some ideological elements survive from past social formations, that some cognitive systems do not form part of the superstructure and that in any case at least in socialist societies the superstructure has an active influence on the base; secondly, the doctrines of socialism in one country and of the centrality of the Soviet Union in the development of world communism; thirdly, the absolute priority of the Party as an institution in Soviet society and especially in leading the Soviet Union to communism. With this second set of ideas, the underlying values also seem to diverge from classical Marxism. Many of the distinctive theses of Soviet historical materialism are grounded in the need to justify the Soviet Union's position as a world power, the Party's power within the country and the failure of certain features of Soviet society to change as radically as expected.

Soviet sociology's basic theoretical concepts, statements, assumptions and research foci are essentially derivative of the theses of Soviet historical materialism which I have just outlined. For example, the recent stress on the power of ideas, especially of moral ideas that have been chosen by the Party towards the end of creating new kinds of communist institutions and people, stems from the beliefs in the nature of communism, the weakening of the base–superstructure model and the priority of the Party. Similarly, the Soviet concept of 'non-antagonistic contradictions' is a product of the idea that the fundamental social fissure, that between classes in different relations to the means of production, no longer exists: while there are still divisions within Soviet society (town and country, intellectual and manual labour, men's and women's roles), only the existence of classes in the full sense demands an explosive, revolutionary type of development.

Several points about this basic Soviet sociological theoretical framework should be noted. First, to return to the themes of chapters two and three, in trying to understand Soviet sociology, we do not need to take a stand on the relationship which exists between Soviet sociology and the mass culture of the Soviet people. Everything I say about the internal structure and scientific status of Soviet sociology stands, whether the Soviet people categorise and explain their experience in the terms of historical materialism or in completely different terms. What evidence there is suggests, as we might expect, that some ideas of historical materialism have entered the Soviet people's ordinary language, others remain foreign, and many ideas common in ordinary life are alien to historical materialism.

Secondly, many of the specifically Soviet aspects of Soviet historical materialism had an origin which tells us much about the Party's control over the acceptability of concepts and statements. The intervention by 'the Greatest Philologist in the World' (Kolakowski, 1971, p. 191) in Soviet linguistics (Stalin, 1950) had an impact on historical materialism that lasted beyond 1956. Stalin's essay on linguistics contains the canonical versions of some of Soviet historical materialism's central ideas: that, for example, some cognitive systems (including ordinary language) are not part of the superstructure, that the superstructure's role is one of 'actively assisting its base to take shape and consolidate itself, and doing everything it can to help the new system finish off and eliminate the old base and the old classes' (pp. 408–9), and that revolutions must be 'by means of an explosion' only when a society is 'divided into hostile classes', not when they are 'on the initiative of the existing power' and with the support of the masses in a society without hostile classes (pp. 425–6).

Thirdly, despite the close internal relations between Soviet values and the Soviet theory of society, we cannot conclude that there will be no changes in the Soviet sociological paradigm. Irrespective of any changes induced by empirical research, changes in the basic values and theory might be occasioned by changes in the social situation with which the Party is faced. Such movements are sanctioned by the Marxist emphasis on the necessity of theory to change with history. They would also be mediated by existing Soviet sociological concepts, thus avoiding any crude empiricist assumptions of sociological concepts mirroring social change, such as we have encountered above.

Fourthly, emphasis on Soviet values' legitimate role in acting as a criterion of choice of Soviet sociological theory does not prevent us from holding that Soviet sociology may also be biased in the negative sense noted in section 4.2 point (e). Perhaps Soviet sociology cannot study certain areas, discuss and use certain concepts, or publish certain results for reasons to do with the bare facts of the nature and locus of power in the Soviet Union, not because they fall outside the theoretical framework of Soviet historical materialism. Furthermore, appeal to political authority should not settle the disputes that are possible within the Soviet sociological paradigm. *Prima facie*, the fact, if it is such, that Soviet sociology cannot study the main economic and political organisations, the system of economic management, the unions, and the party and governmental apparatuses, is an example of pernicious bias. For there is nothing in Soviet theory which allows these institutions to be conceptualised as non-existent (as are antagonistic classes, for example) or unimportant. I will return to the issue of what Soviet sociology cannot talk about.

Finally, most Soviet theorists would accept that there is an exclusive Soviet sociological paradigm and that it is thoroughly imbued with Soviet values. Thus Ilichev, head of the Party's Ideological Commission, said in 1962:

Some of our opponents in the West try to present as a shortcoming what is an enormous merit of Marxist–Leninist science – its unity and monolithic nature. . . It seems not to occur to the bourgeois critics that the merits of sociology, and for that matter of any other science, lie not at all in diversity of points of view. Depth and correctness in reflecting objective reality, foresight as to the ways and laws of its development, and richness in practical results – these are the integral qualities of true science (quoted in Fischer, 1967b, pp. 278–9).

Whereas my account of this homogeneity – insofar as it can be understood rationally – depends on a philosophical analysis of the role of values in filling the lacunae left in criteria of theoretical choice by the underdetermination of theory by reality, it could be adequately explained in Soviet terms by means of the base–superstructure model. For sociology is still considered part of the superstructure, and it is therefore to be expected that a socialist sociology will be homogeneous and radically different from that to be found in capitalist societies.

So, what have been the central problems studied by theoretical and empirical sociology in the Soviet Union? We can derive various answers from different commentators:

(1): (Osipov and Yochuk, 1967, pp. 304–5): 1. Studies of the work situation, such as the problems of automation, in general analysing the 'processes of transforming work into the primary life requirement and the development of social consciousness'. 2. Studies of Soviet personality, including problems to do with education and morality, directed towards the formation of a new kind of communist person. 3. Problems to do with the alteration of the social structure in the process of building communism, including the eradication of the remaining social differences in Soviet society. 4. Problems to do with family life in Soviet society, including the nature of family life in relation to living space and to material and social conditions, and the usage of leisure time and the role of women. 5. 'The transfer of Socialist State functions to public self-governing organisations'.

(2): (Fischer, 1967c, p. 340): Fischer states that items 3 and 5 on the list attributed to Osipov and Yochuk fall under what would be termed 'political sociology' in the West. He denies that any significant work is being produced by Soviet social scientists on political sociology. Fischer allows that the other three items are being tackled by Soviet social science, with sociology concentrating on the sociology of work.

(3): (Hollander, 1967, pp. 314–22): Hollander mentions studies on the usage of leisure time, workers and their attitudes, and marriage and the family, which would fall within, respectively, items 1, 2 and 4 of Osipov and Yochuk's list. He also discusses public opinion poll studies in the Soviet Union. Like Fischer, he omits items 3 and 5.

(4): (Lane, 1971, pp. 87–99 and 107–20): Lane uses detailed Soviet studies of ethnic and sexual discrimination, of social mobility, of the causes of children's job and educational aspirations and their actual attainments, and of the sources of parental aspirations for their children.

(5): (Weinberg, ch. 5): 1. Time budget research, concentrating on how people spend their non-working time and how misuse of time can be avoided. 2. Research on the nature and structure of work. 3. Studies of social structure and stratification, increasingly concentrating on intra-class differences (between, for example, skilled and unskilled workers, manual and intellectual labour). 4. Problems to do with marriage, the family, daily life, divorce and the role of women. 5. Studies of urban development, city planning and urban-rural relations. 6. Criminology and the study of juvenile delinquency. 7. The sociology of religion.

We can also look for some of the problem areas that Soviet sociology has not confronted. There is general agreement that Soviet sociology has not worked on political sociology, that is, on the power and structure of political organisations and on political processes, except perhaps at the local level. Additionally, Western commentators mention the following gaps in research:

(1): (Feuer, 1967, pp. 272–4): 1. Generational conflict. 2. Anti-semitism. 3. Problems associated with the cult of personality.
(2): (Hollander, 1967, p. 324): 4. The rehabilitation of Stalinism's victims. 5. Problems of old age. 6. Problems of political participation. 7. The causes of capitalistic 'survivals'.
(3): (Lane, 1971, pp. 79ff. and 101–6): Lane says that there has been no Soviet research on: 'subjective' stratificational distinctions – e.g., whether material inequalities correlate with deference between groups; individuals' perceptions of their own class position, and of the character and number of social classes; correlations between spouses' occupational statuses; and differential group attitudes to wage inequalities.

These two lists are no doubt incomplete and different commentators would transfer items from one list to the other. Yet they show how historical materialism structures the permissible problem areas, and concepts and statements within those areas, for Soviet sociology. Similarly, they provide at least some understanding of the two areas of the unsayable in Soviet sociology: that which is unsayable because it cannot be conceptualised in historical materialist terms and that which is unsayable because of the intrusion of negative political bias.

It appears that Soviet sociology focuses on problems of work and of consciousness. Within the framework of historical materialism, concentration on the theory of work stems from the basic place that labour has in Marxist ontology. Even the many Soviet studies of leisure tend to be aimed at promoting the collectivism and efficiency of work. Moreover, it is industrial labour, the work of the urban proletariat, that is central to historical materialism. This stress on the concept of industrial labour explains Soviet sociology's pervasive concern with industrialisation – with, for example, the eradication of differences between town and country – irrespective of any immediate practical needs that this focus serves for the Party. Soviet sociology of work is also structured by another distinctive Soviet historical materialist problem. For work is seen as a basic medium for re-socialising the Soviet people; it is the decisive front on which the new Soviet person is to be created, by, for example, the development of collectivist work processes. As Weinberg puts it:

Sotsiologiia v SSSR has stated that the basic task of sociological research on labour consists in establishing what influence the present production activities of different people have on the formation of socialist and communist relations (e.g., the new society) and on the development of the individual (e.g., the 'new man') (1974, p. 60).

The various Soviet sociological studies of consciousness (of morality, religion, education, law etc.) are also set firmly in the context of Soviet historical materialism, in its belief in ideological survivals and in the active power of the superstructure. They too are conceived in terms of the Soviet project of creating the Soviet person. The roots of the theory of ideological survivals in historical materialist categories are particularly clear. Certain beliefs and patterns of thought, which according to Soviet theory should have disappeared with the passing of capitalist property relations, are explained as 'survivals'. This approach can have more content than at first appears, as when Aptekman (1967) studies the correlations between workers' religious beliefs and the degree of collectivisation in work organisation. Similarly, the existence of crime is studied and explained in terms of the backwardness of consciousness as compared with the objective conditions of socialist society.

Yet there remain a whole series of issues thrown up by Western sociological theories which cannot be conceptualised in historical materialist terms. For example, Soviet sociology cannot pose the issue of whether Soviet society is totalitarian, in a sense which would classify fascist and socialist societies together in opposition to representative democracies, because the Party is defined as the organised expression of the proletariat, that is, the mass of the people. Likewise, Soviet sociology cannot take seriously theories of a common 'industrial society' towards which the Soviet Union and advanced Western countries are converging, because it holds the nature of property relations to be the most important social variable. And Soviet sociology cannot formulate many of the problems that interest a Western student of class who turns to the Soviet Union, for it is axiomatic to Soviet sociology that there are no antagonistic classes, given that, with the partial exception of the peasantry, all strata have identical relations to the means of production. Even the research into intra-class differences, which Weinberg mentions, is carried out within the historical materialist framework. As the Soviet sociologist Shkaratan posed the issue in 1970:

during the transitional period from capitalism to socialism, and during subsequent development, the working class (while unified by a common relationship to the means of production, by a leading role in the societal organisation of labour, and by common sources of the basic means of existence) is still internally differentiated in many ways (quoted in Weinberg, 1974, p. 70).

I am not suggesting that the only role of values in Soviet sociology is to act as an extra criterion of theory choice in a way which chapter four held to be necessary for all social science. There are three general ways in which Soviet sociology might be biased in a negative sense. First, results which could be formulated in historical materialist terms might be suppressed if they were politically embarrassing. Thus, widespread sexual or ethnic discrimination might be discovered, or it might be found that the most common value orientation of young Soviet workers is their family or making money. Secondly, the very study of certain areas might be banned, despite their centrality to historical materialism. This would seem to explain the neglect of political sociology. Thirdly, political authority might pronounce on the areas for legitimate disagreement which exist in Soviet sociology, not least because Soviet sociology, in common with all social science, contains the concept of negation, so that if it can state p, it can also state not-p. For example, the debate in Soviet urban sociology about whether urban–rural differences should be eliminated by building many middle-sized towns or a few large cities, might be settled in this way. An interesting question, which shows the difficulty of applying philosophical categories to concrete cases, is whether the neglect of the cult of personality is to be explained because this issue cannot be coherently stated in historical materialist terms or because of irrational external political pressure. On the one hand, it runs contrary to historical materialist tenets to explain the features of an epoch in terms of an individual's personality; on the other hand, the Party leadership itself after all originated the term.

Detailed analytical study would also be needed to decide how we are to conceptualise pre-1956 theoretical work in terms of value intrusion, given that there is a strict analogue to the negative role of values in social science, in theoretical and purely philosophical disciplines. Was Stalinist historical materialism ideological in a negative sense or merely unempirical? If, as seems likely, the former is correct, to what extent was it ideological in a negative sense? None of these issues can be answered *a priori* or by intuition. Similarly, we cannot predict to what extent Soviet sociology will become more negatively ideological in the future.

Nor do I rule out the possibility that there are areas of concern common to Soviet and Western sociological theories. Many Soviet

193

sociological studies find their parallel in the West. For example, the sociology of work looks at labour efficiency, and the sociology of the family investigates the causes of divorce, the birth rate and housing needs. Many techniques in practical methodology, such as statistical analysis and game theory, are also shared. A full account is needed of how these apparently similar interests fit into radically different theoretical frameworks. Thus, Soviet work on the sociology of the family which I have just mentioned studies the 'development of and differences between the family under capitalism, socialism and communism' and 'the liquidation of conflict within the family so that the family might successfully carry out its role in educating the "new man" ' (Weinberg, 1974, pp. 71–2). But we still cannot exclude *a priori* a partial overlap between Soviet and Western sociology. We must just note the impotence of philosophy of science to give an account of this overlap without retreating to an unacceptable empiricism.

If Soviet sociology operates with an exclusive paradigm, then, on a Kuhnian view, we should be able to point to its strengths. For an exclusive paradigm sustains a period of normal scientific research, during which the bases of the paradigm are articulated and developed, and the paradigm's main problems are studied in great depth. When we examine Soviet sociology's fundamental problem areas, we notice the centrality of issues such as, in the sociology of work, the possibilities of and difficulties in breaking down both the division of labour (especially that between manual and intellectual labour) and the town–country division; in its studies of consciousness, the relations between ideas and modes of production, and the means of directing social relations and even human personality by a self-conscious ideological programme. These issues are barely touched by Western sociology. Moreover, there is no reason why they should not be studied empirically within the Soviet paradigm, as indeed most already have been. That is, there is no reason why Soviet sociology should not evolve relatively empirical generalisations, explanations and predictions, which might in turn reflect back critically on the more fundamental statements of the Soviet sociological system.

Similarly, as Gellner argues, Soviet anthropology's historical materialist and evolutionist foundations have yielded a useful typology of societies, in contrast to functionalism:

As it contains five or more types, and as the individual types within it are more specific and have a greater theoretical content, on average, than the all-purpose single type used by functionalism, it might even be said that Marxism is richer, more scientific, more exposed to risk, more suggestive of new problems and discoveries, than functionalism (1974b, p. 1166).

194

Moreover, so Gellner claims, the empirical problems encountered in applying the typology to various non-Western societies have led to refinement of the typology itself.

Yet we would not want the Soviet sociological paradigm to be the only sociological theory. As I have noted, there are a series of theoretical issues and approaches, even with respect to Soviet society itself, which cannot be formulated by Soviet sociology. The fact that more extensive theoretical and empirical content would be yielded by a diversity of sociological paradigms suggests that Kuhn's methodology of exclusive paradigms is not applicable to social science. But this point goes beyond the dangers of empirical narrowness. Soviet sociology is based on and reinforces a distinctive set of values. Were it the only sociology we possessed, we would be poorer not just in theoretical and empirical understanding, but also in the possibilities of moral thought and action.

Conclusion

I have argued that social study can model itself on natural science, if natural science is understood along post-empiricist lines. The naturalistic social science which emerges from post-empiricism pursues generalisations, explanations and predictions, adopting a non-hermeneutic approach to meaning, within the framework of a number of theories based on different moral and political stances. I have remained agnostic on several crucial issues. I have not speculated about which direction social study might or ought to take in the future. Nothing I have said gives me any basis for guessing which substantive social scientific theories will flourish. Nor have I tried to prove the impossibility of a non-naturalistic approach to social study. Much work remains to be done on non-naturalistic methodology. Where non-naturalism models itself on textual analysis, we need combinations of competences that are rare in Anglo-American philosophy – most obviously, in epistemology and the theory of literary criticism. It is a sad fact that the philosophy of social science seems to invite garrulous and vacuous contributions on subjects which are not yet well understood; it is an exciting fact that there is so much left to investigate in this area.

I have also avoided evaluating the post-empiricist philosophy of science on which my book hinges. This topic is essentially beyond the bounds of my work and it would be mere dilettantism to attempt it in a few pages. However, I should indicate that – while I believe post-empiricism to be an important advance on empiricism – we have continuously encountered a fundamental problem in post-empiricism. This problem has a host of names, including that of truth, relativism, falsification, commensurability and cross-theoretical comparison.

Whatever we call it, the problem is this. Post-empiricism holds that the meaning of a term – and, therefore, to an extent the truth-status of statements in which the term appears – is in part determined by its relationship with other terms in its home theory. This mutual dependence of theoretical items is suggested by calling a theory 'holistic'.

196

But, then, it becomes difficult to understand how there can be cross-theoretical debate. For it looks as though we are committed to at least one of two different types of relativisms, which for convenience I will call 'meaning' and 'truth' relativism. If we pursued the discussion to a deeper philosophical level, where we analysed the relationship of meaning and truth, we might have to conclude that there is only one type of relativism. But the analytical delineation of two types of relativism is a useful starting point.

Meaning relativism holds that the meanings of items in different theories differ, even if those items are physically identical, because the meanings of terms and statements are given by internal relations within a theory. There is, therefore, no sense in which purportedly rival theories are in conflict with one another. In particular, two different theories, T_1 and T_2, cannot contain statements which are genuinely in contradiction with one another. T_1 cannot state that p and T_2 that not-p, where p is understood identically by both; though, of course, T_1 can contain the physical item 'p' and T_2 the physical item 'not-p'. When the Marxist says that the state is the executive committee of the bourgeoisie and the liberal appears to deny this, they do not really mean the same thing. Hence, there is no way of choosing between different theories.

A brisk counter to meaning relativism is to deny that there is a genuine problem here, certainly not a problem of truth or relativism. For if different theories are about different things, if they are incommensurable rather than incompatible, then we are free to hold all theories without bothering with questions of cross-theoretical choice. The non-relativist can further assert against meaning relativism that we *know* that different theories of childhood, class, inflation, the family, the state, etc. are about the same thing. If this assertion is true, as I am sure it is, then meaning relativism must be false.

But the relativist need not be unduly bothered by this line of argument. For he can accept the implication thrown at him in the attempt at a *reductio* of his position: science as the collection of a host of theories about different things, between which there is no possibility of debate and all of which we are therefore free to hold, conforms with the spirit of the relativist's case, not that of his opponent. Moreover, he can ask for justification of the bare assertion of knowledge that different theories can be about the same thing; after all, we reached meaning relativism from premises shared by a non-relativist who rejects empiricism. The problem for the non-relativist working with a post-empiricist philosophy of science becomes, then, to give an account of his knowledge.

Truth relativism holds that even if we can show that statements in different theories can mean the same thing, there is no way of deciding between T_1 and T_2, if T_1 states that p and T_2 that not-p. For it is always possible to adjust the other statements in the theories, so that T_1 can defend p, and T_2 not-p, even in the light of observational evidence.

Under both types of relativism, truth becomes warranted assertability *within* a theory. P is true within a theory if it meshes with the other statements in the theory and with observation of the world through that theory's conceptual apparatus. It is a mistake to think that all kinds of relativism threaten all notions of truth. The relativism which post-empiricism tends to sustain threatens cross-theoretical truth. A reasonably strong and empirical notion of intra-theoretical truth is easily stated by post-empiricism, as I argued in 4.6.b.

Even though social science has generally been characterised by intra-theoretical debate and development, we cannot rest content with an intra-theoretical conception of meaning and truth. A Feyeraben-dian licence to hold any theory we want precludes the possibility of rational debate between theories. But we *know* that there has been rational debate between theories. Any serious attempt to convince us otherwise ought to be rejected with as much scorn as any serious attempt to convince us that we do not know other people, material objects and time to be real. At many points in my book, I have certainly assumed that different theories can be about the same thing and can conflict with one another. I assumed that Orwell and Young and Willmott are talking about the same slum-dwellers' discontent, that Western and Soviet theories are about the same Soviet reality, that religious and social scientific accounts of religion can conflict, and that there are different views of human nature. More generally, I criticised ethnomethodology for its relativism, I held that actors' and social scientists' theories can conflict, and I assumed that a science is defined by its subject matter, so there can be several paradigms of the same subject matter.

The empiricist account of cross-theoretical debate involves an observation language, with terms and statements in an isolatedly immediate relationship with the extra-linguistic world, as a common basis for choice between theories. Two theories can make different statements about the same thing because empirical theories contain implications about the world which can be stated in the common observation language. It is possible for T_1 to state that p and T_2 that not-p, where p is a statement in the observation language. Choice between T_1 and T_2 is, then, rationally influenced by finding out whether or not p corresponds with the world.

The post-empiricist point that there are no absolute observation statements, not least because all terms and statements are theory-laden, precludes the empiricist approach to relativism. But post-empiricist attempts to give an account of cross-theoretical debate have so far been unsuccessful. As I noted in 3.4.c, to demand that there should be shared senses across theories is almost trivially too strict. Yet to hold that different theories may share reference or item-identification is not useful unless they also share a common scheme of senses (i.e. a translation manual) which will allow the one theory to talk about the world to others. In some cases, two theories might employ transparently intertranslatable frameworks, perhaps through containing common sub-sets of statements. However, this typically does not occur with social scientific theories which we want to consider rivals in at least part of what they claim (e.g. behaviourist and Freudian psychology, Marxist and functionalist sociology).

The most promising post-empiricist approaches to relativism have, in fact, required retreats towards empiricism. For example, some writers[1] are trying to give an account of theoretical levels which, though not absolutely pre-theoretical, may at least be common to different theories. There may be a continuum of levels, with some terms being common to most theories at a certain point of time, some terms being common to a few theories, some being common to only two theories, and some being entirely theory-specific. Two theories can say conflicting things about the same thing, therefore, if they share linguistic elements which are common to them. The task of delineating these different levels seems very difficult, however. It is implausible that statements which two theories might wish to dispute could contain no terms carrying implications specific to one of the theories. In any case, the relevance of these considerations for social science is suspect. For, if there are such shared terms, they are presumably terms which were candidates for empiricism's observation language: 'red', 'table', 'six', etc. The prospect of deriving statements composed entirely of these terms from social scientific statements is remote; as unrealistic as empiricism's project of translating all language into sensory or material object terminology.

Post-empiricism may have to evolve a new understanding of truth if it is to conceptualise cross-theoretical debate in its own terms. The classical correspondence notion of truth holds that statements are true in virtue of a correspondence with the world which is independent of language. This notion underpinned empiricism, but is clearly unsuitable for post-empiricism's contextual account of linguistic meaning. Yet coherence theories of truth have typically been unable to state the empirical possibilities of language; in particular, they cannot show

---

[1] See e.g. Williams (1977).

how a statement can be rejected in virtue of its clash with the world. Ideally, post-empiricism needs a combined correspondence and coherence account of truth, whereby theories as a whole stand or fall in virtue of a correspondence or lack of it with the world. This view would also commit us to a thoroughgoing epistemological and ontological realism: there would be no distinction between items of a theory in terms of their status *vis-à-vis* the world.

At present, however, there is no sign of a plausible post-empiricist concept of truth. We are left with science's commitments to the reality of the external world, the fact that science informs us about the world and the possibility of cross-theoretical debate. These commitments can reasonably be included in what I have called the defining methodology of science. We can be certain that if post-empiricism ultimately fails to give an account of these commitments, it will come to appear as unsatisfactory a philosophy of science as empiricism seems now.

References

〜〜〜

Abel, T. (1968). 'The Operation Called *Verstehen'*, in E. H. Madden (ed.), *The Structure of Scientific Thought*, London.

Achinstein, P. (1968). *Concepts of Science*, Baltimore.

Adorno, T. W. (1967). *Prisms*, London.

Agassi, J. (1964). 'The Nature of Scientific Problems and Their Roots in Metaphysics', in M. Bunge (ed.), *The Critical Approach to Science and Philosophy*, London.

Ainsworth, M. D. S. (1971). 'Further Research into the Adverse Effects of Maternal Deprivation', in Bowlby (1971).

Albert, H. (1964). 'Social Science and Moral Philosophy', in M. Bunge (ed.), *The Critical Approach to Science and Philosophy*, London.

Almond, G. A. (1966). 'Political Theory and Political Science', *American Political Science Review*, 60.

Alston, W. P. (1964). *Philosophy of Language,* Englewood Cliffs.

Althusser, L. (1969). *For Marx*, Harmondsworth.

Althusser, L. (1971). *Lenin and Philosophy*, London.

Althusser, L. (1975). Parts I and II of Althusser and E. Balibar, *Reading Capital*, London.

Apel, K. O. (1967). *Analytical Philosophy of Language and the Geisteswissenschaften*, Dordrecht.

Aptekman, D. M. (1967). 'The Vitality of the Baptismal Ceremony under Modern Soviet Conditions', in A. Simirenko (ed.), *Soviet Sociology*, London.

Ardener, E. (1971). Introduction to Ardener (ed.), *Social Anthropology and Language*, London.

Austin, J. L. (1962). *How To Do Things with Words*, Oxford.

Ayer, A. J. (1967). 'Man as a Subject for Science', in P. Laslett and W. R. Runciman, (eds.), *Philosophy, Politics and Society*, third series, Oxford.

Barber, W. J. (1970). *A History of Economic Thought*, Harmondsworth.

Barbour, I. G. (1968). (ed.), *Science and Religion: New Perspectives on the Dialogue*, New York.

Bernstein, R. J. (1976). *The Restructuring of Social and Political Theory*, Oxford.

Bottomore, T. (1956). 'Some Reflections on the Sociology of Knowledge', *British Journal of Sociology*, 7.

Bottomore, T. (1969). *Critics of Society*, London.

References

Bottomore, T. (1975). *Marxist Sociology*, London.

Bowlby, J. (1971). *Child Care and the Growth of Love*, Harmondsworth.

Briskman, L. B. (1972). 'Is a Kuhnian Analysis Applicable to Psychology?', *Science Studies*, 2.

Brodbeck, M. (1971a). 'Explanation, Prediction and "Imperfect" Knowledge', in Brodbeck (ed.), *Readings in the Philosophy of the Social Sciences*, London.

Brodbeck, M. (1971b). 'Meaning and Action', in Brodbeck (ed.), *Readings in the Philosophy of the Social Sciences*, London.

Brodersen, A. (1967). 'Soviet Social Science and Our Own', in A. Simirenko (ed.), *Soviet Sociology*, London.

Bronbenbrenner, M. (1971). 'The "Structure of Revolutions" in Economic Thought', *History of Political Economy*, 3.

Brown, A. H. (1974). *Soviet Politics and Political Science*, London.

Brown, R. (1968). *Explanation in Social Science*, London.

Burtt, E. A. (1925). *The Metaphysical Foundations of Modern Physical Science*, London.

Butterfield, H. (1949). *The Origins of Modern Science*, London.

Butterfield, H. (1951). *History and Human Relations*, London.

Clemmer, R. O. (1972). 'Resistance and the Revitalisation of Anthropologists: A New Perspective on Cultural Change', in D. Hymes (ed.), *Reinventing Anthropology*, New York.

Coats, A. W. (1969). 'Is There a "Structure of Scientific Revolutions" in Economics?', *Kyklos*, 22.

Collingwood, R. G. (1969). *An Essay on Metaphysics*, Oxford.

Collingwood, R. G. (1970). *An Autobiography*, Oxford.

Cox, W. H. (1976). *Cities*, Harmondsworth.

Cunningham, G. (1973). *Objectivity in Social Science*, Toronto.

Dagenais, J. J. (1972). *Models of Man*, The Hague.

Dahl, R. (1965). *Modern Political Analysis*, Englewood Cliffs.

Dahrendorf, R. (1968). *Essays in the Theory of Society*, London.

Davidson, D. (1963). 'Actions, Reasons and Causes', *Journal of Philosophy*, 60.

Douglas, J. D. (1971). 'Understanding Everyday Life', in Douglas (ed.), *Understanding Everyday Life*, London.

Douglas, M. (1970). Introduction to Douglas (ed.), *Witchcraft Confessions and Accusations*, London.

Duhem, P. (1954). *The Aim and Structure of Physical Theory*, Princeton.

Dunn, J. (1978). 'Practising History and Social Science on "Realist" Assumptions', in C. Hookway and P. Pettit (eds.), *Action and Interpretation*, Cambridge.

Durkheim, E. (1952). *Suicide*, London.

Durkheim, E. (1964). *The Rules of Sociological Method*, London.

Durkheim, E. (1971). *The Elementary Forms of the Religious Life*, London.

Durkheim, E. and M. Mauss (1963). *Primitive Classification*, London.

Earle, W. (1952–3). 'The Standard Observer in the Sciences of Man', *Ethics*, 63.

Easthope, G. (1974). *History of Social Research Methods*, London.

Easton, D. (1971). *The Political System*, New York.

Edel, A. (1961). *Science and the Structure of Ethics*, Chicago.

References

Edel, A. (1964). 'Social Science and Value', in I. L. Horowitz (ed.), *The New Sociology*, New York.

Engels, F. (1873). Letter dated 20th June to A. Bebel in Marx and Engels (1973).

Engels, F. (1882). 'Bruno Bauer and Early Christianity' in Marx and Engels (1972).

Engels, F. (1884). Preface to the first German edition of Marx (1973b).

Engels, F. (1885). 'On the History of the Communist League' in Marx and Engels (1973).

Engels, F. (1887). 'Juristic Socialism' in Marx and Engels (1972).

Engels, F. (1890). Letter dated 27th October to C. Schmidt in Marx and Engels (1973).

Engels, F. (1891). Introduction to Marx 'The Civil War in France' in Marx and Engels (1973).

Engels, F. (1975). *Anti-Dühring*, Moscow.

Evans-Pritchard, E. E. (1965). *Witchcraft, Oracles and Magic Among the Azande*, Oxford.

Evans-Pritchard, E. E. (1967a). *Nuer Religion*, Oxford.

Evans-Pritchard, E. E. (1967b). *Theories of Primitive Religion*, Oxford.

Evans-Pritchard, E. E. (1972). *Social Anthropology*, London.

Feuer, L. S. (1967). 'Meeting the Soviet Philosophers', in A. Simirenko (ed.), *Soviet Sociology*, London.

Feyerabend, P. K. (1975). *Against Method*, London.

Fiori, G. (1970). *Antonio Gramsci*, London.

Firth, R. (1959). 'Problem and Assumption in the Anthropological Study of Religion', *Journal of the Royal Anthropological Institute*, 89.

Fischer, G. (1967a). 'Sociology', in Fischer (ed.), *Science and Ideology in Soviet Society*, New York.

Fischer, G. (1967b). 'The New Sociology in the Soviet Union', in A. Simirenko (ed.), *Soviet Sociology*, London.

Fischer, G. (1967c). 'Empirical Research of Soviet Sociologists', in A. Simirenko (ed.), *Soviet Sociology*, London.

Floud, J. J. (1969). 'Karl Mannheim', in T. Raison (ed.), *The Founding Fathers of Social Science*, Harmondsworth.

Fortes, M. (1959). *Oedipus and Job in West African Religion*, Cambridge.

Foucault, M. (1970). *The Order of Things*, London.

Foucault, M. (1971). *Madness and Civilisation*, London.

Foucault, M. (1974). *The Archaeology of Knowledge*, London.

Freud, S. (1949). *New Introductory Lectures on Psychoanalysis*, London.

Gallie, W. B. (1955–6). 'Essentially Contested Concepts', *Proceedings of the Aristotelian Society*, 56.

Garfinkel, H. (1967). *Studies in Ethnomethodology*, Englewood Cliffs.

Geertz, C. (1964). 'Ideology as a Cultural System', in D. Apter (ed.), *Ideology and Discontent*, New York.

Gellner, E. (1974a). *Legitimation of Belief*, Cambridge.

Gellner, E. (1974b). 'The Soviet and the Savage', *Times Literary Supplement*, 18th October.

de George, R. T. (1966). *Patterns of Soviet Thought*, Michigan.

de George, R. T. (1967). 'Philosophy', in G. Fischer (ed.), *Science and Ideology in Soviet Society*, New York.

Giddens, A. (1976). *New Rules of Sociological Method*, London.

Goffman, E. (1973). *Asylums*, Harmondsworth.

Goldmann, L. (1973). *The Human Sciences and Philosophy*, London.

Goodman, N. (1970). 'Seven Strictures on Similarity', in L. Foster and J. W. Swanson (eds.), *Experience and Theory*, London.

Gouldner, A. W. (1972). *The Coming Crisis of Western Sociology*, London.

Graham, L. R. (1967). 'Cybernetics', in G. Fischer (ed.), *Science and Ideology in Soviet Society*, New York.

Graham, L. R. (1971). *Science and Philosophy in the Soviet Union*, London.

Grave, S. A. (1967). 'Common Sense', in P. Edwards (ed.), *The Encyclopaedia of Philosophy*, vol. 2, London.

Grice, H. P. (1967). 'Meaning', in P. F. Strawson (ed.), *Philosophical Logic*, Oxford.

Gunther, M. and K. Reshaur (1971). 'Science and Values in Political "Science" ', *Philosophy of the Social Sciences*, 1.

Habermas, J. (1972). *Knowledge and Human Interests*, London.

Haggett, P. and R. J. Chorley (1970). 'Models, Paradigms and the New Geography', in Chorley and Haggett (eds.), *Socio-Economic Models in Geography*, London.

Hale, K. (1972). 'Some Questions about Anthropological Linguistics: The Role of Native Knowledge', in D. Hymes (ed.), *Reinventing Anthropology*, New York.

Harré, R. and P. F. Secord (1972). *The Explanation of Social Behaviour*, Oxford.

Harrod, R. (1971). *Sociology, Morals and Mystery*, London.

Hawthorn, G. (1976). *Enlightenment and Despair*, Cambridge.

Hempel, C. G. (1959). 'The Function of General Laws in History', in P. Gardiner (ed.), *Theories of History*, New York.

Hempel, C. G. (1971). 'The Logic of Functional Analysis', in M. Brodbeck (ed.), *Readings in the Philosophy of the Social Sciences*, London.

Hesse, M. B. (1970). *Models and Analogies in Science*, Notre Dame.

Hesse, M. B. (1972). 'In Defence of Objectivity', *Proceedings of the British Academy*.

Hesse, M. B. (1974). *The Structure of Scientific Inference*, London.

Hesse, M. B. (1978). 'Theory and Value in the Social Sciences', in C. Hookway and P. Pettit (eds.), *Action and Interpretation*, Cambridge.

Hick, J. (1964). (ed.), *Faith and the Philosophers*, London.

Hollander, P. (1967). 'The Dilemmas of Soviet Sociology', in A. Simirenko (ed.), *Soviet Sociology*, London.

Hollis, M. (1970). 'The Limits of Irrationality', in B. R. Wilson (ed.), *Rationality*, Oxford.

Hollis, M. (1975). 'My Role and Its Duties', in R. S. Peters (ed.), *Nature and Conduct*, London.

Hollis, M. (1977). *Models of Man*, Cambridge.

Holloway, D. (1974). 'Innovation in Science – the Case of Cybernetics in the Soviet Union', *Science Studies*, 4.

References

Holm, J. (1977). *The Study of Religions*, London.

Homans, G. C. (1964). 'Bringing Men Back In', *American Sociological Review*, 29.

Homans, G. C. (1967). *The Nature of Social Science*, New York.

Hook, S. (1962). (ed.), *Religious Experience and Truth*, London.

Hookway, C. (1978). 'Indeterminacy and Interpretation', in C. Hookway and P. Pettit (eds.), *Action and Interpretation*, Cambridge.

Hudson, W. D. (1968). *Ludwig Wittgenstein: The Bearing of his Philosophy upon Religious Belief*, London.

Hymes, D. (1972). 'The Use of Anthropology', in Hymes (ed.), *Reinventing Anthropology*, New York.

Jarvie, I. C. (1972). *Concepts and Society*, London.

Jarvie, I. C. and J. Agassi (1970). 'The Problem of the Rationality of Magic', in B. R. Wilson (ed.), *Rationality*, Oxford.

Judy, R. W. (1973). 'The Economists', in H. G. Skilling and F. Griffiths (eds.), *Interest Groups in Soviet Politics*, Princeton.

Kamenka, E. (1972). *The Ethical Foundations of Marxism*, London.

Keat, R. and J. Urry (1975). *Social Theory as Science*, London.

Kolakowski, L. (1971). *Marxism and Beyond*, London.

Kolakowski, L. (1972). *Positivist Philosophy*, Harmondsworth.

Körner, S. (1970). *Categorial Frameworks*, Oxford.

Kuhn, T. S. (1963a). 'The Essential Tension: Tradition and Innovation in Scientific Research', in C. W. Taylor and F. Barron (eds.), *Scientific Creativity*, New York.

Kuhn, T. S. (1963b). 'Scientific Paradigms', in S. B. Barnes (ed.), *Sociology of Science*, Harmondsworth.

Kuhn, T. S. (1968). 'Science: The History of Science', in D. L. Sills (ed.), *International Encyclopedia of the Social Sciences*, vol. 14.

Kuhn, T. S. (1969). 'The New Reality in Art and Science', *Comparative Studies in Society and History*, 14.

Kuhn, T. S. (1970). *The Structure of Scientific Revolutions*, London.

Kuhn, T. S. (1971). 'Notes on Lakatos', in R. C. Buck and R. S. Cohen (eds.), *Boston Studies in the Philosophy of Science*, vol. 8, Dordrecht.

Kuhn, T. S. (1972a). 'Logic of Discovery or Psychology of Research?', in I. Lakatos and A. Musgrave (eds.), *Criticism and the Growth of Knowledge*, Cambridge.

Kuhn, T. S. (1972b). 'Reflections on my Critics', in I. Lakatos and A. Musgrave (eds.), *Criticism and the Growth of Knowledge*, Cambridge.

Labedz, L. (1958). 'The Soviet Attitude to Sociology', in W. Z. Laqueur and G. Lichtheim (eds.), *The Soviet Cultural Scene*, London.

Labedz, L. (1967). 'Sociology as a Vocation', in A. Simirenko (ed.), *Soviet Sociology*, London.

Lakatos, I. (1972). 'Falsification and the Methodology of Scientific Research Programmes', in Lakatos and A. Musgrave (eds.), *Criticism and the Growth of Knowledge*, Cambridge.

Lane, D. (1970). 'Ideology and Sociology in the U.S.S.R.', *British Journal of Sociology*, 21.

References

Lane, D. (1971). *The End of Inequality?: Stratification under State Socialism*, Harmondsworth.

Laserson, M. M. (1971). 'Russian Sociology', in G. Gurvitch and W. E. Moore (eds.), *Twentieth Century Sociology*, New York.

Leach, E. R. (1976). *Culture and Communication*, Cambridge.

Lecourt, D. (1975). *Marxism and Epistemology*, London.

Lessnoff, M. H. (1974). *The Structure of Social Science*, London.

Lévi-Strauss, C. (1974). *The Scope of Anthropology*, London.

Lewis, J. (1975). *Max Weber and Value-free Sociology*, London.

Lipsey, R. G. (1974). *An Introduction to Positive Economics*, London.

Louch, A. R. (1972). *Explanation and Action*, London.

Lukács, G. (1971). *History and Class Consciousness*, London.

Lukes, S. (1972). 'Methodological Individualism Reconsidered' in D. Emmet and A. MacIntyre (eds.), *Sociological Theory and Philosophical Analysis*, London.

Lukes, S. (1973). *Emile Durkheim*, London.

Lukes, S. (1974). *Power*, London.

Luxemburg, R. (no date). *The Mass Strike, the Political Party and the Trade Unions*, London.

MacCallum, G. (1972). 'Negative and Positive Freedom', in P. Laslett, W. G. Runciman and Q. Skinner (eds.), *Philosophy, Politics and Society*, 4th series, Oxford.

MacIntyre, A. (1969). *Marxism and Christianity*, London.

MacIntyre, A. (1970). 'The Idea of a Social Science', in B. R. Wilson (ed.), *Rationality*, Oxford.

MacIntyre, A. (1972). 'Is a Science of Comparative Politics Possible?', in P. Laslett, W. G. Runciman and Q. Skinner (eds.), *Philosophy, Politics and Society*, 4th series, Oxford.

MacIntyre, A. (1973). *The Unconscious*, London.

MacKay, D. M. (1960). 'On the Logical Indeterminacy of a Free Choice', *Mind*, 69.

MacKay, D. M. (1971). 'Freedom of Action in a Mechanistic Universe', in M. S. Gazzaniga and E. P. Lovejoy (eds.), *Good Reading in Psychology*, Englewood Cliffs.

McHugh, P. (1971). 'On the Failure of Positivism' in J. D. Douglas (ed.), *Understanding Everyday Life*, London.

Malcolm, N. (1967). *Dreaming*, London.

Malinowski, B. (1926). 'Magic, Science and Religion', in J. Needham (ed.), *Science, Religion and Reality*, London.

Mannheim, K. (1921–2). 'On the Interpretation of *Weltanschauung*' in Mannheim (1968).

Mannheim, K. (1922). 'Structural Analysis of Epistemology' in Mannheim (1953).

Mannheim, K. (1924). 'Historicism' in Mannheim (1968).

Mannheim, K. (1927). 'Conservative Thought' in Mannheim (1953).

Mannheim, K. (1928–9). 'The Problem of Generations' in Mannheim (1968).

References

Mannheim, K. (1932). 'American Sociology' in Mannheim (1953).

Mannheim, K. (1950). *Diagnosis of Our Time*, London.

Mannheim, K. (1953). *Essays on Sociology and Social Psychology*, London.

Mannheim, K. (1956). *Essays on the Sociology of Culture*, London.

Mannheim, K. (1967). *Systematic Sociology*, London.

Mannheim, K. (1968). *Essays on the Sociology of Knowledge*, London.

Mannheim, K. (1972). *Ideology and Utopia*, London.

Mannheim, K. and W. A. C. Stewart (1969). *An Introduction to the Sociology of Education*, London.

Martins, H. (1972). 'The Kuhnian "Revolution" and its Implications for Sociology', in T. Nossiter, A. Hanson and S. Rokkan (eds.), *Imagination and Precision in the Social Sciences*, London.

Marx, K. (1844). 'Introduction to a Contribution to the Critique of Hegel's Philosophy of Right' in Marx and Engels (1972).

Marx, K. (1847). 'Wage Labour and Capital' in Marx and Engels (1973).

Marx, K. (1852). 'The Eighteenth Brumaire of Louis Bonaparte' in Marx and Engels (1973).

Marx, K. (1973a). *Economic and Philosophic Manuscripts of 1844*, London.

Marx, K. (1973b). *The Poverty of Philosophy*, Moscow.

Marx, K. and F. Engels (1848). 'The Communist Manifesto' in Marx and Engels (1973).

Marx, K. and F. Engels (1972). *On Religion*, Moscow.

Marx, K. and F. Engels (1973). *Selected Works*, London.

Marx, K. and F. Engels (1974). *The German Ideology*, London.

Masterman, M. (1972). 'The Nature of a Paradigm', in I. Lakatos and A. Musgrave (eds.), *Criticism and the Growth of Knowledge*, Cambridge.

Melden, A. I. (1961). *Free Action*, London.

Merton, R. K. (1964). *Social Theory and Social Structure*, London.

Mikulak, M. W. (1964). 'Philosophy and Science', *Survey*, 52.

Miliband, R. (1977). *The State in Capitalist Society*, London.

Mill, J. S. (1865). *A System of Logic*, vol. 2, London.

Mitchell, B. (1973). *The Justification of Religious Belief*, London.

Montefiore, A. (1966). 'Fact, Value and Ideology', in B. Williams and Montefiore (eds.), *British Analytical Philosophy*, London.

Morgenbesser, S. (1972). 'Is it a Science?', in D. Emmet and A. MacIntyre (eds.), *Sociological Theory and Philosophical Analysis*, London.

Mulkay, M. J. (1972). *The Social Process of Innovation*, London.

Myrdal, G. (1955). *The Political Element in the Development of Economic Theory*, London.

Myrdal, G. (1970). *Objectivity in Social Research*, London.

Nagel, E. (1961). *The Structure of Science*, London.

Needham, R. (1972). *Belief, Language and Experience*, Oxford.

Neurath, O. (1962). *Foundations of the Social Sciences*, Chicago.

Ollman, B. (1971). *Alienation: Marx's Conception of Man in Capitalist Society*, Cambridge.

Orwell, G. (1975). *The Road to Wigan Pier*, Harmondsworth.

References

Osipov, G. and M. Yochuk (1967). 'Some Principles of Theory, Problems and Methods of Research in Sociology in the USSR: a Soviet View', in A. Simirenko (ed.), *Soviet Sociology*, London.

Outhwaite, W. (1975), *Understanding Social Life*, London.

Palermo, D. S. (1971). 'Is a Scientific Revolution Taking Place in Psychology?', *Science Studies*, 1.

Partridge, P. (1968). 'Politics, Philosophy, Ideology', in A. Quinton (ed.), *Political Philosophy*, London.

Passmore, J. A. (1953). 'Can the Social Sciences be Value-free?', in H. Feigl and M. Brodbeck (eds.), *Readings in the Philosophy of Science*, New York.

Pears, D. F. (1970). (ed.), *The Nature of Metaphysics*, London.

Peters, R. S. (1969). *The Concept of Motivation*, London.

Phillips, D. L. (1973). *Abandoning Method*, San Francisco.

Phillips, D. Z. (1965). *The Concept of Prayer*, London.

Pitkin, H. F. (1972). *Wittgenstein and Justice*, London.

Popper, K. R. (1950). 'Indeterminism in Quantum Physics and in Classical Physics', I and II, *British Journal for the Philosophy of Science*, 1.

Popper, K. R. (1952). *The Open Society and Its Enemies*, vol. 2, London.

Popper, K. R. (1961). *The Poverty of Historicism*, London.

Popper, K. R. (1972). *Conjectures and Refutations*, London.

Powell, D. E. and P. Shoup (1970). 'The Emergence of Political Science in Communist Countries', *American Political Science Review*, 64.

Putnam, H. (1975). *Mind, Language and Reality*, Cambridge.

Quine, W. V. O. (1961). 'Two Dogmas of Empiricism' in his *From a Logical Point of View*, New York.

Quine, W. V. O. (1969). *Word and Object*, Cambridge, Mass.

Quinton, A. (1975). 'Has Man an Essence?', in R. S. Peters (ed.), *Nature and Conduct*, London.

Radcliffe-Brown, A. R. (1965). *Structure and Function in Primitive Society*, London.

Remmling, G. W. (1975). *The Sociology of Karl Mannheim*, London.

Rickmann, H. P. (1967). *Understanding and the Human Studies*, London.

Roberts, G. K. (1972). *What is Comparative Politics?*, London.

Robinson, J. (1968). *Economic Philosophy*, Harmondsworth.

Rudner, R. (1966). *Philosophy of Social Science*, Englewood Cliffs.

Runciman, W. G. (1970). *Sociology in its Place*, Cambridge.

Runciman, W. G. (1972a). *A Critique of Max Weber's Philosophy of Social Science*, Cambridge.

Runciman, W. G. (1972b). 'Describing', *Mind*, 81.

Runciman, W. G. (1973). 'Ideology and Social Science', in R. Benewick, R. N. Berki and B. Parekh (eds.), *Knowledge and Belief in Politics*, London.

Ryan, A. (1970a). *The Philosophy of John Stuart Mill*, London.

Ryan, A. (1970b). *The Philosophy of the Social Sciences*, London.

Ryle, G. (1964). *Dilemmas*, Cambridge.

Schapere, D. (1966). 'Meaning and Scientific Change', in R. G. Colodny (ed.), *Mind and Cosmos*, Pittsburgh.

Scheffler, I. (1967). *Science and Subjectivity*, New York.

References

Scriven, M. (1959). 'Truisms as the Grounds for Historical Explanation', in
P.Gardiner (ed.), *Theories of History*, New York.

Searle, J. R. (1972). *Speech Acts*, Cambridge.

Simirenko, A. (1967a). 'The Concept of Industrial Society Under Criticism by
Soviet Sociologists', in Simirenko (ed.), *Soviet Sociology*, London.

Simirenko, A. (1967b). 'An Outline History of Soviet Sociology with a Focus on
Recent Developments', in Simirenko (ed.), *Soviet Sociology*, London.

Simirenko, A. (1967c). Introduction to Part 5 of Simirenko (ed.), *Soviet Sociology*, London.

Simon, H. A. (1971). 'The Effect of Predictions', in M. Brodbeck (ed.), *Readings
in the Philosophy of the Social Sciences*, London.

Skinner, Q. (1972). ' "Social Meaning" and the Explanation of Social Action',
in P. Laslett, W. G. Runciman and Skinner (eds.), *Philosophy, Politics and
Society*, 4th series, Oxford.

Skinner, Q. (1973). 'The Empirical Theorists of Democracy and their Critics',
Political Theory, 1.

Skorupski, J. (1973). 'Science and Traditional Thought', *Philosophy of the Social
Sciences*, vol. 3, nos 2 and 3.

Spiro, M. E. (1968). 'Religion: Problems of Definition and Explanation', in M.
Banton (ed.), *Anthropological Approaches to the Study of Religion*, London.

Stalin, J. (1950). 'Marxism and Linguistics' in *The Essential Stalin*, London.

Strawson, P. F. (1968). 'Freedom and Resentment', in Strawson (ed.), *Studies
in the Philosophy of Thought and Action*, London.

Stretton, H. (1969). *The Political Sciences*, London.

Tambiah, S. J. (1973). 'Form and Meaning of Magical Acts', in R. Horton and
R. Finnegan (eds.), *Modes of Thought*, London.

Taylor, C. (1967). 'Neutrality in Political Science', in P. Laslett and W. G.
Runciman (eds.), *Philosophy, Politics and Society*, 3rd series, Oxford.

Taylor, C. (1971). 'Interpretation and the Sciences of Man', *The Review of
Metaphysics*, 25.

Taylor, I., P. Walton and J. Young (1975). *The New Criminology*, London.

Taylor, L. and P. Walton (1971). 'Industrial Sabotage: Motives and Meanings',
in S. Cohen (ed.), *Images of Deviance*, Harmondsworth.

Theen, R. H. W. (1971). 'Political Science in the USSR', *World Politics*, 23.

Thomas, K. (1970). 'The Relevance of Social Anthropology to the Historical
Study of English Witchcraft', in M. Douglas (ed.), *Witchcraft Confessions
and Accusations*, London.

Thompson, E. P. (1977). *The Making of the English Working Class*, Harmondsworth.

Trevor-Roper, H. R. (1967). 'The European Witch-craze of the Sixteenth and
Seventeenth Centuries' in his *Religion, the Reformation and Social Change*,
London.

Truman, D. B. (1965). 'Disillusion and Regeneration: The Quest for a Discipline', *American Political Science Review*, 59.

Urry, J. (1973). 'T. S. Kuhn as Sociologist of Knowledge', *British Journal of
Sociology*, 24.

von Wright, G. H. (1971). *Explanation and Understanding*, London.

References

Weber, M. (1949). *The Methodology of the Social Sciences*, New York.

Weber, M. (1957). 'Science as a Vocation' in *From Max Weber*, London.

Weber, M. (1968). *Economy and Society*, New York.

Weinberg, E. A. (1974). *The Development of Sociology in the Soviet Union*, London.

Whyte, W. F. (1969). *Street Corner Society*, Chicago.

Wiatr, J. J. (1964). 'Political Sociology in Eastern Europe', *Current Sociology*, 13.

Williams, B. A. O. (1972). *Morality*, Harmondsworth.

Williams, N. R. (1977). *Some Reflections on Meaning and the Growth of Science*, unpublished Ph.D. thesis, Cambridge University.

Winch, P. (1958). *The Idea of a Social Science*, London.

Winch, P. (1970). 'Understanding a Primitive Society', in B. R. Wilson (ed.), *Rationality*, Oxford.

Winch, P. (1972). *Ethics and Action*, London.

Wisdom, J. (1957). 'Gods' in his *Philosophy and Psychoanalysis*, Oxford.

Wittgenstein, L. (1967a). *Lectures and Conversations on Aesthetics, Psychology and Religious Belief*, Oxford.

Wittgenstein, L. (1967b). *Zettel*, Oxford.

Wittgenstein, L. (1972). *Philosophical Investigations*, Oxford.

Wolfe, T. (1973). Introduction to Wolfe and E. W. Johnson (eds.), *The New Journalism*, London.

Wolin, S. S. (1968). 'Paradigms and Political Theories', in P. King and B. C. Parekh (eds.), *Politics and Experience*, Cambridge.

Wright Mills, C. (1963). *Power, Politics and People*, New York.

Wright Mills, C. (1973). *The Sociological Imagination*, Harmondsworth.

Young, M. and P. Willmott (1966). *Family and Kinship in East London*, Harmondsworth.

Znaniecki, E. M. (1971). 'Polish Sociology', in G. Gurvitch and W. E. Moore (eds.), *Twentieth Century Sociology*, New York.

Index

211

DATE DUE